OP

Operational Values in Psychotherapy

Operational Values in
Psychotherapy

A CONCEPTUAL FRAMEWORK OF INTERPERSONALITY

by Donald D. Glad, Ph.D.

with portions contributed by VIRGINIA M. GLAD, Ph.D.

and ROBERT H. BARNES, M.D.

NEW YORK

OXFORD UNIVERSITY PRESS / 1959

Copyrighted materials are quoted by permission of publishers of the following articles and books:

'An operational conception of psychotherapy,' by D. D. Glad, *Psychiatry*, 1956: 19, 371–82, The William Alanson White Psychiatric Foundation. *Psychotherapy, Practice and Theory*, by C. Berg, copyright, 1948, Norton. *The Psychiatric Interview*, by H. S. Sullivan, copyright, 1954, Norton. *Client-Centered Therapy*, by C. R. Rogers, copyright, 1951, Houghton Mifflin. *Introduction to Therapeutic Counseling*, by E. H. Porter, copyright, 1950, Houghton Mifflin. *A Primer For Psychotherapists*, by K. M. Colby, copyright, 1951, Ronald. *Introduction to Clinical Psychology*, by L. A. Pennington and I. A. Berg (Eds.), copyright, 1948, Ronald. *Personality and the Behavior Disorders*, by J. McV. Hunt (Ed.), copyright, 1944, Ronald. *The Theories of Harry Stack Sullivan*, by P. Mullahy (Ed.), copyright, 1952, Hermitage House.

Quotations of less than 100 words are acknowledged by bibliographical reference.

PRINTED IN THE UNITED STATES OF AMERICA

Dedicated to

Lynn, Dawn, Toni, *and* Lyle

Preface

You can no more master psychotherapy by reading only than win a woman with your eyes alone. The moment you feel you understand her, she displays new postures and other fascinations. I am reminded of Carroll's whimsey: ' 'Twas brillig, and the slithy toves did gyre and gimble in the wabe; all mimsey were the borogoves and the mome raths outgrabe.' In a sense, my purpose is to translate such whimsey into operational terms. This book presents a series of operational analyses of four value systems in psychotherapy to the end that the arts of healing human behavior may become explicitly defined and the methods repeatable. Yet this operational proposal is a tentative question rather than a definitive answer. In the search for conceptual simplicity and operational clarity it will be necessary to wander the woods of many fancies, sometimes blithely tripping the paths of faith but often falling on the face of doubt. The slithy toves indeed do gyre and gimble in the wabe. Yet there are well beaten paths through this whimsical wood. Psychotherapy is not shooting at the moon with bubble gum; it has powerful, though ill-defined, tools which can direct human energies into constructive channels.

The task of science is to clarify, conceptualize, and develop operational efficiency for the management of natural events. In a science concerned with human values, this operational task has intimacy with everyone's beliefs and shames: operational psychotherapy must engage itself with philosophy, religion, kitchen resentments, bathroom soliloquies, bedroom affections, lusts, and death. In such a perspective the definition of operational values in psychotherapy is as broad as human life. My horizon is more circumscribed: to consider some significant value systems which are conceptualized in psychotherapy theory and to describe their operational dimensions. Four such value systems will be expressed in operational form: psychoanalysis, interpersonal psychiatry, dynamic relationship therapy and client-centered phenomenology will be examined and fitted to an operational struc-

vii

ture. The value systems of clients and patients will be examined in cognate terms, to the end that effective changes in behavior may be expressed as an interaction of interviewer and client values. I have adapted the term *interpersonality* (see p. 210) to express this notion of interactive values in psychotherapy.

The book is intended to be a preliminary engagement between science and art in the production of useful values and behavior. It is a tentative answer to an essential question in psychotherapeutic science. The question itself — In what ways are the values of psychotherapy amenable to operational definition and application? — provides the scientific foil against an artistic shield.

My principal indebtedness is to four great psychotherapists and to many colleagues. Freud, Sullivan, Rank, and Rogers need no acknowledgment. Some conceptual tools are modified from Kurt Lewin and C. W. Morris. Most of my students have contributed in some way. My clients in psychotherapy have been essential. Colleagues, students, or assistants whose contributions do not appear in the bibliography are as follows:

Psychologists: Margaret Thaler Singer, Muriel Parrott, P. Stuart Boyd, Harold W. Keely, and E. Frederick Thompson.

Psychiatrists: John O'Hearn, Robert Stubblefield, Stonewall Stickney, Albert Silverman, Cotter Hirschberg, and Tulio Estrada.

The opportunity to pursue the conceptual and empirical work presented here was provided successively by Franklin G. Ebaugh and John J. Conger at the University of Colorado Medical Center, by Lawrence W. Miller at the University of Denver, and by F. H. Zimmerman at the Colorado State Hospital. Lewis Bernstein, of the Veterans Administration Hospital, has provided similar support for the contributions of my wife.

The present form of the book was stimulated by constructive reactions from several classes in psychotherapy at the University of Colorado Medical Center, the University of Denver, and the Colorado State Hospital. Particularly, however, critiques by Robert H. Barnes, Dexter M. Bullard, Virginia M. Glad, Alvin R. Mahrer, George W. Nimms, and David McK. Rioch have, in my opinion, improved the clarity of the volume. The editorial staff of Oxford University Press, particularly Douglas C. Ross, Jr., and Katharine O. Parker, have contributed much to its technical excellence. Kenneth G. Chinburg, psychiatrist, with whom I am associated in private practice, has helped by providing illustrative patient material and by critically reading the entire manuscript. That my obligation to Virginia M. Glad and Robert H. Barnes is more than editorial is shown by their listing as contributing authors.

Finally, the secretarial-editorial contributions of Helen Burns, Jessie Greensley, and George Nimms through several preliminary drafts of the book have been essential. Jack Canepa executed the final form of the illustrations. Allen H. Roberts assisted on the bibliography and index.

Denver   D.D.G.
October 1958

Foreword

It is a considerable pleasure to me to write a foreword to Dr. Glad's book on *Operational Values in Psychotherapy*. It seems to me that although we have, for sometime now, given lip service to the need for reducing psychotherapy to communicable operations, we have not only failed to make much progress in this direction but have continued to practice certain defensive techniques, neatly designed to preclude any disciplined regulation of our field. Most teachers of psychotherapy, from time to time, issue pronouncements to the effect that psychotherapy is highly individual and that useful techniques of one man are not necessarily useful to another. We have, furthermore, been notably reluctant to expose our psychotherapy to study by third persons. One cannot deny that there are charming rationalizations for this, but nonetheless, little has been accomplished.

I assume that Dr. Glad will be accused of reducing our sublime art to fragments of relatively simple operations. This may be true. Nonetheless, he has set up operations which, with some degree of probability, are parts of the psychotherapies. If the numbers of the operations agreed upon can be increased, if the functional relationships of these operations to the process of psychotherapy can be convincingly demonstrated, the change from art to science will be furthered. The main consideration now is that this beginning has been made, as other beginnings are being made on the same subject. I am pleased to see them all, and fervently wish them useful development.

James Galvin, M. D.,
Director, Colorado Psychopathic Hospital

Contents

PART ONE

Explorations in Human Values, Science, and Psychotherapies

A science of psychotherapies is intimately concerned with human values. However validly the integrity of science demands objective methodology, psychotherapeutic science must grapple with the poignantly subjective lives of both clients and therapists. To consider the problems in developing scientific lawfulness in the modification of personal-social misery, Part I addresses itself to the interrelation of human values, scientific method, and psychotherapeutic operations as these relate to effective changes in human behavior.

> . . . though we both
> seek the Grail,
> You would trudge
> the highway,
> And I would blaze
> a trail.[1]
>
> UNKNOWN

1. Human Values and Psychotherapy Theories [2]

How people change their values and behavior is still a privately intuitive matter. Techniques and processes of ameliorating human misery in psychotherapy remain in the penumbra of objective science and in the center of such artistic subtleties as unconscious relationships between interviewer and client. Such operational elusiveness, such scientific obscurity must somehow be explicitly and publicly penetrated. A practice which provides the procession of human values emerging from the consulting rooms of psychotherapy must somehow be susceptible to explicit description, repeatability, and objective validation.

This volume presents an operational analysis of psychotherapy and group leadership. It is designed to specify the operational consequences of psychotherapy theories in such a way that essential forms of treatment may be compared, objective analyses of processes of change in human behavior made, and validated methods for resolving personal misery explicitly communicated.

There are many good ways of being human. The wisely just and gentle father who guides his sons to a comparable manhood is a

---

[1] Quoted from memory and an unknown source of long ago. I have been unable to identify the author of this stanza but consider it so apt as to require inclusion.

[2] Modified from the author's symposium paper at the Fourth Interamerican Congress of Psychology, Rio Piedras, Puerto Rico, December 27, 1956.

towering beacon for others. The friendly, pleasant comrade who shares your interest, parries your errors, and delights in your warmth is as engaging as the hearth-fire of home. The many-visioned artist or scientist who lonely carves the naked cliffs of truth or beauty hand-hews the path that others follow. The man of understanding who knows and sees your world through your eyes, who finds your world good and does not take it from you, delights your sense of self and yields you pleasure in other selves you then can understand. Yes, there are many good ways of being human; good — but different — ways. How I will be human in a human society depends on which good way I choose or where I am led by those who influence me.

These several 'good adjustments' suggest the reason for a treatment of four approaches to psychotherapy and leadership. Civilization in its culture varieties is demonstration enough that personality may be successfully modified. The many ways of culture and personalities within culture suggest that people are malleable. Yet the same proposition about personality modification through psychotherapy or group leadership has been slow in acceptance. Such laggard resistance to the obvious may result from the fact that some more generic process of personality change is suggested by a 'many good adjustments' proposal. Perhaps, Guy-Fawkes-like, such an idea provokes the fear that kings and willing parliaments will be destroyed and new ones raised to take their places. Such fears are unrealistic and it might be hoped that a simpler, more efficient form of theory will improve upon (and make more testable) dynamic propositions. Yet, it appears that what has stemmed from Freud, Rank, Sullivan, and Rogers, to name a few, will hardly be destroyed, but rather made more lucid — lawful really — by simpler and more complete ways of looking at behavior change.

THEORETICAL VALUE-FORMS AND PERSONALITY CHANGE

Research beginnings and informed opinions are converging toward the proposal that the particular method of therapy or leadership produces its own value-form in clients treated by it. Alexander (2) says, 'Methodical psychotherapy is to a large degree, nothing more than the systematic, conscious application of those methods by which we influence our fellow men.' Rosenthal (88) has shown that patients who improve in psychotherapy adopt the moral values of their therapists. Of six patients who improved, there were value changes about sex, aggression, and discipline; the patients changed toward conforming with the values of their therapists. In six patients who were unimproved, no such convergence of patient and therapist values occurred. Wolff (110) canvassed opinions of a variety of psychotherapists to discover if they thought their value systems influenced the form of patient change. It appears from Wolff that therapists so believe; theoretical value systems tend to be adopted in successful treatment. The author has directed exploratory studies (21, 35, 39, 42, 48, 56, 64) which provide some evidence that both normally adjusted and clinically ill persons in 'psychotherapy groups' behave in ways that are consistent with a particular psychotherapy theory as expressed in the leader's method.

There is evidence and opinion that both change in psychotherapy and personality process in groups of normal people will depend upon the theory of psychotherapy or leadership and the kind of personality outcome the theory anticipates.

Fiedler's (23, 24) interesting data show the quality of the interpersonal relation between client and interviewer to be the same for competent therapists, regardless of their theories. He has found that skillful therapists participate fully in the patient's communication and convey a sense of sharing in the patient's feelings. This description sounds quite like a warm, accepting friendship where one feels well-loved and understood. It should provide a common baseline for effective learning through which the patient may modify himself in ways that the therapist values. So, one might wonder whether Fiedler has provided definition of the therapy relation as a favorable opportunity for learning.

Interactions Among Personality and Theoretical Values

It has frequently been said that some patients who make no progress at all with one therapist improve quickly with another. Such comments are more likely to come from the second rather than the first therapist. It is possible that such differences in change with one therapist rather than another depend on whether the therapist and patient begin with a relatively common philosophy so that the therapist can understand and communicate acceptance. Rosenbaum et al. (87) provide relevant evidence. They show that lack of therapeutic progress is related to religious belief; those patients who are most religious are least likely to benefit from psychotherapy. When one considers the agnosticism of much personality science, it may be wondered whether the divergence of therapist and client on such essential values might reduce the likelihood of changing a religious person. A therapist with a religious value system might be much more effective for such people.

Rogers (84) makes a similar observation about the success of client-centered counseling. He notes that clients who are relatively democratic in their attitudes are most likely to benefit from the democratically client-centered approach. Rank's therapeutic philosophy has always eschewed the common man, supposing that only those who are struggling between their wishes to belong or to separate are likely candidates for *dynamic relationship therapy*.[1] The author's impression of colleagues who benefit from psychoanalysis is that those who originally express relatively paternalistic attitudes become comfortable in such paternalism as a result of psychoanalytic treatment. This observation is consistent with the analytic proposal that psychosexual 'maturity' increases treatability.

There are empirical and logical reasons to suppose that personality modification will be toward the value system which the therapist or the group leader provides. Conversely, there are indications that the personality will be modified most effectively by help in a direction it is already headed, or toward a value-form it nearly fits. Accordingly, this book presents the reader with an assessment of personality concepts and psychotherapists' methods from four theories of psychotherapy. So far as possible, Freud's psychoanalysis, Sullivan's interpersonal psychiatry, Rank's dynamic relationship therapy, and Rogers's phenomenology will be distilled into operational form.

PSYCHOTHERAPY THEORIES DEFINE THERAPIST METHODS: A personality theory becomes a value system for the person who espouses it. Both by inclination and training, the therapist or leader develops behavior patterns which express his theory. The therapist who applies a theory of psychotherapy both has adopted and has been trained in methods which are operational applications of his theory of human behavior. Therefore, personality theories can be stated in the form of characteristic operations in psychotherapy and leadership. The psychoanalytic therapist will behave in ways that are expressions of this theory; he will apply psychoanalytic operations. A group leader holding a psycho-

[1] The term *dynamic relationship therapy* will be used for the theory and method of Otto Rank (77, 78, 79, 103).

analytic conception of personality and group processes will behave in ways that are expressions of psychoanalysis. These characteristic ways of therapist and leadership behavior can be described and illustrated in the form of operations that are typical of psychoanalysis. By contrast, the psychotherapist holding a client-centered philosophy of treatment will behave in ways that are expressions of his empathic philosophy. A group leader with such a phenomenological approach to personality growth will tend to express this metaphysic in the form of empathic operations that are the expressions of his theory. Thus, it becomes possible to provide descriptions of the methods of various approaches to psychotherapy and leadership as derivatives of the theories.

It is possible to investigate the effects of theoretically systematic operations after making such operational definitions. We can test the hypothesis that a theory defines methods which produce theoretically consistent reactions in patients and other people.

PSYCHOTHERAPY THEORIES DEFINE PERSONALITY STRUCTURES: Such assessments of the relationship between theory and method provide the basis for defining the personality constellation and value system of the patient or group member in terms of theoretical value systems. Criteria can be developed for assessing the degree to which a personality is already integrated in one or another theoretically consistent way. Psychoanalytic *paternalism*, interpersonal psychiatric *socialization*, dynamic relationship *creativity*, and phenomenological *empathic individuality* are relatively different kinds of personality integrations. Such personality value-forms are defined by psychotherapy theories and provide a basis for examining the effectiveness of personality 'improvement' as a joint function of the therapist's theoretical method and the client's theoretical value-integration. More simply, John, who is already a fairly understanding, democratic person with relatively little need to be artistically creative, firmly parental, or socially effective, would become 'well-adjusted' most rapidly in the democratically understanding atmosphere of client-centered counseling. Conversely, Dave, who yearns to use his own ideas and follow paths where few have ventured, may fear the desolation of rejection which such meanderings might bring. Dave would develop most quickly in his own directions by dynamic relationship therapy, designed as it is to reduce the threat of rejection and to increase the acceptance of creative individuality.

These propositions are shown in Figure 1. It will be noted that the client whose values are similar to the values of a particular theory is located close to that theory in the diagram. The figure shows that the degree of personality change required for a psychoanalytically integrated patient to become adjusted in psychoanalytic therapy is minimal in comparison to the degree of change essential for the same client to become well under client-centered treatment. Furthermore,

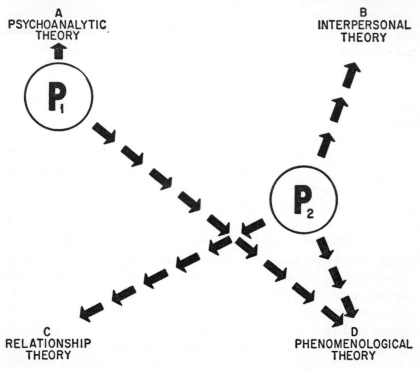

Fig. 1.

Spatial diagram of the joint propositions that (1) personality modification results from an acceptance of the value system characteristic of the therapist's or leader's theory, and (2) that rapidity of 'improvement' depends upon the degree to which the client or group member is close to the form of good 'adjustment' prized by the theory of treatment.

Conceptualizing the distances among the four theories in terms of the amount of change required to reach theoretical 'adjustment,' it is proposed that person one (P_1) would have to change very little to become 'adjusted' in the psychosexual maturity sense of psychoanalysis, but would have to change considerably to become 'adjusted' in the empathically democratic sense of client-centered phenomenology. Similarly P_2 might rapidly 'adjust' in phenomenological terms by client-centered methods, would take longer to change toward interpersonal psychiatric socialization values as a result of interpersonal treatment, and would have to change enormously to become a creative individual as the result of dynamic relationship methods.

the client who already tends toward empathic, understanding self-acceptance will rapidly improve in client-centered treatment, would take longer to adjust in interpersonal psychiatric treatment, and be recalcitrant to dynamic relationship therapy. Some research support of this proposal about the interactions of behavior-value integrations and theoretical interpretations will be reviewed in Chapter XI.

In further definition of what this book is about, consider again the interrelated propositions that (a) psychotherapy theories tend to have special value systems as to the nature of 'good adjustment,' (b) such theories tend to produce psychotherapy and leadership operations which are expressions of such value systems, and (c) personality consequences of being treated or led by operations derived from theoretical value systems are likely to be consistent with the theoretical definitions of good adjustment.

It has been suggested: How people behave is related to their philosophies of life or value systems. Comparative studies of theoretically systematic psychotherapy operations indicate that personalities are modified in the directions prized by the particular theory (35). It appears that exposure to theoretically consistent operations leads the clients or research subjects to adopt the value system inherent in the psychotherapy theory (64).

Psychoanalysis values psychosexual maturity as the 'best adjustment.' This is achieved in part by an identification with a same-sex parental figure. Such psychosexual maturity provides means for controlling affectionate and aggressive drives in socially valuable ways. A relatively authoritarian, wisdom-giving 'parentalism' is the characteristic behavior-value integration prized by psychoanalytic theory.

Interpersonal psychiatric theory values the proposition that 'no man is an island unto himself.' A *socially integrated* adjustment results from interpersonal affection, acceptance of the socially agreed upon, and skill in giving security to others. Such behavior-value integration would plausibly result in affectionate, conventional, and friendly equalitarian behavior.

Rankian dynamic relationship theory proposes that *creative individuality* will be achieved by an emotionally successful acceptance of one's right and privilege to leave the paradisiacal womb and build one's own more stately mansions. Acceptance of this belief should result in unusual, perhaps creative, but certainly unconforming behavior-value reactions.

Client-centered phenomenology emphasizes the acceptance of one's right to be understood in his personal individuality. Such self-acceptance is accompanied by empathic respect for the selfhood of others. Such self-other respect should be expressed in comfortable understanding and an *empathically independent* acceptance among democratic equals.

I have tried to epitomize the value systems and some plausible outcomes of four approaches to psychotherapy. These vignettes provide a basis for considering how personality, group processes, and perhaps society may be influenced by such philosophical values.

Such proposals may provoke the question: Will the theory and method of one approach to psychotherapy have different effects from the theory and method of another approach? They provide a basis for the further question: Is it possible to apply theoretically derived methods which may produce congruent reactions in normally adjusted people? That is, will methods of interviewing, leadership, or teaching consistent with any particular theory of personality produce behavior congruent to the theory?

Investigations to be reviewed have attempted to provide ways of assessing such questions (34, 37). From systematic analysis of both theoretical positions and published transcripts of psychotherapy, the author has derived an operational conception of psychotherapy (cf. Part III). This operational conception provides means for investigating how personality modifications may be made in clinical psychotherapy or in normal group processes, and how such modifications may relate to both theoretical premises and empirical outcomes.

THEORETICALLY SYSTEMATIC OPERATIONS

The following is a brief sketch of some theoretically systematic operations and some preliminary results of such operations with both clinical and normal groups of clients and patients.

Operations of Psychotherapists

Some characteristic ways in which therapists are likely to respond to a patient are as follows:

An excerpt of patient behavior from Colby (12) may be used as a basis for constructing illustrative therapist responses from four points of view.

PT: 'It's silly to feel that way, I know. Well, what it is is a day dream I've had for years. In it I think of myself as a queen like Cleopatra who is surrounded by a sort of harem of big, handsome men. All these men are my slaves. Some are in chains. They do anything I want them to. For the first time a couple of weeks ago you were one of the men.'

PSYCHOANALYTIC THERAPIST

One of the many ways that a psychoanalytic therapist might respond to this could be in terms of an inquiry about the transference. He might say: *'Do any of these men remind you of your father?'* [1] Such an inquiry would be likely to lead to associations about the patient's experiences and fantasies involving father and the therapist.

INTERPERSONAL THERAPIST

An interpersonal therapist would be more likely to respond to the patient's security-operations, or social expression, and the perceptual distortions involved in the fantasy. He might say: *'I wonder if you're trying to control me by thinking of me as your slave?'* Such a therapist remark would produce an emphasis upon interpersonal maneuvers and the social implications of one's behavior.

DYNAMIC RELATIONSHIP THERAPIST

A dynamic relationship therapist would be likely to respond to the patient's immediate emotional meaning about the therapist. He could say something like this: *'I wonder if that means you like me very much, but you're afraid I don't allow you much freedom?'* This expression from the therapist emphasizes the meaning of the relationship to the therapist in terms of affection and the wish to escape such a bondage of love.

CLIENT-CENTERED THERAPIST

A client-centered therapist could say: *'You feel sort of embarrassed about such fantasies.'* This emphasis upon the client's feelings calls attention to the emotional meaning of his experience and would be likely to lead to increased ability to experience feelings without threat.

It will be seen that each theory emphasizes different aspects of the client's behavior. Such differences in emphasis are systematically con-

---

[1] Many of the illustrative quotations from clients and therapists in this book will not be referenced. In such cases they are either fictitious examples constructed for the particular purpose or they are drawn from the author's clinical and research experience.

sistent with the theories, and might be expected to result in the client's modifying his value system in the direction prized by the theory.

Group Leadership Operations

We may now illustrate theoretically systematic operations in group leadership, and how each theory of therapy might be applied in defining leadership techniques. An example of behavior from a training workshop in community relations will provide a basis for taking several different theoretical looks at leadership possibilities.

> LEADER: 'Could you tell us a little more about what you mean by "the attitudes the way they are?"'
>
> DELEGATE 4: 'Well, I mean the white children don't want the Negro children to come in, and they freeze them out if they do, and the Negro children can't be convinced that they'll have a good time or will be welcomed if they do come over for the activity.' [Lippitt, 65]

PSYCHOANALYTIC LEADER

From a psychoanalytic approach the leader might treat this in many ways. Let us assume, however, that he interprets the delegate's remark as symbolizing some kind of wish to avoid sexuality. Such a hypothesis would relate simply to an unconscious premise that sexually different kinds of people should not play together. On such a basis the psychoanalytically oriented leader might remark: *'Different kinds of children just don't seem to be able to play together comfortably,'* or more directly, *'Maybe it's dangerous to put different kinds of children in the same group.'*

INTERPERSONAL PSYCHIATRIC LEADER

From an interpersonal psychiatric approach the leader may respond to the social expression meaning of the delegate's remarks, or to the perceptual distortion expressed by the delegate. The interpersonal leader might comment about the delegate's social role: *'I wonder if you're trying to avoid doing anything about the problem?'* Or he might comment on some kind of perceptual distortion: *'Do other people find that Negro and white children can't get along together? I haven't found it so.'*

DYNAMIC RELATIONSHIP LEADER

From a dynamic relationship approach, the leader might respond to the implicit feeling which the delegate is expressing toward the leader.

He might say: *'You're a little irked at me for not seeing the problem'* or alternatively, *'You want me to agree with you.'*

CLIENT-CENTERED LEADER

From a client-centered approach the leader might empathize with a number of aspects of the delegate's problem. He might express the delegate's perplexity and distress: *'That makes it pretty difficult and upsetting for you if the children don't get along.'* Or he might re-express the delegate's perception of the problem: *'Really then, it seems that both the white and the Negro children refuse to be friendly.'*

Systematic Implications

These samples of how therapists from several theoretical viewpoints are likely to respond to their clients, and how leaders may apply congruent operations to the management of normal group processes, will be extended into a series of systematic operations representing the variety of things a therapist or leader is most likely to say or do from any particular theoretical approach.

Such a systematic extension provides a basis for investigating the characteristic modes of response of patients or other group members in a theoretically oriented process of modifying behavior. Research in psychotherapy processes and in the effects of particular forms of group leadership can be readily implemented on such a basis.

The results of several exploratory studies suggest that both clinically ill and normally adjusted people tend to respond to theoretically derived operations in ways which are consistent with the parent theory. To illustrate:

1. A leadership method from psychoanalysis for the treatment of chronic alcoholics resulted in both a high rate of 'remission' and theoretically characteristic acceptance of the 'ego-ideal' (18, and cf. Ch. XII, pp. 293–4.

2. A leadership method from interpersonal psychiatry has consistently produced increases in socialization and pleasant feelings toward others (21, 42, 48, 64).

3. A leadership method from dynamic relationship theory has resulted in both dependent and autonomous reactions (8, 37, 48).

4. A leadership method from client-centered theory has been fairly consistent in increasing comfortable independence (18, 48, 84).

Thus, there is tentative evidence that methods of interviewing or group leadership derived from particular theories of psychotherapy tend to modify personality functioning in the directions expected by the theory. This is likely to be true not only of psychotherapy with patients, but also of normal members of groups in other kinds of situations. Such suggestive evidence leads to the possibility of developing methods of therapy and leadership which will evoke the kinds of personality reactions most needed for particular problems.

Certainly there are needs in society for the wise paternalism to be expected from psychoanalytic approaches; there are many needs for the social conjunctivity which interpersonal psychiatric methods enhance; the creative nonconformity expected from dynamic relationship therapy is essential to an emergent society; and the empathic individuality anticipated from client-centered leadership is perhaps the *sine qua non* of democracy in action.

II. Science of Psychotherapies

Inquiry evokes investigation, but doctrine stifles thought. Since this book is intended to contribute to the development of a science of psychotherapies, it is in the form of a constant quest rather than a finished answer to the questions it must raise. Even a question, however, to be of any value, must be incisive — what do we want to know? Questions about psychotherapy and leadership can be organized about several topics.

This chapter introduces the following questions: (a) *Theoretical:* How does a theory affect the behavior of the therapist and the client? (b) *Process validity:* What aspects of 'therapeutic' transactions are relevant to the processes of 'improvement'? (c) *Descriptive methodology:* How can the psychotherapeutic transaction be described in such ways that the theoretical explanation and the process validity questions may be assessed? (d) *Science and helping:* In what ways may an art of helping profit from a science of psychotherapies?

Questions invite answers, but a living science is a perpetual question. This book presents no final answers. It assumes that there is no key to Omar's door of knowledge — that the door itself is a mirage obstruction to a doctrinal corridor along which 'in' and 'out' are the only possible directions. Assuming such a man-made nature of 'fact' and 'information,' the author invites the reader to remain perplexed throughout this book — and thereafter — expecting that questions will invite answers in the form of further questions and acknowledging that the Holy Grail of psychotherapy knowledge is able to appear to one as

15

a urinal, to another as a milk pitcher, and to a third as a hermitage. The substance of the 'true Grail' may be discerned among its several forms.

CRUCIAL QUESTIONS ABOUT PSYCHOTHERAPIES

Scientific perplexities about psychotherapy and leadership need to be stated before they can be examined. To be most useful, such problems should be raised as incisive questions even though the answers are timid. Consider some of the ways in which the question, What is psychotherapy? may be asked.

A neurotic might lament, 'Will this do me any good?'

A psychotic might object, 'What are you trying to do to me?'

A student, trying to learn about psychotherapy, could inquire, 'How can I make sense out of this mass of feelings, illustrations, and concepts?'

The clinical psychotherapist often ponders, 'How can I help this patient over his insecurity?'

The scientist will propose a larger problem, 'How can psychotherapy be conceived and organized in such a way that incisive questions may be raised and approaches to solution developed?'

The neurotic's, the psychotic's, and the student's questions are all parts of the scientist's inquiry. The therapist's problem is closely related. While this book is about all of these questions, it will be organized around the scientific problem.

'Will This Do Me Any Good?'

The neurotic's lament can be translated into several research inquiries:

1. Does client X become client X'?[1] Do changes occur in the client while he is in treatment?

2. Under what conditions does client X become client X'? What are the necessary conditions to produce change in the client?

3. Is the change that occurs a worthwhile one? Does the value system of the therapist (improvement) correspond to the value system of the client (get better)?

[1] As proposed by Victor C. Raimy, personal communication.

'What Are You Trying to Do to Me?'

The psychotic's objection provokes other research perplexities:

1. Is consciously accepted motivation to change essential for improvement? Or more simply, does the patient have to know that he wants to get well before psychotherapy can help?

2. Does the patient have to understand what is happening in order for psychotherapy to have an effect?

3. What performance measures can be developed for defining and measuring personal and social adjustment?

'How Can I Make Any Sense out of This?'

The student's inquiry raises other questions. It seems legitimate that a practice that provides such relief of human suffering as psychotherapy appears to do should make some kind of integrated sense. Appel (4) says that '. . . there is something basically effective in the process of therapy in general which is independent of the methods employed.' 'Something basically effective' summarizes much of the student's puzzle. What is that something? This problem may be rephrased in the form of some organizational questions:

1. In what ways is psychotherapy effective?

2. Is there something basically effective about the process of psychotherapy in general?

3. Are there any particular aspects of psychotherapy which have specific effects?

4. How may the field of psychotherapy be organized that it will seem less chaotic?

'How Can I Help This Patient Over His Insecurity?'

The psychotherapist's pondering raises still other questions:

1. Am I a suitable *kind of person* for this client's needs?

2. Will the way I manage *my relationship* to the client help him in any way?

3. Are there special techniques that *I can apply* effectively to this kind of problem?

The scientific problem encompasses the neurotic's, the psychotic's, the student's, and the psychotherapist's questions by asking: 'How can psychotherapy be conceptualized and organized so that incisively relevant questions may be raised and answered?' The several, separate inquiries may be examined in relation to this organizational and research question. To illustrate the larger problem, let us examine one result of 'successful' group leadership in psychotherapy.

Ellen was a 19-year-old college sophomore whose marriage had suffocated from six months of stifling in the warm, protective atmosphere of her widowed mother's home. Ellen still lived at home with her wonderful mother, always had, and of course could not consider anything else. She was a mildly anxious girl, devoted to mother, and desperately afraid of spiders. In a therapy group of six college students she talked warmly about her mother. Later she reported dreams of the Queen of Hearts hovering over a dark pool and gradually changing into a black widow spider. The possibility was raised that her fear of spiders was somehow related to an unwelcome feeling of being oppressed by mother's affection. A few days later Ellen picked a small spider off of the floor to demonstrate that her fear had vanished. But soon she began to wonder aloud, 'What does it mean when you're afraid to step on the cracks in a sidewalk?' Other members of the group recited the childhood verse:

> Step on a crack,
> Break your mother's back.

Ellen denied having heard this before, but soon dropped her fear of the sidewalk cracks and announced that she intended to kill herself. With some help she gave up her suicidal threat and gradually came to accept that mother's love was honeyed venom. As the school year merged into summer she arranged a job away from home and was delightedly planning an emancipation summer on her own.

This example provides no answers. Hopefully, it may illustrate some questions. It is intentionally drawn from the author's earliest experience with psychotherapy in order to vivify the question, 'Is there something basically effective regardless of the method?' Certainly something changed in this client over six months of three group meetings per week. Client X became client X'. Change occurred. *Was it improvement?*

Whether change equals improvement may be a matter of opinion. More particularly, improvement is defined by the value system of the person making the judgment. As this girl's therapist, the author was pleased with her change. In his opinion she was better adjusted. In all likelihood, Ellen's mother was distressed with such an 'improvement.' Mother lost the constant devotion of her daughter. From the social point of view represented intensely by Ellen's mother, the change was disastrous. Even Ellen was not entirely satisfied with the change. She was happier, she was more independent, she was no longer afraid of spiders; but on the other hand she could no longer accept the blanket of mother's affection.

Assuming that something useful did happen to Ellen, how can the process of change be understood? Does it make any kind of economical conceptual sense? The summary is obviously selective in theoretical terms. These events have a strong psychoanalytic flavor. A different series of happenings might have been chosen to illustrate a sequence of learning processes. Another sequence might have supported the Rankian theory of a struggle between dependent and independent needs. A selection of the insecurity aspects and the improvement in interpersonal operations might have illustrated the interpersonal psychiatric conceptual system. How can Ellen's process of improvement be explained most economically and efficiently?

It might be wondered what happened to Ellen during and following her summer emancipation. The author does not know what became of her. Perhaps she's back in mother's arms. Perhaps her body lies safe in the beautiful lake near which she implemented her growing up. Quite possibly she found it necessary to see a psychiatrist in the autumn to repair the damage that unskilled group therapy had wreaked upon her. If so that psychiatrist might have questioned vigorously whether change equals improvement. No one making an evaluation of this case would question whether change occurred. Several could question whether change of the kind described is necessarily *improvement*. And so the question again, 'Is there something basically effective about the process of psychotherapy?'

A small part of this question may be answered firmly: Client X became client X'. Other aspects of this particular case remain uncertain.

SOME QUESTIONS SEARCHING FOR ANSWERS

Let us summarize these unanswered questions:

1. *Is change necessarily improvement?* This is uncertain, since the usefulness of change appears to depend on the point of view of the person making the evaluation, and on when the evaluation is made.

2. *Is change a function of the psychotherapy method?* Possibly, but

the changes in Ellen could also have been a function of time, with the psychotherapy unrelated to the change. Alternatively, the change may have been a result of other things that were happening in Ellen's environment. It may have been that Ellen's mother was becoming more wholesome for her, or that Ellen had fallen in love with a life-guard who planned to work at the lake during that summer.

3. *Is change a function of the relationship to the psychotherapist?* This is also possible, since something vaguely definable as psychotherapy had been provided by a relatively accepting, understanding person. This, however, is only one of many available hypotheses as to how change may have been induced.

4. *If change has occurred, how may it be conceptualized?* Do psychoanalytic, self-concept, relationship, interpersonal, or other types of conceptual systems provide the most efficient synopsis of the psychotherapy data?

We may now examine in detail the various facets of these proposed uncertainties about the application and investigation of psychotherapy. The question is, how can we systematically conceptualize psychotherapies in such a way as to examine therapy processes which may effect personality readjustment? One approach is to analyze what practitioners of effective psychotherapies do and arrive at methods for representing and classifying such therapist behavior and client reactions. Such synopses may point directions for the investigation and understanding of therapeutically induced readjustment.

TOWARD A SCIENCE OF PSYCHOTHERAPIES

The basic problem in psychotherapeutic science is essentially two-fold: How psychotherapy may be organized in such a way that the behavior — or operations — of the interviewer may be made explicit and repeatable; and how relevant personality reactions of the client may be observed and quantified in such a way that psychotherapy processes may be examined and understood.

This problem is considered in terms of how to describe the behavior of both therapist and client, and how to relate behavior observations to psychotherapy concepts. It has been assumed that the best frame of reference for defining relevant variables of therapist and client behavior should be available in successful psychotherapies.

Consequently the behavior of the therapist as a function of his theory is examined from four theoretical approaches. From this examination an operational outline of therapist behaviors will be developed. Such operations will be used to define those aspects of the client's behavior which are plausibly relevant to a psychotherapeutic process.

A Primer of Psychotherapeutic Inquiry

The present work is a primer of psychotherapy. It proposes a basic organization and synthesis of the behaviors of therapists, group leaders, and clients as these are represented by the *psychoanalytic*, the *interpersonal*, the *dynamic relationship*, and the *phenomenological* theories of psychotherapy. The author assumes that the background of the reader in his special field, whether it be psychiatry, psychology, psychiatric social work, or counseling, will be important to his grasp of this material. This work is intended to be a synthesis of operations in four approaches to psychotherapy. As such a synthesis it may bring together many of the things the reader already knows, and provide a basis for organizing questions, learnings, and investigations. The purpose is threefold: (a) to provide a synoptic organization of psychotherapy theories; (b) to provide the therapist with an organization of therapy concepts and techniques as a contribution to technical skill; and (c) to provide the investigator with operational definitions and technical methods which may be applied to the pursuit of knowledge about psychotherapy processes and outcomes.

Some definition of *psychotherapy* is an essential basis for this integrative process. Specificity of definition, however, is foolhardy in view of the wide range of possibilities. It is possible to appraise how psychotherapy is defined. Criteria for selecting those aspects of the domain that are most likely to yield to valid investigation can be proposed. Yet we cannot presume at the moment that any point of view is most valid. Let us consider some definitional possibilities and evaluate where these are likely to lead.

Hathaway (50) proposes that definitions range from the assertion '. . . that there is only one type of psychotherapy . . . any other approach is a covering up or ameliorative procedure . . .' to the other extreme, where psychotherapy becomes '. . . any predominantly psychological procedure, personal or environmental, that is assumed to be contributory to mental hygiene or personal adjustment. With this broader definition, better living conditions, better food, and the like all become psychotherapeutic procedures insofar as they have psychological implications.' Furthermore, there is difficulty in relating individual and group psychotherapy in any systematic way. Raimy (76) notes that '. . . group therapists polarize themselves into those who . . . strive to make group therapy identical with individual therapy, and those others who see the group as a means for stimulating and learning adequate social techniques in a real life setting.' Such points of view suggest the domains which require study and research. Yet with such a range of possibilities some limitation is essential to a manipulable organization of the problem. We shall define psychotherapy for this purpose as *any psychological method which is intended to improve the personal or social adjustment of individuals who are aware that the therapist is offering psychological help.* We shall further limit the definition by restricting the present work to psychotherapies which can be classified as psychoanalytic, relationship, phenomenological, or interpersonal psychiatric.

INDIVIDUAL PSYCHOTHERAPY AND GROUP LEADERSHIP: Personality change as a result of individual interviews or group leadership may occur in somewhat different ways and through pertinent variations in technique; yet it seems feasible to conceptualize such personal and group interview processes similarly. Ruesch and Bateson (89) propose that interpersonal and psychotherapeutic events in general may be conceptualized similarly by considering the individual within the framework of a social situation. A cognate liaison may be made between individual and group psychotherapy methods. We may examine the activities of the therapist as he functions in the interview in terms of his interpersonal operations. We may examine the behavior of the client as he relates to himself and others in an individual or group interview situation. If we conceive of psychotherapy as an interpersonal relation, it becomes possible to focus upon the smallest possible segment — one therapist and one client — or upon a larger unit — one or more therapists and several clients. Hence this book will not include a systematic consideration of group versus individual psychotherapy. That there are crucial differences seems likely. For conceptual simplicity, however, this question will be neglected and the author will assume that illustrations of psychotherapy operations and processes may be taken from both group and individual sources.

Four Proposals

THE THEORETICAL PROPOSAL: The form of the therapist's theory has characteristic effects in determining the structure of the client's process of change.

THE PROCESS VALIDITY PROPOSAL: Certain aspects of the psychotherapy transaction are more relevant to 'improvement' than other aspects. Such relevancies can be defined by skillful, objective investigation of theory, techniques, and processes of change in client 'adjustment.'

THE DESCRIPTIVE METHODOLOGY PROPOSAL: Technical-conceptual tools are essential to any sophisticated and fruitful investigation of psychotherapy processes.

THE SCIENCE AND HELPING PROPOSAL: Theoretical-objective knowledge will contribute to the effectiveness with which psychotherapists help their clients.

These are the essential proposals involved in the several questions we have raised. They can be restated more cautiously in inquiring form:

What relationships are there among psychotherapy theories, therapist activities, and client behavior and change? In what ways do theories explain psychotherapy? What effects do theories have upon the operations of psychotherapists? How do such theories and operations affect the behavior and improvement of the client?

What aspects of the psychotherapy transaction are relevant to development of clinical skill and investigation of theory, techniques, and processes? How should the client be described? What aspects of the relationship between therapist and client need to be considered? What aspects of therapist's activities should be included? What aspects of the environment should be described?

What methods of representation and analysis of the psychotherapy transaction can be applied or developed for investigative purposes? How may the therapist's personality and activities in psychotherapy be conceived as reliably repeatable operations? How may the client's behavior and change be represented and measured? How may the relationship between client and therapist be measured and analyzed? How may such methods be applied to the examination of process, outcome, and theoretical understanding?

What value for clinical psychotherapy will a systematic picture of the psychotherapy transaction provide? Will it make any difference to the practitioner's ability to help a person in need?

The Importance of Systematizing Psychotherapies

Intense concern is expressed in the literature about the lack of systematic knowledge in the psychotherapies. There is considerable agreement that no consistent organization of the field has emerged. Powdermaker and Frank (74) note that '. . . the literature is singularly free from objective observations and validated conclusions on the actual events during the psychotherapeutic processes with individuals and with groups.' The basis for this lack of objectivity and system is characterized by Kubie (59) as '. . . vagueness as to what constitutes the essential forms of treatment to be compared.' Some serious scholars consider that relevant objective measurements are theoretically and practically premature. For example, a Group for the Advancement of Psychiatry (GAP) report on Research in Individual Psychotherapy (47) suggests that it is '. . . theoretically almost impossible to achieve [quantitative analysis], and one reminds oneself how much of psychotherapy is still undefinable and inarticulate, and how much of the process is dependent on the unverbalized and even unconscious interaction between the therapist and the patient.' The GAP report continues, 'One must still ask whether . . . measurements being used are indeed concerned with the fundamental processes at work in psychotherapy, or whether they deal with relatively superficial, isolated artifacts of the therapeutic procedure.' This report does not maintain the nihilistic position implied in the quotations, but suggests that clinical case study directed toward development of hypothetical constructs may provide a basis for later systematic and experimental investigation. This plea for clinical hypotheses as the major research focus of a field that has made little quantitative progress in seventy-five years of brilliant clinical intuition has the white look of surrender! This book will consider such problems as questions rather than barriers. We may ask, How may objective observations be made? How may the essential forms of treatment be conceptualized in operational terms? How may unverbalized or unconscious interactions between therapist and client be examined? How may objective measurements of fundamental processes be made? '. . . We know so little about the process of helping that the only proper attitude is one of maximum experimentalism. The state of theory and its relation to technique is obviously chaotic whatever our pretensions.' (Meehl, 66).

In this chapter many problems about psychotherapy will be elaborated. Subsequent chapters will propose ways of looking at such problems and suggest methods of attacking them. We now turn to a systematic assessment of problems in theory, process validity, descriptive methodology, and a science of helping.

THE THEORETICAL PROPOSAL

The form of the therapist's theory has characteristic effects in determining the structure of the client's process of change. A theory, like the map of a battle plan, is a synoptic picture of functional relationships among observable, inferred, and predicted aspects of events. A theory is intended to simplify the complexities of what is observed, to provide a coherent explanation of how these observations fit together, and to predict what will happen if conditions are changed.

A *psychoanalytic synopsis* of the case of Ellen might be as follows: She is a hysterical personality with primarily phobic symptoms; she uses the ego defenses of denial and displacement. She denies that her mother's love is covertly sucking and venomous but displaces this meaning upon a spider, which she can legitimately fear and which symbolizes precisely those aspects of her mother that she fears and hates. The second development — fear of sidewalk cracks — represents a similar ego defense, but a greater acceptance of hostility toward mother. Ellen still denies her hostility, yet fears that she will express it in an uncontrolled way — that is, she fears she will injure her mother. Since direct awareness of her hatred is so distressing, she transforms it into a phobia about a denied recollection from childhood. 'I fear stepping on the cracks in the sidewalk, because this means attacking mother, and I cannot tolerate such a thought.' Her next development — that of threatening suicide — is a response to her acceptance that she does detest mother. This threat is a plea for someone to love and to protect her even though she is a 'bad girl' who hates, and has lost the affection of, her mother. When she finds that other people are accepting and interested despite her 'badness,' she becomes free to assume some independence from mother and a closer relation to other people. This explanation of Ellen's movement in therapy makes a certain kind of coherent sense and predicts that her next development may include a mature love affair.[1]

The psychoanalytic summary also suggests a theoretical bias in the selection of the details which are reported from sixty hours of group therapy. This bias is intentional since it achieves an adequate synopsis and explanation of the process. But is this structure of explanation necessarily the most efficient? That the method of group psychotherapy was psychoanalytically oriented is also suggested by a brief report. Something in the therapist's personality and behavior, the client's problems, or the prevailing *zeitgeist* led to the evocation of this kind of client productivity rather than to some other kind. It appears that the therapist believed in psychoanalytic theory and may have selectively evoked and retained psychoanalytically cogent information. Such beliefs and selective biases need to be examined in relation to the efficiency of a theory.

THEORETICAL REASONING MAY BE CIRCULAR: Circular reasoning may appear to prove a theory. An analysis of several studies (35, 39, 42, 48) indicates that therapist operations which are derived from particular theories tend to evoke client responses which are consistent with the theoretical source. The therapist's client-centered emphasis upon the client's verbalized feelings, e.g. 'You feel pretty unhappy,' results in expressions of anxiety, independence, and superiority. These reactions are consistent with client-centered theoretical expectations.

The therapist's interpersonal psychiatric emphasis upon social behavior (rather than feelings) produces other characteristic reactions. The interpersonal therapist might say, 'You're being rather critical.' By contrast, the client-centered interviewer could say, 'You mean you feel annoyed about that?' Typical reactions to an interpersonal psychiatric emphasis upon social behavior include relatively little anxiety and an excess of critical, friendly, and sociocentric reactions. Generally, there is an increase of socialization and a reduction of apparent anxiety. These reactions are consistent with the interpersonal psychiatric emphasis upon security operations to avoid anxiety and upon increasing social effectiveness to resolve the sense of insecurity. Such results as these suggest that a theory of psychotherapy produces therapist operations consistent with the theory and theoretically consistent behavior in the client. Such consistency in the client's response be-

---

[1] Assuming, of course, that oedipal material not provoked or worked through in the group was implicitly managed by the client.

comes proof of the theory from which the therapist's operations and the client's reactions were originally derived.

THEORIES TEND TO PROVE THEMSELVES: The tendency of theoretically defined operations to produce consistent evidence requires special attention in psychotherapy. Where data are strongly dependent upon the human observer as an instrument of research, the observer's and the therapist's theoretical and personal predilections are likely to structure observations in several ways. In the first place, the therapist will behave in a selective fashion. He will do those things that seem useful to the client according to his theory of therapy, e.g. interpret Ellen's fear of spiders as a displacement of fears in relation to mother. As a consequence of the therapist's selective behavior, the client will also respond selectively and produce to some degree the kind of reactions the therapist expects. An observer who shares the frame of reference of the therapist is likely to observe and retain for analysis those aspects of the therapist-client interaction which are most systematically consistent with the chosen reference frame, e.g. *displacement* rather than *conditioning generalization*. Finally, the data will be analyzed in reference to the theory which produced and selected them in the first place, thus completing the circular process of theory proving itself.

To guard against such circularity, this book approaches psychotherapy operations and processes from four different theoretical positions and attempts to systematize therapy operations and client behavior independently of the theoretical sources from which they are derived. At the same time the theoretical kinships of such operations are kept clear in order to provide a basis for comparative testing of hypotheses derived from separate sources.

Furthermore, theories of psychotherapy have generated therapist techniques. Theories define how a therapist should respond to a client and what aspects of the client's functioning are important to an understanding of the process of improvement. Thus, decisions about how to describe the therapist, the client, and their relationship in psychotherapy may be specifically dictated by the theoretical sources, e.g. the client's verbalized feelings, the social meanings of his behavior, the symbolic meanings of his dreams, or his inferred feelings about the therapist.

THE PROCESS VALIDITY PROPOSAL

Certain aspects of the psychotherapy transaction are more relevant to 'improvement' than other aspects. Such relevancies can be defined by skillful, objective investigation of theory, techniques, and processes of change in client 'adjustment.' Effective therapy presumably induces change in the client. This change, if therapeutic, is toward better adjustment; the client gets along better. It is reasonable that, in describing psychotherapy, we examine it successively from several vantage points, focusing upon (a) the client, who is expected to change; (b) the therapist's operations, which may be expected to induce change; and (c) the criteria for evaluating the presence and nature of an 'improvement.' Since one's personal adequacy is not entirely under one's own control, it is necessary to consider the client's change in psychotherapy as a function of the therapist's personality and behavior and in terms of the reaction of other people to the client's change. If a client feels better and expresses himself as 'happier,' the therapist may assume this to be evidence of improvement. On the other hand, it could be evidence of a *flight into health* to escape the indignity of emotional illness, or it could be a polite way of saying 'I want to leave therapy without offending you.' Change may occur in the way the client feels about himself without necessarily indicating that he is better adjusted socially — he may be happily delusional. In any event, the *change* may be a result of therapy whether the 'happiness' is a hermit's paradise in a cave, a dynamic defense against a sense of loneliness, a social façade to cover a sense of inadequacy, or a genuine improvement in integration. Even when improvement has occurred, it is not uncommon for the patient to feel better and to think himself to be more socially competent, yet to be unable to adjust to his pathogenic environment any better than he did before he entered treatment.

The client's feeling better is no necessary indication of improved social competence. Perhaps he feels better because he has been in treatment for some months and relieved of the difficulties to which he has been accustomed. The relief of stress from a cruel environment may make it possible for him to feel better independently of any process in psychotherapy. Or perhaps he has not improved enough to handle 'real life.' Family and friends may object to the boisterous sociability that supplants an unassuming depression. Thus it is necessary to consider at least three criteria of improvement; (a) the client's sense of adequacy, (b) his environmental effectiveness, and (c) the point of view of significant people in the client's life space. Does he have the feeling that he is 'better' as a result of psychotherapy? Is he more effective in work and interpersonal relations? Can people with whom he lives and works accept him more easily? The therapist may observe that the patient is doing well in the therapeutic environment. But this is a partial observation.

The criterion for effective living is not, How effective is the client in psychotherapy? but, How adequate is he outside of treatment? These are questions about the outcome of psychotherapy. It is necessary to describe outcomes from the point of view of the client, from the point of view of an impartial observer's estimate of the client's effectiveness, and from the point of view of significant people with whom the client interacts.

To explain how psychotherapy occurs it is necessary to describe it in such a way that a meaningful picture of the psychological process may be provided. Descriptively this can be limited to the question, Under what conditions does psychotherapy occur? Psychotherapy involves one or more clients and one or more professional therapists. The conditions of psychotherapy may be described grossly as a relationship between at least one therapist and one client. In this relationship the client or clients are to be affected in their adjustment. But what constitutes such a relationship? A variety of aspects must be considered.

The Client's Contribution

Primary concern is about what happens to the client; therefore, we shall begin with the client's contribution. The kind of person the client is, the kinds of problems he brings, his typical reactions, etc., will contribute to the kind of relationship that develops. His personality may be described selectively from several theoretical positions, e.g. an *oral character* or a *passive aggressive*. He may be described in several aspects of his functioning, how he thinks and feels, e.g. 'confused'; how he behaves socially, e.g. a 'boor'; the kinds of ego-defenses he uses, e.g. 'over-compensation'; or his typical security operations, e.g. 'political maneuvering.' He may be described as he experiences himself (benevolent); as he expresses himself (pious goodness); as he functions socially (advice giver); as he affects other people (annoyance); or as other people experience him (self-ordained Pope). Descriptions of the client may vary in the way they represent the same aspect of the behavior, e.g. in the vernacular, 'he's a complainer'; in social-role terms, 'he is dependent'; in self-concept terms, 'he feels inferior'; in psychoanalese, 'he is fixated at the oral-biting level.' Ideally, description should be in terms that are most relevant to the psychological processes in treatment. Therapeutically relevant description is an aim rather than an accomplishment. The kinds of descriptions which *may be relevant* must be considered. Finally, the client must be described in temporal terms — at what points in the treatment process do particular kinds of reaction occur.

The Therapist's Contribution

We may shift to the contribution of the therapist in the psychotherapy relationship. What constitutes the therapeutic environment? What are the consequential characteristics of people with whom the client interacts in therapy? The particular therapist, the particular membership of a therapy group, even the physical setting in which treatment occurs, may contribute to the quality of the relationship. Hopefully some aspects of the treatment environment may be more consequential than others. We shall take as our guide those aspects of the therapist and setting which four theories of psychotherapy emphasize.

The required extent for description of the therapist should be generally less than the extent required for describing the client. That is, the therapist responds in relatively defined and controlled ways, while the client responds extemporaneously. Theoretically it might be conceived that *how the client experiences the therapist* is the important contribution that the therapist makes. While *it may be* essential for a therapist to *feel* kindly toward a client in order to be effective, *it is possible* that he need only to *behave* in a kindly fashion in order to have the same effect. It would be economical to limit description of therapist behavior to those aspects which have an effect upon the client. So far, however, how the client experiences the therapist is a problem for investigation rather than an answerable question. Therefore, it seems necessary to describe those aspects of therapists' behavior which are likely to be experienced by clients, and to provide bases for investigating the client's experience as a function of the therapist's activities.

The client's response may be a function of the therapist; what the therapist talks about; how he talks; and his expressive behavior while talking or silent. How does the therapist express himself? What does he express himself about? How does the client experience and respond to the therapist's expression? Such questions are likely to include the functional importance of the therapist in the client's process of change. In order to provide a basis for assessing the functional importance of the therapist, a variety of operations available in psychotherapy literature will be examined and defined. The four theoretical approaches to be assessed provide a rich variety of therapist operations. A systematic analysis and synopsis of the ways in which therapists express themselves, the ways in which they represent the client's functioning, and the ways in which they relate to the client will be described as an operational conception of psychotherapy (cf. Chapters VIII, IX, X, XI, XII).

Evaluating Determinants of Change

In the case of Ellen it was noted that change occurred. We questioned whether the change was necessarily a function of how Ellen felt, or whether how she felt may have been related to changes in her mother, or to her falling in love. The question, What happened? could be answered at only an impoverished level. We were even unable to say that the change was primarily in Ellen. We could not insist that the group psychotherapy was the effective agent in her change, and we were able to question whether change was necessarily improvement.

The problem of describing improvement in psychotherapy, then, requires successive attention to: (a) *the client's behavior* in therapy, to assess the psychological processes in change; and outside of therapy, to assess the results or outcome of the process; (b) *the operations of the therapist* or other group members, as these may affect the client's experience and produce a psychotherapeutic process; (c) *the viewpoint of observers,* both professional and social, as such observers evaluate the worthwhileness and permanency of the client's changes. That change occurs has been demonstrated in many studies of psychotherapy. Dymond (17), for example, has shown in a comparison of fifteen treated and twenty-two untreated applicants for client-centered counseling that there is a significant increase in positive self-descriptions as a result of psychotherapy, and that this change is maintained six months later. Whether such change is necessarily 'improvement' from every point of view is uncertain. Glad et al. (39) have demonstrated that improvement in self-esteem is not necessarily related to improved social competence or acceptance by others. Clients may 'improve' in their own evaluation of their adequacy while they are deteriorating in social effectiveness. The worthwhileness of a particular kind of change depends on the point of view of the person making the judgment.

Change in the client must be described from several points of view, which may be summarized as:

1. *Therapy Process:* The client's behavior in therapy as a function of the therapy situation.

2. *Therapy Outcome:* The client's behavior in his post-treatment environment.

3. *Therapy Focus:* Which aspects of client functioning do change? Does he feel differently? Does he behave differently? Does he have a different impact upon other people? Is he more generally effective?

4. *The Observer's Judgment:* According to whose opinion has change occurred? According to what personal or social criteria is change definable as improvement?

We may summarize the process validity question in terms of how the client expresses, how he functions, how he affects, how he experiences himself and others, and how others experience him. The therapist may be described in terms of how he expresses himself, what he expresses himself about, how he functions in the relationship, and how he is experienced by the client. What is the nature of the functional relationship between client and therapist? This is the essence of the process validity question.

THE DESCRIPTIVE METHODOLOGY PROPOSAL

Technical-conceptual tools are essential to any sophisticated and fruitful investigation of psychotherapy processes. How may data of psychotherapy be represented and analyzed in such a way as to provide a simplified, efficient explanation of the processes involved? Several approaches to this question suggest promising results. Methods to date, however, have focused upon overly limited segments of the problem or upon overextended totalities. Studies of the quality of self-references in typed protocols from client-centered counseling have neglected to examine the expressive behavior reactions of the client in response to such independent variables as counselor operations.[1] The *situation analyses* of Powdermaker and Frank (74) consider such large units that the functional significance of therapists, other patients, or even the patient focused upon is obscured in the gestalten forest. It

---

[1] In that no comparative analyses of counselor operations have been included.

would appear desirable that research be based upon operational definitions of independent therapist variables and dependent client reaction variables, and include analyses directed toward accounting successively for variance attributable to therapists, clients, and temporal periods. Studies attempting to apply these criteria are becoming available (34, 35, 37, 39, 42, 48).

To provide a basis for assessing the contributions of the therapist, the client, and the psycho-temporal period, an over-all method of quantitative synopsis seems essential. Selectivity enters into any attempt to summarize, so it seems useful to consider further how selectivity occurs and how therapeutically relevant selection may be enhanced. As our psychoanalytic summary of Ellen indicated, observation depends upon the bias of the observer. Such a bias may be personally, methodologically, or theoretically determined. In clinical analysis, selective behavior of the therapist is likely to influence what happens in the first place — the therapist's personality and method will evoke particular reactions in the client. The observer's personal or theoretical bias will determine what he will record from all that happens. From these highly selected 'raw' data the analyzer's predilections will emphasize those aspects which satisfy his sensitivities. Such possibilities of bias suggest the proposition that *therapist activities should be ordered into definable and repeatable operations* which may be studied *in situ* as they occur in clinical service, or introduced as independent variables in controlled experimentation. Such problems also suggest the need for a comprehensive, yet synoptic ordering of the data that emerge, so that client reactions may be examined as a dependent function of what the therapist does. Guides for developing an organization of therapists' operations, and a comprehensive synopsis of client behavior may be found in the activities of therapists in the four different approaches to psychotherapy examined in this book. By classifying therapists' operations in different theories, we can avoid the bias introduced by a single system. By describing client behavior from the frames of reference that four separate theories provide, we can include the majority of aspects of client functioning that are considered consequential to psychotherapy, yet avoid unmanageable complexity.

As an example of the importance of clearly identifying and investigating the effects of the therapist's operations, some research on effects of the therapist's operations is illustrative (35, 48, and cf. Chapters X, XI, XII). Generally such research has indicated that the particular things that the therapist does are likely to contribute to the quality of client behavior. In studies comparing the therapist's emphasis upon the client's *social behaviors, feelings,* and *verbal content,* it was found that the client tends to move into the verbal and expressive vernacular of the therapist. Clients become more socially expressive when their behavior is talked about by the therapist. They show more evidence of feelings when their feelings are referred to. They talk more about themselves when the therapist talks about their selves rather than their objects. They become object-oriented if the therapist talks about their objects rather than their selves. Such movement with the therapist is a highly reasonable finding. At the same time, it underlines the necessity for examining the functional importance of the therapist's operations.

It is possible to order observations about the therapy situation in various ways. Observations can be made about the way the client responds to problem situations, with respect to the kinds of feelings expressed, with respect to the social role and interpersonal techniques, or with respect to ego-defenses and security operations. Any or all such observations can be analyzed as a function of what the therapist does and how he is experienced by the client.

What kind of system of representation or measurement can be developed which will render a maximal description of all plausibly relevant aspects of behavior? The question of *validity* to the process of psychotherapy may be a question primarily of *relevance* and *completeness.* If data are relevant but incomplete, interpretive distortion may occur. If data are comprehensively complete, interpretation is likely to be largely irrelevant. Does it matter, for example, about the blinking of the eyelid or the twitching of the big toe on the left foot? *Interpersonality Synopsis* (37),[1] which is derived from the present work, presents technical methods for representing the interactions of therapist and client. These methods are derived from the range of therapist activities and interpretations included in four approaches to psychotherapy. The aspects of therapist and client behavior emphasized by these four theories are included as the essentials of psychotherapy process which require representation and analysis. Such comprehensive methods may be expected to provide a basis for integrated but efficient investigation of psychotherapy problems.

[1] The book *Interpersonality Synopsis* (37) is a detailed theoretical and technical manual for research in the behavioral sciences by this approach.

A Methodological Illustration

To illustrate how the use of several theories of psychotherapy may contribute to the definition of a comprehensive descriptive methodology, we may use examples developed in Chapter I to construct a cross-theoretical model of the client's personality. This methodology will be used illustratively throughout the book.

It will be recalled (p. 12) that Delegate 4 said: 'Well, I mean the white children don't want the Negro children to come in, and they freeze them out if they do, and the Negro children can't be convinced that they'll have a good time or will be welcomed if they do come over for the activity.' This sample expression was used as a basis for constructing a 'typical' leader response from each theoretical approach.

A *psychoanalytic leader response to symbolic meaning* was couched in terms of the sexual fantasy threat quality of the delegate's remark: '*Maybe it's dangerous to put different kinds of children in the same group.*' This leader response suggests at once (a) an emphasis upon the fantasy-symbolic implications of the delegate's remark and (b) that anxiety and threat about sex are involved in this symbolism. In terms of its contribution to a methodology for summarizing psychotherapy process, it emphasizes the symbolic aspects of behavior and the importance of accounting for tensional aspects of the client's behavior, that is:

Psychoanalytical Emphasis

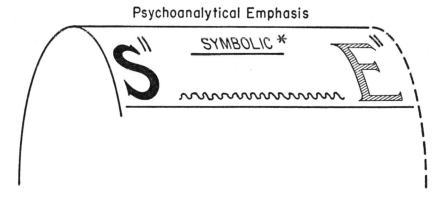

Fig. 2.

* Where S" refers to the symbolic, or fantasy *Self;* E" refers to the symbolic or fantasy Environment, and the notation ⌒⌒⌒ indicates a feeling of tension, anxiety, or threat.

A *client-centered leader response to the verbal content* was presented in terms of empathic re-expression or understanding of the delegate's directly verbalized feeling. The client-centered leader said in one example: *'That makes it pretty difficult and upsetting for you if the children don't get along.'* This leader response emphasizes at once that (a) this is essentially what *you* have expressed or this is *your verbalized feeling* and (b) the situation is unpleasant for you. This type of response adds another mode of emphasis to a methodology for summarizing psychotherapy process. It emphasizes the importance of the client's own verbalized meaning and the importance of recognizing the self-concept aspects of the client's behavior, that is:

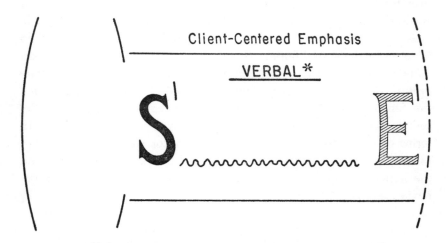

Fig. 3.

* Where S′ refers to the talked about or verbalized Self; E′ refers to the talked about, or verbalized Environment, and the notation 〰〰 again indicates tension.

An *interpersonal psychiatric leader reponse to the expressive behavior* interpreted the meaning in terms of interpersonal values: *'I wonder if you're trying to avoid doing anything about the problem?'* This leader response suggests at once (a) an emphasis upon the expressive social meaning of the behavior and (b) withdrawal, or avoidance of the situation. As a theoretical contribution to a methodology for synopsis of psychotherapy it emphasizes the *social value* of expressive behavior.

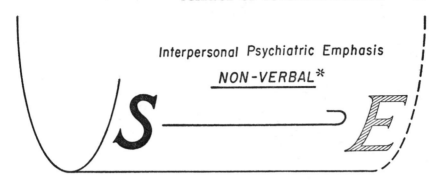

Interpersonal Psychiatric Emphasis

NON-VERBAL*

Fig. 4.

* Where S refers to the expressively behaving Subject or Patient, E refers to the 'real' Environment, and the notation ──➲ represents the social-expressive meaning of withdrawal.

A dynamic relationship leader response suggested that the delegate was implicitly expressing a feeling about the leader himself: 'You're a little irked at me for not seeing the problem.' This response defines a different way of describing behavior; an inferred feeling about the present relationship, and an additional quality of expression, anger, or irritation, as follows:

NON-VERBAL

Inferred Relationship*

Fig. 5.

* Where D indicates delegate, L indicates leader, and ∿∿∿- indicates tension toward a negatively valued object, i.e. anger or irritation toward the leader.

An interpersonality synopsis model may be generated by collecting these several modes of leadership emphasis and qualities into a common diagram and notational system. Figure 6 presents such a model.

The interpersonality synopsis model becomes a method by which the therapist's expressive behavior and modes of emphasis may be rep-

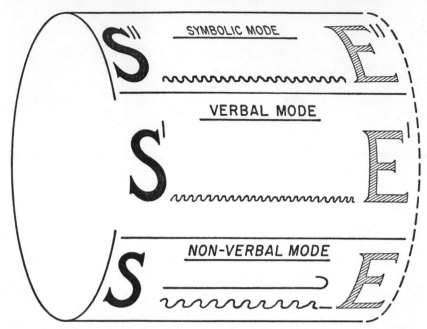

Fig. 6. Spatial and Qualitative Summary of Some Principal Aspects of Theoretical
Group Leader Emphases.

resented, by which the client's or patient's behavior in psychotherapy
may be summarized, and into which the several theories of personality
modification may be cast for purposes of research and clinical analysis.
This model becomes a part answer to the question, What methodology
can be developed that will provide a theoretically and clinically relevant picture of the process of personality modification?

Our review of descriptive methodology problems has indicated that
characteristic values in the therapist's personality, method, and theory
are likely to have selective effects. Such selection may produce biases
in the phenomenon produced, the data selected for representation, and
the conceptual structure imposed as explanation. While selectivity is
essential to the development of theoretical efficiency, it seems scientifically necessary to provide a basis for explicit rather than accidental
determination of how a synopsis is to be made. It is proposed that a
systematic definition of the operations of psychotherapists from four
different theoretical approaches should provide a sufficient variety of
therapist method to allow adequate flexibility in therapist operations.
It is further proposed that the client should be described in the variety

of aspects emphasized by these same four theoretical approaches as a basis for synopsizing the probably relevant aspects of client behavior.

THE SCIENCE AND HELPING PROPOSAL

Theoretical-objective knowledge will contribute to the effectiveness with which psychotherapists help their clients. Psychotherapy practice and psychotherapy research are interdependent. Psychotherapy theory with its insistent questioning has developed from the brilliant insights of clinical practitioners. Effective research in psychotherapy is most likely to derive from theoretically defined problems investigated by clinically skillful researchers. Psychotherapeutic skill is partly dependent upon personal and clinical maturity; yet, it is equally dependent upon a systematic organization of knowledge about psychotherapy processes and upon technical adequacy in applying such knowledge. On this basis it is proposed that the problems of psychotherapy research and practice are relatively interdependent. It may be assumed that one may apply psychotherapy as a precision instrument to the degree that he has a clear organization of the gestalt and particulars of psychotherapy method and process. It is equally plausible that one may investigate psychotherapy process in an effective way on the basis of an organization and specification of operational, observational, and theoretical aspects of the psychotherapy domain. The present approach is designed to represent psychotherapy as a gestalt of interpersonality expression and the particulars of therapist-client interactions. An articulate explication of methods and data of psychotherapy should provide for self-awareness and precision in psychotherapy practice. An organization of the kinds or aspects of behavior that are likely to occur in the psychotherapy client should increase the therapist's flexibility and sensitivity in observing and understanding the client. Thus, the clinical psychotherapist should be able to increase his skill in providing appropriate methods for special problems and in observing more adequately the client's responsiveness and progress. It is not supposed that clinical skill in psychotherapy can be developed from conceptual and technical mastery of the organization presented here. It is only proposed that this organization of theory and data may provide a basis for developing therapeutic effectiveness. We know little about psychotherapeutic specifics for particular problems. We do not even know with certainty how psychotherapy works in general. There is some opinion and 'research' suggesting that psychotherapy doesn't work at all (Eysenck, 19). Hence the contribution of this book to therapeutic skill in clinical practice should be considered as background to conceptual and technical development.

SUMMARY

Although there are many more questions than answers in psychotherapy, the leading theories should provide a basis for relevant investigation and optimally effective practice. The problems may be summarized in relation to theory, validity, method, and practice.

Therapy method derives from theory. Further development of theory in a scientific direction derives from systematic application of psychotherapy methods in research. As a result of the interdependency of therapy method and theory, research is likely to be partial and biased, with theories tending to prove themselves in circular fashion. To modify such circularity it is suggested that an organization of psychotherapy methods from several different theoretical approaches may provide a comprehensive yet theoretically relevant outline of operations and observational techniques.

The aspects of the psychotherapy transaction that need to be described as a basis for relevant research can be defined by the practice of adherents to various theoretical schools. The psychoanalytic, the interpersonal psychiatric, the client-centered, and the dynamic relationship approaches to psychotherapy have provided the raw data for the organization presented here.

The validity problem includes an assessment of which aspects of the client should be observed in psychotherapy and in the extratherapeutic environment, which aspects of therapy need to be ordered into operationally defined and repeatable activities; and of how the interactions of therapist and client over a psycho-temporal period can be described.

The descriptive methodology problem requires representation of the operations of the therapist, the behavior of the client, and a relevant synopsis of what happens in the psychotherapy process. Such an operational differentiation is essential to analysis of psychotherapy process *in* clinical *situ,* or to the design of research involving the controlled presentation of independently defined variables of psychotherapy. The development of a relevant synopsis of therapist and client behavior in psychotherapy is essential to unbiased recording and analysis of either clinical or research protocols.

The practice of psychotherapy is considered to be dependent upon the same background of theory, validity, and method as is essential to psychotherapy research. It is proposed that a mastery of such essentials should contribute to the development of clinical skill.

III. Interrelations of Theories, Operations, and Personality Modifications [1]

To provide some theoretical and operational trail markers, in this chapter we shall illustrate in detail how the relationships of the therapist's concepts, his method growing out of such concepts, and the client's personality may be examined in such a way that the functional interactions of theories, operations, and personality changes may be discerned. To provide such trail markers for later sections of the book, we shall first consider the interactive effects of theory and clinical experience in sharpening theoretical constructs and precisely defining therapists' methods. Following this general discussion, a detailed illustration of psychoanalytic constructs and therapists' operations will be contrasted with interpersonal psychiatric concepts and methods of responding to a patient. This will serve as preliminary technical illustration of the method used throughout the book. Finally we shall consider the potential consequences of psychotherapy theories in modifying the values and behaviors of clients. This value integration assessment will foreshadow the theoretical analyses of theory-therapist-patient interactions to be presented in Chapters X, XI, and XII.

Psychotherapy as a science is characterized by a startling absence of systematic observations or controlled research. Several reasons for this scientific poverty may be summarized as:

1. The problem of *subtlety* — '. . . much psychotherapy is still un-

---

[1] The introductory part of this chapter is a modification of a portion of the author's paper, An operational conception of psychotherapy, *Psychiatry,* Nov. 1956, *19:* 371–82.

definable and inarticulate . . . and dependent on the unverbalized and even unconscious interaction between the therapist and the patient' (47).

2. The problem of *subjectivity* — psychotherapy literature remains relatively '. . . free from objective observations and validated conclusions on the actual events during the psychotherapeutic process with individuals and with groups' (74).

3. The problem of *operational elusiveness* — which may be described as '. . . vagueness as to what constitutes the essential forms of treatment to be compared . . .' (59).

Because psychotherapy is subtle, its operations elusive, and its investigation subjective, a basic research need is for an objective, operationally defined, and repeatable account of what psychotherapists do. The present book proposes an examination of psychotherapy which will lead to operational definitions of interviewer and leader activities and provide a basis for studying interpersonality processes in individual and group interviews as they occur *in situ* or as they may be manipulated in controlled research.

Definitions of interviewer methods have been proposed from several viewpoints, i.e. client-centered verbal categories have been developed and applied in research (Seeman, 90; Snyder, 90; Porter, 79); some operational categories of dynamic psychiatry have been proposed (Coleman, 13; Colby 12; Wolberg, 109); and Strupp (101) has applied Bales's (5) *Interaction Process Analysis* categories to the comparison of client-centered and interpersonal psychiatric operations. Such specifically theoretical or systematic bases for categories of interviewer operations have value for a science of psychotherapies, and have served as catalysts for the development of the integrated structure for psychotherapy research and practice to be presented in this book.

The present approach is intended to provide an operational conception of functional categories of interviewer behaviors. A systematic structure for classifying expressive, value judgment, referential, inferential, and interpretive operations will be proposed following a review of theories.

PRELIMINARY ASSESSMENT OF PSYCHOTHERAPY OPERATIONS

A major problem in defining interviewer operations is to determine which aspects require, and are susceptible to, definition. Fiedler's assessment (23, 24) of the therapeutic relationship suggests that various systems of psychotherapy are similar in defining a relationship that is therapeutic. On the other hand, Strupp's (101) studies indicate that the interviewer's *verbal operations* vary as a function of theoretical persuasion.

The client-centered group supposes that an *empathic* attitude on the interviewer's part is the *sine qua non* of effective therapy; the orthodox analytic position supports an *impassive* attitude, while neo-analytic approaches, for example the interpersonal (33), presume that *any mood or expressive behavior* suited to the situation, except frivolity, is permissible. Studies deriving from the *Interpersonality Synopsis* indicate that variations in what the interviewer *refers to* evoke characteristic reactions (35, 93); that variations in the interviewer's personality or *expressive behavior* influence client responses (94); and that operations typical of particular *theoretical* positions evoke theoretically consistent client reactions (35, 36). Rosen (86) has illustrated that the *level at which symbolism is interpreted* dramatically affects the therapeutic process. The foregoing points of view and research results suggest that a variety of aspects of the interviewer's behavior should be conceptualized and stated in operational terms. Certain aspects are readily amenable to such definitions while others may be difficult or impossible to define. The quality of the therapeutic *relationship,* emphasized in contemporary literature as psychotherapy's basic ingredient, is probably not a separable aspect. It seems more plausible that the relationship quality is a resultant of several or many other aspects which can be defined.[1]

As a basis for developing the most plausibly relevant operations in psychotherapy it seems reasonable that several theoretical approaches would be fruitful. That is, assuming that each theory of psychotherapy has some bearing upon the problem, the author considered that several

[1] Similarly, the gross descriptions 'autocratic' and 'democratic' in leadership methods and their psychotherapy cognates 'directive' and 'nondirective' can be operationally defined in more particular form rather than allowed their status of psychological profanities and blessings.

theories might provide an adequately comprehensive base. The four theoretical approaches that are most active in contemporary psychotherapy service were chosen to provide this background.

As an introduction to an operational analysis of what the adherents of four psychotherapy theories do in practice, it seems useful to consider briefly the interrelations of theory and operations in a somewhat generalized sense.

INTERRELATIONS OF THEORY AND OPERATIONS

Psychotherapy theory formalizes understanding of how change is effected in client adjustment. Such formalized understanding is partly a result of earlier observation of how changes have apparently been produced. As a result of the explanation, certain aspects of the therapist's behavior tend to be emphasized while other aspects are reduced or discarded. The emphasized aspects are likely to be those which are theoretically cogent. The discarded aspects are likely to be those which seem theoretically irrelevant to the client's improvement. Thus, for example, psychoanalysis has developed from the use of hypnotic catharsis, through the interminable recovery of childhood memories, to a current emphasis upon the interpretation of ego-defenses. Observation has led to revision in psychotherapy theory, and revision in theory has further modified clinical practice. Thus, client-centered counseling has developed out of the Rankian dynamic relationship emphasis upon the self, through a relatively neutral nondirective reflecting or rephrasing of the client's responses, to an emphasis upon empathic understanding by the counselor. Such changes in the therapist's operations result from a constant feedback between therapy theory and therapy technique. Rank's dynamic relationship therapy is said to have developed from his experience in predetermining the end of a therapy series. He was attempting to make psychoanalysis more efficient by setting a termination date fairly early in the process. Under these conditions Rank observed that all of his patients responded with birth symbolisms; presumably, they re-experienced the *birth trauma* in symbolic form. This observation led Rank to infer that patients experience conflict between their desires to be independent and free and their fear of losing wholeness or unity with the therapist (symbolic mother). This conceptualization led to modifications in technique designed to make the *current experience in therapy* the major therapeutic agent. Thus, Rank shifted from the psychoanalytic historical-genetic-transference approach to an emphasis upon the meanings of the client's experiences in the immediate therapy relationship. Such concomitant developments in theory and technique illustrate the interplay and feedback of theory and operation. Theory is developed to explain observations. The explanation highlights certain technical features of therapy and thereby modifies both the therapist's method and the client's likely range of responses.

Feedback between theory, operation, and client response is an essential to the development of technical progress. In order to verify experimentally a clinical hunch (or hypothesis), the variables noted in the clinical experience need to be refined and applied under controlled conditions. Thus it becomes possible to identify functional relationships between therapist operations and client behavior. We noted earlier, however, that such circularity may lead to a scientific scotoma.

Uncritical acceptance and doctrinal application of a theory may lead to biases in a clinical situation where the therapist's operations are applied in unsystematic fashion and observations are made without sufficient controls. A further source of error in the process of scientific explanation may result from failure to consider the variety of operations which may produce a grossly similar result, e.g. 'improvement,' or the variety of results which may be obscured in an overgeneralized conception of 'improvement.'

At the present time there is a considerable variety of therapies which lay claim to therapeutic validity. That therapy method makes little difference in the generalized outcome of 'success' has been widely heralded in both clinical and research publications (Fiedler, 23; Appel, 4; Eysenck, 19). Only when the additional question, 'Success of what kind?,' is raised, does it become plausible to consider the special influences of particular methods.

That the kind of change in personality may be specific to the kind of method employed is an explicit proposition of operational research in psychotherapy. It is considered highly probable that results of psychotherapy which are vaguely described as 'successful outcome,' 'improvement,' or 'remission' can be differentiated into the variety of changes in personality adjustment that occur as part functions of the variety of theories and methods employed. A corollary to this proposition is that *the nature of psychotherapy process is diverse.* One process may be engendered by one method, and some other process induced by a different method. By analogy, an organization of a body of knowledge arrived at by a coherent overview of the field, with principles and data articulated into a gestalt, is different from an encyclopedic collection achieved by rote memorization of the material. Or, to change the analogy, no matter how favorable the conditions are for a student to learn in a French class — e.g. a positive relationship to the petite mademoiselle teaching the course — these conditions, enhancing for learning French, are unlikely to produce increments in the student's knowledge of algebra. Similarly, the method of therapy employed is likely to have specialized effects upon personality outcomes; the client will learn to change in the directions the therapist suggests, if the client has positive feelings about the therapist. Thus, *Improvement in what?* rather than *Improvement in general?* seems to be the important question. *Success* may be a misleading overgeneralization which obscures rather than clarifies the investigation of psychotherapy process.

An organization of psychotherapy in terms of several theories is intended (a) to provide a broad basis for conceptualizing the activities of the therapist and therapeutically relevant aspects of client functioning, and (b) to provide a framework from which it becomes possible to consider a variety of 'successful' processes and outcomes in treatment. By examining psychotherapy from four viewpoints, most of the kinds of things that therapists do, and the theoretical kinships of such doings, can be represented. Also, most of the aspects of client behavior which may be relevant to a variety of processes of change can be included in such a broad framework.

These four theories were chosen on the basis of (a) their contemporary popularity, since they appear to be most commonly employed at the present time, and (b) their collective versatility, since they appear to include most of the kinds of therapist operations and client emphases that successful psychotherapies in general include.

GENERAL PLAN FOR EXAMINING THEORY-OPERATION INTERACTIONS

The approach to the problem of relating theories, operations, and client change will include the following: (a) a brief synopsis of those aspects of the theory that directly influence therapist operations; (b) excerpts from psychotherapy protocols presented in such a way as to represent as wide a variety of operations derived from the theory as possible; and (c) the variety of therapist operations and client behaviors, illustrated by protocol excerpts, summarized into functional categories.

Following the separate presentation of psychoanalytic, interpersonal psychiatric, dynamic relationship, and client-centered approaches, a generalized taxonomy of psychotherapy operations will be derived. This taxonomy will provide a basis for a presentation of illustration and exploratory research in the problem of personality consequences of psychotherapy theories and operations.

An Illustration of Relations Between Theories and Operations

As a preview of the process of relating theory and operations in psychotherapy, a synopsis of similarities and differences between psychoanalytic and interpersonal psychiatric concepts with their operational consequences follows. The reader may find such a synopsis difficult at this point, but should return to it after having read Chapters IV and V on psychoanalytic and interpersonal psychiatric theory and operations. The outline includes a brief statement of each of several cardinal propositions, followed by a summary of therapist operations to which these concepts lead.

SUMMARY COMPARISON OF PSYCHOANALYSIS AND INTERPERSONAL PSYCHIATRY

PSYCHOANALYTIC	INTERPERSONAL

I. *Motivation in General*

Common proposition: Biological or physical energy taken for granted.

Biological drives basic motives; two primary types: (a) pleasure striving and (b) destructive striving.	Biological drives for satisfaction considered inconsequential. The need for security in interpersonal relations and the drive toward social maturity are the essentially human motives.
Social motives derivative from reality requirements to express basic drives in socially acceptable form.	

DERIVED OPERATIONS IN PSYCHOTHERAPY

Focus attention upon inner conflicts arising from libidinal strivings in opposition to reality requirements.	Focus attention upon interpersonal meanings in terms of (a) threats to security and (b) strivings toward socially valid behavior.
Example: The psychoanalytic	

PSYCHOANALYTIC

therapist might say to a client: 'Perhaps you're angry at me because you're afraid it's unmanly to show affection?'

INTERPERSONAL

Example: The interpersonal therapist might respond to a similar meaning with: 'Is it possible that you're so critical because you're afraid I don't accept you? We might wonder how you could *legitimately* get approval from others.'

A. NATURE AND ROLE OF ANXIETY

Common proposition: Anxiety is principal motive for defense maneuvers.

Consists of a danger signal that unsuccessfully repressed ego-alien drives are struggling for expression.

Consists of fear of lack of affection from others — a threat to interpersonal security or a fear of loss of approval.

DERIVED OPERATIONS IN PSYCHOTHERAPY

Focus upon associations that relate to the anxiety so that the repressed drives may be recognized and integrated into the conscious ego.
Example: 'What other thoughts do you have about the exam? What are you denying?'

Promote awareness of the anxiety and the security-operations evoked by it so that socially more effective attitudes and skills may be developed. Provide acceptance to the patient so that he may learn that the fear of rejection is inappropriate.
Example: 'I notice your voice trembled when you mentioned how well you did in that exam. I gather that you're uneasy. Did something happen that you're afraid I won't approve?'

B. NATURE AND ROLE OF HOSTILITY

Originally conceived as destructive (Thanatos) instinct. Commonly considered now as a reaction to frustration of pleasure striving.

A security-operation to reduce anxiety. An attacking reaction in the presence of threats to security since hostility is a more tolerable experience than anxiety.

DERIVED OPERATIONS IN PSYCHOTHERAPY

Provide opportunity for client to express hostilities in cathartic fashion. Develop ego strength for

Investigate security threats and sources of anxiety. Reduce hostility by improving security-operations

Psychoanalytic	Interpersonal
recognizing and successfully coping with hostile feelings. *Example:* 'Of course you're angry — why shouldn't you be? It's perfectly all right to be angry here.'	and by providing acceptance for the client. *Example:* 'Just before you got angry a moment ago, did you notice any thoughts or feelings you didn't talk about?'

II. *Personality Structure*

Common proposition: Self-system and ego are somewhat similar, referring to characteristic modes of behavior and awareness. Levels of consciousness are relatively similar, with (a) *unconscious* similar to *dissociated,* and (b) *preconscious* similar to *selectively inattended.* On the other hand, the contents of the unconscious are not similarly conceived.

Personality conceived in somewhat mechanical interaction terms as structural parts: id, ego and super-ego. (a) Pleasure principle is primary law of the id. (b) Reality principle is the primary law of the ego. The ego is the executive function for warding off the repressed and for maneuvering with reality. (c) Ethical and ideal principles are primary in the super-ego. The super-ego is acquired by identifying with parental figures and thereby adopting a system of social values and ideals. (d) Ego-defenses are conceived primarily as techniques for coping with internal pressures and for securing some pleasure in an unrewarding reality.	Personality conceived as a relatively enduring configuration of energy, including: (a) the self-system, developed from a succession of reflected appraisals. The self-system derives from acceptance of others' opinions as to the kind of person one is; (b) significant others who contribute to the self-system and influence current meanings of interpersonal processes; and (c) security-operations which are behavioral means of protecting the self-system from anxiety, and techniques of seeking approval from others.

DERIVED OPERATIONS IN PSYCHOTHERAPY

(a) *Free-association* to circumvent the ego-defenses and facilitate awareness of unconscious conflicts. *Example:* 'Tell me everything that comes into your mind.'	(a) *Focusing* upon and inquiring about inattended or dissociated meanings or behaviors. Calling attention to anxiety-reducing operations. *Example:* 'I thought your eyes became a little moist. Was there something there you felt bad about?'

PSYCHOANALYTIC

(b) *Dream analysis* to develop awareness and acceptance of unconscious motivations.

Example: 'Tell me everything that the golden horseshoe nail reminds you of.'

(c) *Resistance analysis* to develop awareness of ego-defenses and permit development of more effective ego techniques.

Example: 'Perhaps you're not able to talk today because you have some disturbing thoughts about me.'

(d) *Transference analysis* to develop awareness of the irreal quality of one's inappropriate generalization of past meanings into present relations. The nebulous and therefore irrelevant role of the analyst emphasizes the irreality of the transference neurosis and promotes its dissolution.

Example: 'What do you mean, I won't allow smoking in here? I've been smoking all the months you've been coming. I wonder who really imposed the *no smoking* rule.'

INTERPERSONAL

(b) *Synopsizing* information or dreams so that the central meaning is clear.

Example: 'I wonder if the golden horseshoe nail dream suggests your feeling of superiority, and your other feeling of being kicked around.'

(c) *Describing, challenging, reasoning about,* and *valuing* security-operations observed, in order to provide consensually valid understanding of what is effective or ineffective and provoke movement toward more effective interpersonal skills.

Example: 'It seems to me that you have copied your mother's delusions and made some improvements on them.'

(d) *Clarification* and *specification* of parataxic distortions. Requiring precision in thinking and talking about meanings. Pointing up the real as compared to the fictional distortion aspects of the real interpersonal situation.

Example: 'I distinctly recall having said, "You must have suffered from your brother's kidding you about your ears." I did not call you a "donkey." I'm not your brother.'

(e) Providing new experiences in reflected appraisals by challenging the consensually invalid aspects of the self-system and supporting the valuable or socially valid aspects.

Example: 'Certainly you've had trouble being friendly to people. You were afraid of them. But you seem more interested in them now

PSYCHOANALYTIC	INTERPERSONAL

and will probably be more friend-ly.'

III. *Parallel Concepts in Adjustment Techniques*

A. REGRESSION

Common proposition: A return to earlier forms of behavior.

Conceived as a return of libidinal cathexes to earlier fixations, with behavioral derivatives consistent with the psychosexual fixations.	Conceived of as a revival of more primitive security-operations in the face of perceived failure in present functioning.

DERIVED OPERATIONS IN PSYCHOTHERAPY

Focus upon and interpret 'free-associations' about infantile experiences in order to loosen the infantile fixations. *Example:* 'The way you seem to be blissfully enjoying these hours lately, I wonder if I seem like a mother to your infancy?'	Exploration of sources of failure in present functioning and support of the ability of the patient to develop more effective interpersonal skills. *Example:* 'Perhaps you do feel like giving up and being a baby, but you don't need to if you try to handle your boss in more reasonable ways.'

B. DENIAL AND INATTENTION

Conceived as a refusal to respond to certain aspects of the self or environment in an attempt to disregard ego-alien wishes which impinge upon consciousness.	Lack of awareness of behavior or content which is more comfortably disregarded.

DERIVED OPERATIONS IN PSYCHOTHERAPY

Analytic method in general with special reference to dynamics of hysteria.	Calling attention to or describing the inattended aspect, as: 'Did I notice the eyes became a little moist?'

C. REPRESSION — DISSOCIATION

Common proposition: Exclusion from awareness of unacceptable aspects of the self.

Conceived as the ego's warding off and keeping in the unconscious any erotic or destructive impulses	Conceived as a security-operation against the threat that one is unacceptable to significant others.

PSYCHOANALYTIC

which have not been comfortably accepted.

INTERPERSONAL

Exclusion from the self-system of excessively damaging or traumatic experiences and meanings.

DERIVED OPERATIONS IN PSYCHOTHERAPY

Analytic method in general, but especially resistance analysis and dream analysis.

Example: 'Certainly it's more comfortable to enjoy your infancy here than it is to think and talk about unpleasant experiences.'

Providing a fully accepting atmosphere. Calling attention to minimal cues of dissociation such as sudden change in topic or voice tone. Encouraging and inquiring into peripheral thoughts.

Example: 'Of course I accept your story about the grocery bill, but your voice quavered a little when you mentioned that you finally got it straight. Is there anything else you wanted to say about it?'

D. PROJECTION — PARATAXIC DISTORTION

Common proposition: Distortion of the true qualities of another person.

Attributing to another those aspects of the self which one is unable to accept as part of himself.

Seeing others in the present as having the characteristics of historically significant others.

DERIVED OPERATIONS IN PSYCHOTHERAPY

Allowing the patient to develop projections in the transference neurosis and to experience the evidence that it is himself rather than the analyst who produces these meanings.

Example: 'I suppose that your father punished you pretty severely for smoking — and it seems that I'm like he was.'

Being displeased with and firmly correcting the patient's distortions. Helping the patient to experience that the therapist is a new and different person.

Example: 'I am not your father — and you may smoke any time you please. Here, have one of mine.'

E. IDENTIFICATION — REFLECTED APPRAISALS

Taking over attitudes and values of parental figures as a maneuver to implement oedipal repression and defend against attack. Identification with the parent in order to

Seeing oneself as others see one; becoming oneself by accepting the judgment of others about oneself. On this basis reflected appraisals would lead to an imitative (identi-

PSYCHOANALYTIC	INTERPERSONAL
avoid external punishment and controls.	fication-like) development if significant others were to make a 'like me' appraisal.

DERIVED OPERATIONS IN PSYCHOTHERAPY

Incidentally providing the patient with an acceptable identification figure. By positive transference the patient might be expected to identify with a parent as a function of using the therapist vicariously in this meaning.	Providing the patient with many opportunities to be evaluated by the therapist. Helping the patient to develop a consensually valid and mature self-system on the basis of respect and approval from the therapist.
Example: 'Somehow it seems to you that I'm all good and your father was all bad. At least I punish you by requiring you to be prompt, and I control you by insisting that you tell me everything. Isn't that a little like your father's making you read and report on "good" books?'	*Example:* 'I know your father must have made you feel insignificant with his criticism of your reading. But it's obvious that you've become a very literate and intelligent person regardless of what he thought.'

F. SUBLIMATION — SYNTAXIS

Common proposition: Socially valid, effective, and satisfying behavior.

Redirecting libido from direct pleasure seeking into channels where substitute gratification is available in socially acceptable form.	Learning the consensually valid reality of the interpersonal world and developing interpersonal skills consistent with it and satisfying therein.

DERIVED OPERATIONS IN PSYCHOTHERAPY

Analytic method in general, but especially 'transference analysis.'	Interpersonal method in general, but especially the correction of parataxis and promotion of consensually valid communication.

G. TRANSFERENCE — PARATAXIS

Common proposition: Attachment of meanings about historically remote figures to current figures.

Attaching libido and derived meanings of earlier fixations to analyst in an attempt to avoid remembering infantile experiences. The repetition-compulsion princi-	Endowing contemporary figures with fictional images of significant figures from the past. Behaving as though old learnings are completely relevant to current experience.

PSYCHOANALYTIC   INTERPERSONAL

ple is involved in transference re-
enactment.

DERIVED OPERATIONS IN PSYCHOTHERAPY

Transference analysis to develop
awareness of the irreal quality of
one's inappropriate generalization
of past meanings into present relations. Emphasizing the irreality of
transference by the nebulous and
therefore irrelevant role of the analyst. Interpreting transference enactment as resistance to the recall
of infantile experiences.

Example: 'Isn't it possible that
your father was really trying to
help you when he criticized your
reading *Tarzan?* I've been pretty
critical of some of the things
you've said, but you thought I
was helping.'

Clarification and *specification* of
fictional (parataxic) distortions.
Requiring precision in thinking
and talking about meanings. Pointing up the socially real as compared to the parataxic distortion
aspects of the interpersonal situation.

Example: 'It's likely that many
people would disagree with your
thinking I'm the most wonderful
person in the world. But I realize
that one is likely to feel very grateful to someone who listens to their
terrifying experiences.'

This outline comparison of relationships among concepts and operations suggests the method which has been used in the four theoretical
chapters that follow. In order to indicate relationships between theory
and operation, a systematic review of central concepts in each theory
provides a basis for examining the operations of therapists within the
theory. The reader should review the foregoing outline after having
read Chapters IV and V.

PERSONALITY CONSEQUENCES OF PSYCHOTHERAPY THEORIES [1]

Such selective differences in emphasis might plausibly be expected
to produce differences in the kind of personality change to which one
or the other theory would lead.

That hypotheses tend to prove themselves was suggested by William
James many years ago. Some years earlier another pragmatist said,
'By their fruits ye shall know them. Do men gather figs from thistles

[1] Modified from the author's presidential address to the Rocky Mountain Psychological Association, Grand Tetons National Park, June 12, 1956.

or grapes from thorns?' While there is little reason to doubt that scientific data are artifacts of particular methods applied by scientists, it does appear plausible that no hypothesis can be demonstrated as valid unless it has some relevance to the phenomenon which it is designed to investigate. Men gather figs from fig trees and grapes from vineyards because of differences in the two sources. A similar proposition about the consequences of psychotherapy theories requires consideration; namely, that the results of psychotherapies and leadership methods will differ as a function of the theory of personality and the modus operandi of each theory in action. If psychotherapy theories tend to prove themselves, such a tendency is psychologically and socially consequential.

An operational analysis of psychotherapies (34, 36) and the investigation of behavioral consequences of particular operations applied in psychotherapy research, to be reviewed in later chapters (cf. especially Chapters VIII, IX, X, XI), vivifies this question. A considerable body of exploratory evidence tends to indicate that leadership and psychotherapy operations derived from one theoretical system have behavioral consequences which are different from the effects of operations derived from another theory. That is, the theory in action appears to produce behavioral reactions which are consistent with particular theoretical expectations. It seems essential to examine this proposition and to consider its implications.

EXTENT AND IMPLICATIONS OF PSYCHOTHERAPY THEORIES

The reader will recognize that psychotherapy theories include conceptualizations of (a) personality organization, (b) goals for personality modification consistent with the theory, and (c) — implicitly at least — criteria for successful resolution of the problems treated. It has been suggested in several studies that client behavior is a part function of theoretically derived therapist operations. What the therapist or leader does will have discernible effects on how the client or the group behaves. Such empirical outcomes have profound implications for a behavioral science. They suggest, at least, that the kind of personality or social consequence of psychotherapy or group management will be dependent upon the personality theory as it is expressed in operations, goals, and criteria for successful change. What form of personality modification will result from psychoanalytic treatment? Will this be the same personality outcome as a client-centered method produces? Is successful change a unitary phenomenon, or is it one result in interpersonal psychiatry and a different result in dynamic relationship therapy? These questions can be only partly answered from available evidence. Since they are important to the definition of research problems and to the choice of treatment methods, we may explore *probable* relationships among particular theories and anticipated outcomes.

To make this exploration and to introduce the next four chapters, we shall briefly represent each of the four theories of psychotherapy. Particular emphasis will be placed on differences among the theories in goals and criteria for successful treatment.[1]

PSYCHOANALYSIS: The well-adjusted personality is one who has a maximum awareness and acceptance of his primitive erotic-aggressive drives, but who has learned to control and direct these drives in socially effective and personally satisfying ways. In normal development, such good adjustment is achieved in part by successfully identifying with the same-sex parent. In other words, the attitudes, opinions and personality skills of the father or the mother, as the case may be, are accepted as one's own. The well-adjusted young man adopts the mantle of his father.

In maladjustment some failure in the process of becoming a parent-like member of society occurs. The maladjusted personality does not comfortably accept and utilize his primitive drives. His energy is consumed in avoiding self-knowledge. Identification with an appropriate parent is lacking or maladroit.

A part-process of therapy in psychoanalysis is the development of a more successful parental identification. The patient accepts the analyst as a father- or mother-surrogate and identifies with him as '. . . someone who is looked upon as a useful member of human society, who is able to be happy' (cf. p. 67). In making such an identification, the patient accepts his own love-hate affects as legitimate and useful. He accepts the role of a parent-figure who must exercise controls over himself and can legitimately exercise controls over appropriate others.

---

[1] Emphasis upon differences rather than similarities is made for heuristic purposes. The sensitive reader will recognize the necessity for this to be an overemphasis in the interest of contrast.

The picture developed is one of a relatively authoritarian kind of socialized individual. We might call him an emotionally controlled, identified-with-parent, socialized-authoritarian. His criteria for effectiveness and satisfaction are likely to be internal rather than social. His acceptance of other people is likely to be tolerant and utilitarian rather than interested and humanitarian.

Clinical observations of patients in psychoanalysis suggest that they become more comfortably relaxed, they become more parent-like and authoritarian, and they tend to accept their own judgment as a valuable and communication-worthy point of view.

INTERPERSONAL PSYCHIATRY: The socially integrated interpersonal man is one who is comfortable and happy to the extent that he is an accepting and accepted part of his society. Developmentally, such social integration is a product of affectionately efficient mothering. If a child is loved and led into learning conjunctive social attitudes and skills, he becomes an integrated part of the interpersonal process. If he is unloved and berated into the expectation of interpersonal malevolence, he becomes socially disintegrated, giving and receiving rejection and distrust.

The therapeutic process of developing social integration is dependent upon at least three components: (a) the therapist's provision to the patient of acceptance and respect in place of the rejection and derogation the patient has learned to expect; (b) the therapist's helping the patient to relearn his role in the interpersonal process — i.e. the development of socially skillful, integrative behavior is encouraged; and (c) the therapist's presentation of *himself* as a socially valid alternative against which the distorted perceptions from childhood may be compared and corrected. By providing acceptance, understanding and consensually valid correction, the interpersonal therapist promotes the development of interpersonal comfort and involvement in the social process.

The therapeutic product in interpersonal psychiatry, then, can be defined primarily in terms of social integration and effectiveness. As contrasted to the parent-like psychoanalytic product, therapeutic success in interpersonal psychiatry should produce an individual whose adjustment can be defined in terms of social integration. The interpersonal man is one who is comfortable and happy to the extent that he is socially effective and acceptable. He is a friendly person who seeks and gives warmth and understanding. The criterion for success in interpersonal therapy is intensely social and interdependent. The criterion in psychoanalysis is intensely personal and internal.

Methods of group leadership derived from interpersonal psychiatry should produce congruent changes in 'normally adjusted' group members. It seems reasonable that improvement in interpersonal warmth and acceptance, social skill development and a generally well-socialized group should result from interpersonal leadership methods.

DYNAMIC RELATIONSHIP THERAPY: Otto Rank conceptualized neurosis as an ambivalent differentiation of the self from mother-symbols. The neurotic recognizes his difference from others, but suffers fear and guilt as a result of such awareness. The neurotic fears his individuality, yet is caught in a conflict between his desire for creative difference and his need to be a part of mother-society. He both wants and fears to be different; he prefers, yet resists the wish, to be like others. This basic conflict is presumably a residuum of an unsuccessful psychological separation from mother at birth. It comprises a wish to establish creative individuality and the threat of loss of unity with mother and mother-symbols.

Obversely, the well-adjusted personality in the dynamic relationship sense is one who accepts and utilizes his creative selfhood. The artist epitomizes such adjustment. He is different, he is creative; but he pays for any guilt about being different by bringing the products of his genius back to enrich society.

The quality of creative genius adjustment may be emphasized by comparison with interpersonal psychiatry's socialized man. Browning's verse is suggestive:

> Round the cape of a sudden
> came the sea,
> And the sun looked over
> the mountain's rim:
> And straight was the path
> of gold for him,
> And the need of a world
> of men for me.

Rank's creative adjustment is in sharp contrast to Sullivan's social adjustment. Rank would despise the mundane normalcy of Sullivan's interpersonal man. Such clods cannot flower into creative genius. Taft (103) has insisted that the criterion of adjustment in dynamic relationship therapy can never be a social criterion. The dynamic relationship criterion of adjustment is exquisitely individual and creative —never social and conforming.

In successful psychotherapy, the client is expected to be engaged in the ambivalence of reuniting with the therapist and establishing separate selfhood. Theoretically, successful independence can never be achieved without prior satisfaction of the need for unity with another. Hence, the client is encouraged to verbalize and accept his intense relationship to the therapist-mother. Since creative individuality is the therapeutic goal, the client is encouraged to accept and verbalize his need to be different. Technically, both the focus upon the 'living present' and the emphasis upon termination are designed to provide successful experiences in emotional individuality.

It is apparent that dynamic relationship methods of group leadership would lead to different consequences than interpersonal psychiatry. Theoretically, the development of creative individuality rather than social ease and effectiveness would result from the dynamic relationship approach to leadership. Such theoretically definitive differences in anticipated outcomes provide a clear-cut basis for research.

The therapeutic goal is the development of constructive independence. The well-adjusted product of dynamic relationship therapy should be his creatively best self, one who accepts and utilizes uniqueness with a minimum of guilt and without destructiveness toward society.

CLIENT-CENTERED PHENOMENOLOGY: A democratization of Rank's creative individuality is expressed in client-centered, phenomenological theory and method. While Rank despised the common man, Rogers was able to see effective selfhood in everyone. Departing from Rank's relationship focus, Rogers adopted an emphasis upon the self. Behavior and experience are meaningful only from the client's point of view. The capacity to modify one's self and actualize one's possibilities is inherent in every person. The organism strives for self-fulfillment. Such self-realization can be effectively pursued in the presence of an accepting, understanding person such as the client-centered therapist. Thus the principal purpose of the counselor is to provide empathic understanding and genuine — not necessarily verbalized — respect for the client. The therapist's essential equipment is a philosophy of respect for the client's individual worth. This philosophy is implemented by the therapist's assumption of the *internal frame of refer-*

ence. The therapist attempts to see and understand the client's experiences through the client's eyes. He communicates this empathic understanding to the client.

The well-adjusted phenomenological man is one who is able to accept and symbolize all organismic and social processes in conscious awareness. He can experience whatever happens without violation of his self-organization. He is understanding of others because he understands and accepts himself. While not necessarily creative in the Rankian sense, he is consciously and comfortably an *individual* who respects and understands the individuality of others. His relation to the social process is not an insistent belongingness in the interpersonal sense, but an empathic, accepting awareness of the selfhood and individuality of others. Social adequacy is a desirable and expected artifact of personal comfort, but it is a consequence, not a cause.

Phenomenological or empathic methods of group leadership should plausibly lead to different consequences than the psychoanalytic, interpersonal, or dynamic relationship approaches. A group whose leader empathizes with and understands the point of view of the group members provides them with experiences in being understood and accepted. The plausible result should be self-acceptance, empathic awareness of, and respect for the selfhood of others.

SUMMARY

The chapter has reviewed the proposition that psychotherapy theories (a) have characteristic values about personality integration; (b) define characteristic operations for proponents of the theory; and (c) encourage typical expectations about the process of personality change. That *theories tend to prove themselves* has been considered. In raising and exploring this question, we have examined some cardinal propositions from psychoanalysis and interpersonal psychiatry, showing how the hypotheses structure the therapist's response.

We have briefly characterized each of the four theories in terms of how they conceptualize personality, psychotherapy process, and successful outcomes of individual or group interviews. The proposition that the consequences of each theory in action are characteristically idiomatic has been examined. It has been suggested that the following theoretically derived consequences are likely to result from the four approaches to helping people change:

The psychoanalytic patient is likely to become an internally organized, emotionally controlled, parent-like person.

The interpersonal patient will apparently become a socially integrated, accepting, and accepted part of his society.

The dynamic relationship client should become an intensely individual, creative 'island unto himself' with an artistic bridge to the mainland.

The client-centered counselee will develop an internally articulated, comfortable selfhood, prizing his own individuality, and democratically understanding the individuality of another.

The next four chapters will consider, in detail, these points of view.

PART TWO

Psychodynamic Theories, Interviewer Operations, and Client Experiences of Change

Four distinctive theories of psychotherapy are considered for the purpose of developing conceptual backgrounds and operational definitions for methods by which behavior and values may be effectively reintegrated. Part II provides a résumé of psychoanalytic, interpersonal, dynamic relationship and phenomenological approaches to psychotherapy. The principal intention of this section is to define a useful variety of therapists' methods as a basis for the operational syntheses of psychotherapies to be developed in Part III.

And hast thou slain
the Jabberwock?
Come to my arms
my beamish boy . . .
CARROLL

IV. Psychoanalytic Theory and Operations

In psychoanalytic theory and practice, the conception of motivation in terms of conflict between erotic and aggressive strivings leads to the therapist's emphasis upon the client's development of self-understanding and acceptance to the end that aggressive-erotic drives may be modified and expressed in socially acceptable form.

The psychoanalytic conception of personality structure as a dynamic configuration of energy in the service of maximal pleasure, minimal pain, and efficient transactions between internal motives and external environment leads to therapist operations of focusing upon the client's unconscious processes and contents, and upon the client's ego-techniques for maneuvering with reality.

The conception of psychosexual development and fixation leads to operations designed to explore childhood memories and to revive malforming experiences so that such experiences may become memories rather than re-enactments.

Thus the analyst focuses upon: unconscious love and hate conflicts; inferred motives; techniques of self-deception; techniques of maneuvering with reality; valuing attitudes and their sources; and developmental processes and experiences.

The analyst employs operations or techniques of (a) facilitating associations, (b) interpreting resistances and ego-defenses, (c) analyzing dreams, (d) analyzing transference, and (e) interpreting motives. The analyst's expressive role includes either an impassive, distant quality designed to provide a blank screen for transference phe-

nomena, or various forms of 'transference role-taking' designed to modify the patient's transference experience.

OPERATIONS BASED UPON THEORY

The therapeutic operations of the psychoanalytic therapist can be
examined most lucidly in the context of the theory. Hence this chapter
will provide a brief review of psychoanalytic concepts which are essential to a discussion of how psychoanalytic therapists express their theory in operational form. No systematic studies have been made of the
experience of patients in psychoanalysis, yet some personal reports
from patients have suggestive value from the patient's point of view.
Hence this chapter will (a) briefly review psychoanalytic theory in
terms of its bearing upon the psychotherapy transaction, (b) consider
in detail the major methods (or operations) of the therapist, and (c)
illustrate the experience of the psychoanalytic patient.

The psychoanalyst's therapeutic attitude is a result of his conception
of the psychosexual maturity integration of an adequately functioning
personality, the processes that produce maladjustment, the nature of
change essential to healing, and the operations which will implement
the patient's improved functioning.

The most effective personality integration is defined in terms of
psychosexual maturity and includes an accepting awareness of primitive instincts, an effectively socialized and reality-oriented disposition
of these instincts, and a maximum freedom of energy for the pursuit
of satisfaction in the environment.

The processes that produce maladjustment can be summarized as
inordinate degrees of attachment or fixation to infantile modes of adjustment; regressive and inefficient behavior in the face of stress; inordinate amounts of energy devoted to the frustration or thwarting of
primitive drives, with a concomitant lack of pleasure or satisfaction;
and reactions that are inappropriately excessive or minimal to reality
situations.

The process of healing is conceived as a reorganization of the maladjusted processes toward effective personality organization; this includes a loosening of infantile fixations, a reversal of regressive processes, a release of energy which has been devoted to drive thwarting,
the development of skills for obtaining legitimate drive satisfactions,
and the management of behavior in such a way that it expresses psy-

chosexual maturity and becomes appropriate to reality circumstances.

Therapist operations which implement the healing process can be summarized as encouragement of *free-association* to circumvent ego-defenses; *resistance* and *ego-defense analyses* to produce modification of the quality of the ego-defense system and unconscious conflicts; *dream analysis,* to develop awareness, understanding, and acceptance of previously unconscious motivations and ego-defenses; and *transference analysis* to promote awareness of the irrationality and inappropriateness of seeing past meanings in present relationships. In orthodox analytic method the nebulous, *impassive role* of the analyst emphasizes the irrationality of the transference neurosis. In recent technical innovations, the *role-taking* behavior of the analyst is an implement of the same theoretical goal.

AN INTERACTIONAL ROLE DEFINITION OF ANALYST AND PATIENT: This conception of personality process and healing includes an interactional role definition of therapist and patient. The therapist is skilled in providing the unskilled patient with circumstances and understanding which promote personality reorganization. In a sense the analyst says, 'If you become like me you will be well.' This parent-child relationship, with the parent commenting on, explaining, and managing the patient's movement, is consistent with the analytic theory that successful personality development occurs as a part function of identification with an adequate, like-sexed parent. The patient identifies with the analyst as '. . . someone who is looked upon as a useful member of human society, who is able to be happy.' (Schilder, 53).

CRUCIAL ASPECTS OF PSYCHOANALYTIC THEORY

In order to conceptualize the therapist and the client in psychoanalysis it will be necessary to provide a brief elaboration of the general theory of psychoanalysis, detailing the motivational, structural, developmental, maladjustive, and ego-defensive aspects of the theory of personality; and specifying curative functions of the major aspects of psychoanalytic method.

The Biological Instincts of Love and Hate

A theory of motivation is the nuclear essential of any personality theory. What energy or driving forces are postulated? The energy constructs are basic to the rest of the theory. In psychoanalysis the conflicting erotic-destructive or love-hate drives can be seen to determine the rest of the theory's structure.

Biologically derived drives are considered to be the core of motivation. The two drives postulated are the *erotic* instinct, or striving for pleasure, and the *death* instinct, or the striving for destruction. The destructive instinct was originally conceived as a primary drive toward death; it is currently considered to be a reaction to frustration or interference with pleasure strivings. Socialized motives are conceived as derivatives from the reality requirement that pleasure and destructive striving be expressed in socially acceptable form, e.g. dancing or boxing.

Pleasure and destructive strivings are directed toward, or invested in, some object. This notion is expressed as *libidinal cathexis. Libido* is the available amount of energy in the reservoir of erotic drive. Thus, it is possible to think by analogy of *libido* as the amount of *air* blown into a child's balloon as illustrated in Figure 7. The air can be conceived of as the amount of energy in the system, and the disposition of the air expresses other characteristics of the libidinal conception of motivation. Such libidinal interest can be channeled toward and attached to (cathected upon) any kind of object, process or event. Characteristically, libidinal cathexes or emotional attachments are upon the (a) self, (b) objects, and (c) mental products or fantasies. One loves himself, other people and objects, or ideas. Thus the distribution of the air in the balloon in Figure 7-A, represents the notion of cathexis. Libido (energy) is cathected upon oral experiences or genital objects, for example.

Energy Converted Into Personality Structure

The psychoanalytic personality is a dynamic configuration of energy conceived in structural terms.

The id, as shown in Figure 8-A, is characterized by primitive aggressive (−) and pleasure (+) strivings, and is largely unavailable to conscious awareness. This unconscious quality of the id is maintained by various dynamic ego-defenses which are designed to keep a comfortable lid upon the raw, uncouth erotic-destructive impulses. The primary striving of the id is for libidinal satisfaction, for pleasure. In unmodified form such pleasure seeking is unacceptable to consciousness because it conflicts with the requirements of reality.

The ego is an energy system which assumes the executive function

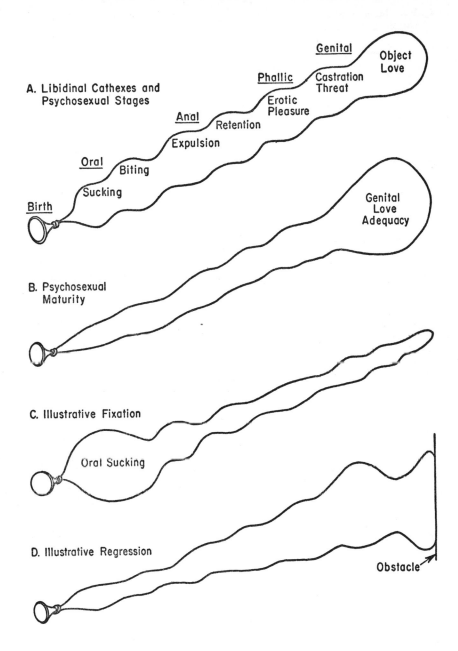

Fig. 7. The Concepts of the Quantitative Nature of the Libido, Cathexis, Psychosexual Development, Maturity, Fixation and Regression as Represented in an Elongated Balloon Analogy.

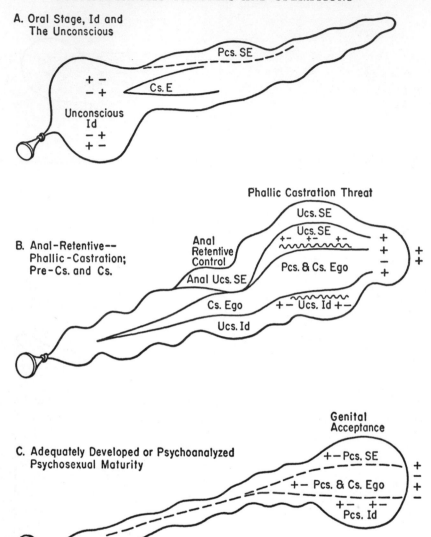

A. Oral Stage, Id and
The Unconscious

Pcs. SE

Cs. E

+ −
− +

Unconscious
Id
− +
+ −

Phallic Castration Threat

Ucs. SE

Ucs. SE

B. Anal-Retentive--
Phallic-Castration;
Pre-Cs. and Cs.

Anal
Retentive
Control

Anal Ucs. SE

+− +− +−   +
+
−
+

Pcs. & Cs. Ego

Cs. Ego

+− Ucs. Id +−

Ucs. Id

+
+
+

Genital
Acceptance

C. Adequately Developed or Psychoanalyzed
Psychosexual Maturity

+− Pcs. SE

+− Pcs. & Cs. Ego

+− +−
Pcs. Id

+
−
+
−

Fig. 8. The Concepts of Id, Ego, Super-ego, and Conscious, Preconscious, Unconscious, in Relation to Psychosexual Development.

of personality. It is the specialized organization of energy which wards
off or transforms unconscious libidinal strivings so that an acceptable
compromise with reality can be achieved. A variety of ego-defenses
or adjustment mechanisms such as repression, denial, reaction-formation, projection, or sublimation become the instruments of the ego

in its continual maneuvering between the primitive insistence of the id and the harsh requirements of reality. The ego functions to maintain a balance between the constant pressures of primitive drives and the sources and forms of satisfaction available in reality.

The reality principle — that is, the transformation of pleasure or aggressive striving into socially acceptable, self-gratifying forms — summarizes the ego's mode of operation.

The super-ego is the ethical or idealizing function of personality. It is developed by identification with parental figures and the adoption of parental social values, ideals, and moral codes.

The super-ego is largely in control of the ego and is in intense opposition or reaction-formation against the immorality of the id's attachments and strivings. The super-ego's criticism of the ego produces a sense of guilt and insufficiency, the roots of which are obscured in the relatively unconscious quality of the super-ego.

Levels of Awareness

There are three levels of awareness postulated by analysis. These include the unconscious, the preconscious, and the conscious. Both the id and the super-ego are largely unavailable to conscious awareness; a person is unable to focus upon and examine his id and super-ego processes. He does not recognize his primitive striving for pleasure or destruction. He recognizes only vaguely the sources of his ethical code or ideals. The preconscious is relatively available to self-inspection. It is possible for a person to become aware of certain aspects of his functioning which are not normally in focus. The ego is largely preconscious and conscious. The conscious is that part of mental contents that is readily in awareness.

Developmental Processes and Problems

In considering the psychoanalytic conception of psychosexual development it will be possible to develop a fairly clear integration of the motivational and structural aspects of personality as these emerge in development. Figure 8 is especially designed to suggest these relationships.

ORAL STAGE, ID, AND UNCONSCIOUS: At birth the human infant is all id. His behavior is completely under the sway of the pleasure principle and he has neither techniques nor occasions for manipulating reality. The world is not differentiated from himself and is relatively at his command. At this point in development, the infant's primary channel for gratification is the mouth — he is completely oral in his libidinal satisfactions. Depending upon how he is treated at the oral stage he will develop expectations of being satisfied — loved and cared for; expectations of being deprived and helpless — neglected by the parent figure; or expectations that the world is undependable — sometimes barren and sometimes giving. These oral experience meanings become largely unconscious or unremembered in later life.

ANAL STAGE, EGO, AND CONSCIOUS: As the infant begins to experience the separateness of himself and the rest of the world, a part of the id energy becomes differentiated into an ego organization — that is, a system of energy is organized for maneuvering with reality in order to gain maximal satisfaction with as little displeasure as possible. This governing energy system has the problem of deciding which pleasures can be achieved immediately, which have to be delayed or rejected entirely, and what sources of satisfaction and means for achieving them are most effective. Experiences associated with toilet training as well as some oral experiences are especially crucial in defining the nature of reality and its relationship to bodily gratifications. The toilet training experience defines some of the conditions under which satisfactions may be achieved. The ego, then, defines the quality of relationship between one's primitive drives and the conditions under which they can be satisfied in the world. Thus the ego is largely conscious or available to consciousness, i.e. preconscious.

PHALLIC STAGE AND SUPER-EGO: As the male child reaches an age at which he becomes aware of the pleasurable possibilities in the genital organs, he is placed in the very dangerous position of being threatened by his interest in this source of pleasure. Since his love object by this time has become the mother, he perceives himself to be in competition with father for her affection. This makes him fear that he will be punished by castration for his interest in mother. Before this he has taken mother as an identification figure. Being closest to mother, he has assumed that he is like her until he discovers that boys have penises and mothers do not. Now he fears that his competition with father will be punished by the loss of this prized erotic possession. Resolution of this castration threat is accomplished by forcing his erotic interest in mother — and other girls — back into the unconscious and by assuming internal controls over his dangerous erotic wish. To implement this accomplishment and at the same time to

obtain some vicarious satisfaction of the repressed wish, the boy identifies with or takes over the socially accessible aspects of his father's
behavior, ideals, and moral standards. In other words, he attempts
to pattern himself after his father in order to protect himself from
father's wrath. This maneuver provides the core of the super-ego, the
internalized parent, which thereafter protects the boy from the father
because the unacceptable erotic interest in mother is forced out of
consciousness and the penis is legitimatized by fitting into the image
of being like the internalized father. At the same time the erotic wish
is vicariously gratified through being like the father, who has affectional access to mother.[1] Thus, in Figure 8-B the phallic castration
threat is shown as unconscious super-ego developed at the point where
the boy resolves the oedipal conflict by identifying with father. Figure
8-B also shows that certain anal unconscious super-ego qualities may
be retained in such a boy from his experiences in toilet training, where
the mother may have contributed her bit to a feminine-cleanliness
value super-ego quality.

In this nontechnical discussion of psychosexual development we
have considered the notions of infantile omnipotence; oral, anal, and
phallic phases of development; fixation; libidinal cathexis; primary
and secondary identification; the oedipus conflict and its resolution;
the development of the ego and super-ego out of an interaction of the
id with reality; and the processes and techniques of repressing unacceptable impulses into the unconscious. A more technical consideration of these is beyond our immediate purpose except as they are
represented in the psychotherapy transaction. It is essential, however,
to consider how psychosexual maturation may go wrong in the dynamics of maladjustment.

Fixation, Regression, and Dynamics of Maladjustment

At any stage in psychosexual development, untoward developments
such as excessive pressures, insufficient or overly sufficient gratifications, or absence of appropriate affectional objects may provoke personality malformations with attendant internal or external difficulties.
Psychoanalytic therapy is, of course, primarily concerned with the
modification of maladjustment. Hence, a brief consideration of the
psychoanalytic theory of neurosis and psychosis is in order. The con-

---

[1] An anal super-ego is equally likely, in which case the arbiter of toilet training
becomes the principal source of ethical values — e.g. the mother.

cepts of repression, fixation, regression and ego-defense are essential to the understanding of neurosis and psychosis. We have already noted that the ego is developed as a system of channels and barriers between the primitive, unconscious id and the requirements of reality.

SUBLIMATION OR REPRESSION? Those impulses which cannot be effectively channeled or *sublimated* into socially effective means of gaining satisfaction are warded off and denied both expression and awareness. The ego determines whether an impulse can be gratified with more satisfaction than pain. If the means of satisfaction are perceived as too painful, the wish is denied or relegated to the unconscious. The process of warding off such unacceptable wishes is called *repression*. However, repression is never quite successful. Denied wishes remain active, continually seeking expression and gratification. Consequently the ego has to mobilize energy to keep such instinctive criminals chained in their subterranean dungeons. This guarding is never quite successful, so the discarded wish may furtively accomplish some excursion into slips of speech, mistakes, dreams, and personality distortions. Anxiety is experienced when the wish gets close to being heard without being recognized and accepted.

FIXATION: Fixation or overinvestment of libido occurs whenever there is an excess of either gratification or deprivation at any particular point in psychosexual development (see Figure 7-C). If pleasure in being fed is inordinate, the person cathects orality; he puts an overemphasis upon the values of and behaviors associated with taking nourishment. Likewise, if there are other irregularities about the food-taking process, such as excessive deprivation, an excessive importance (libidinal cathexis) is attached to the oral activity. While such fixations do not stop psychosexual development, they leave less energy free for succeeding phases and thereby produce less effectiveness in the development of mature modes of adjustment. As a consequence of such psychosexual fixations of libido, reality relationships may be managed ineffectively and excessive frustrations may develop. Such fixations provide bases for *regressive* processes.

REGRESSION: Returning to more infantile modes of behavior is the process of withdrawing libido, interest, or energy from more mature modes of adjustment and reinvesting or cathecting modes of adjustment that have acquired libidinal fixations at a more primitive level (see Figure 7-D). If a person becomes overwhelmed by difficulties at levels for which he has acquired insufficient interests and ego skills, he is likely to withdraw from these more mature levels of adjustment and fall back upon levels that were more important to him. Thus the hysteric regresses to the oedipal conflict, the obsessive compulsive to anal fixations, and the schizophrenic to an oral sucking, deprivation adjustment. Like *fixation*, however, *regression* is a partial rather than a total process. Components of more mature adjustment may be retained in the presence of primarily *regressive solutions* to the failure of the ego. When mature ego-defenses become insufficient, the ego falls back upon less mature and genetically earlier techniques of achieving its compromise between the demands of the id and the requirements of the world.

Ego-defenses

Those methods or techniques which the personality develops for maintaining its balance between id instincts and the reality situation are known as ego-defenses. A complete catalogue of these is not essential to our present purpose. The ego-defense system can be illustrated by oversimplified discussion of *anxiety, repression, denial,* and *sublimation.*

ANXIETY: Although it is not an ego-defense, anxiety is conceptually essential to understanding the ego's functions. It is the danger signal to the ego that something is getting out of hand. A repressed wish is storming the repressive rampart. Anxiety is like the flurry of excitement caused by an unidentified pip on a radar screen. Something alien and dangerous is approaching! We don't know what it is! What do we do now? In such duress the defense command goes into action to protect the base against the dangerous intruder. In other words anxiety is the immediate drive to the mobilization of ego-defenses. Something must be done to keep things comfortable. The ego goes into action to implement and fortify the repressive barrier so that the alien impulse will be warded off or allowed expression in some comfortably disguised form.

REPRESSION: The ego's primary defense system against awareness of ego-alien impulses is called repression. The greater the number of impulses that are denied some kind of acceptable satisfaction, the greater the energy required to repress them. Since repression is an energy structure rather than a wall, it requires energy reserves in proportion to the strength of the drives it is intended to control. Hence, the scope of the repressive function determines the amount of energy available to the ego for other more effectively realistic functions. A major difference between neurotic and psychotic reactions can be conceived in terms of the scope of repression. In neurosis, the ego is weakened and debilitated by excessive demands for energy in the service of repression. In psychosis, repression is defeated by the unconscious id as the instincts and contents of the unconscious overwhelm the ego. Reality as such is no longer coped with when the ego succumbs to the demands of the id.

DENIAL: The technique of denial is a more transparent defense than repression. It is essentially the assertion that 'I refuse to recognize the wish that is plaguing me.' By denial the ego cuts off the reality event or bodily process that is involved in the denied wish. The man who refuses to be aware of the 'well-turned ankle' or the 'curvaceous breast' is saying, 'I cannot allow myself to notice these things because they are dangerously attractive to me.' Such denial is closely akin to both symptom formation and repression. It is close to symptom formation in the sense that hysterical blindness is an easy step away. It is close to repression in that it maintains the wish in the unconscious. As an illustration of the ways in which ego-defenses relate to techniques for dealing with reality, denial demonstrates that the ability to respond to and manipulate reality is limited or deformed by the ego-defense.

The effectiveness of the ego in handling problems of adequate living is reduced as a function of the defensive maneuver to keep the alien wish from expression. Thus, the ego is impaired in two ways as a result of its defensive maneuvers: (a) the amount of available energy or interest (libido) which can be directed toward the reality problem is reduced in proportion to the amount of libido that is bound up in repression, and (b) the effectiveness of the ego's methods for managing reality problems is limited by the degree to which ego-defenses distort or interfere with ego-skills.

SUBLIMATION: That ego-skill which transforms the uncouth primitive striving of the id into efficient or socially effective methods of coping with the physical and social environment is known as sublimation. Every id impulse has some potential source of gratification in the environment if the ego's means of achieving gratification are socially efficient and skillful. Even though sex and aggression are condemned in many expressions, they are lauded in other forms. To the degree that the ego can transform instincts into socially acceptable or efficient modes of expression it has achieved control of the id and has succeeded in mastering reality. Sublimation, then, includes the socialization of id impulses and the means by which the ego gains strength and adequacy in its bargaining with reality. The bargain achieved is that reality forces the personality to make its demands in acceptable form if they are to be honored. The id agrees that it will become ego and will finesse its requirements upon the world in an attractive package. The broker, ego, thus enlists both seller and buyer in his service.

THE ANALYST'S EMPHASES IN RESPONSES TO THE PSYCHOANALYTIC PATIENT

This brief outline of psychoanalytic theory has been intended to focus upon the essential personality concepts which determine how the analytic therapist responds to his patient. The following section will be concerned exclusively with an elaboration of the psychoanalytic therapist's operations (or techniques) in treatment. As an introduction to this operational assessment we may recapitulate the survey of psychoanalytic concepts in terms of their effects upon what the analyst will do in psychotherapy. It has been seen that the analyst's therapeutic attitude is largely determined by his conceptions of the psychosexual maturity nature of effective personality integration. His intention in treatment is to provide circumstances and techniques which will disrupt maladjustive — regressive and defensive — processes and promote the development of a person who is able to accept his traumatic experiences and conflicting instincts in conscious awareness so that he may express his needs in realistically efficient form. Hence, the analyst attends to and manipulates the patient's behavior and verbalizations in psychotherapy with special reference to the many symbolic meanings which are likely to express the psychoanalytic conception of personality.

The psychoanalytic therapist is especially sensitive to:

1. Indications of erotic-destructive energy conflicts and the objects, experiences, or people toward whom such love and hate attachments are made.

2. The unconscious strivings of id impulses and the need for such impulses to be integrated into consciousness.

3. The ego's techniques and energy system for keeping such im-

pulses and conflicts out of awareness and for handling reality in practical ways.

4. The sources and nature of the super-ego to the end that it might be more conscious and mature.

5. The three levels of awareness in that unconscious meanings are considered to be especially important in influencing behavior. It is essential that they become conscious in order for behavior to be modified.

6. Developmental processes, since the effectiveness of the individual depends upon how well he is able to give up his infantile fixations and direct his energies into psychosexually mature forms of gratification. This becomes especially crucial in the problems of *repetition-compulsion* and transference analysis during treatment.

7. Maladjustive processes in terms of repression, fixation, regression, and ego-defenses against anxiety, since these are the crippling maneuvers which the personality has brought into treatment. Modification must be achieved by reintegrating the personality in such a way that the patient can accept himself as a consciously controlled, genitally mature person who does not need infantile satisfactions, who can look at himself without aversion or denial and who can integrate his primitive drives into socially and personally competent expression.

Such personality concepts in psychoanalysis have crucial influence in determining the character of the therapist's operations in providing a curative process. It will be observed that the principal problem is, How can this unhappy, maladjusted *child* become a comfortably accepting and efficient parental figure? How can the intolerable unconscious strivings be integrated into effective energy for conscious ego functioning? The analyst's operations are answers to such questions.

Principal Operations in Psychoanalytic Therapy

Operations implementing psychoanalysis may be subsumed under the topics of: (a) encouragement of free-association, (b) resistance and ego-defense analysis, (c) dream analysis, (d) transference analysis, (e) motivational analysis, and (f) role-taking operations. Since these provide a core outline of the operational problem, they will be illustrated in some detail.

ENCOURAGEMENT OF FREE-ASSOCIATION: In traditional analysis the patient lies on a couch with the analyst out of sight, providing a maximal opportunity for the patient to say whatever comes into awareness. Jones (53) describes Freud as asking '. . . his patients to refrain from concentrating on any particular idea and from consciously guiding their thoughts.' E. Glover (43) says that in free-association 'powerful drives and affective charges of the unconscious system' are allowed 'to operate in as unhampered a way as possible during waking hours.' The analyst '. . . does not argue or persuade, he does not praise or condemn. He does not advise,' he simply enforces the rule that anything that occurs to the patient must be expressed (J. Glover, 53).

Essentially, the patient is instructed to express whatever comes to his mind and not try to put it into any reasonable or logical form. The question may immediately be raised, however, as to how free free-association is. We have noted that the analyst has certain psychological expectations and is at least passively participating in the therapy transaction. Both the patient's expectations from what he knows about psychoanalysis and the quality of the therapist's interventions will impose conditions upon the freedom of associative trends. Ferenczi (53), for example, has proposed that free-association may be used for the purpose of resistance. If the patient produces a series of superficial word associations it provides little basis for dynamic sense. Hence, the patient's use of meaningless associations should be interpreted as resistance.

Thus the encouragement of 'free-association' might be rephrased as the encouragement of associations which provide clues to dynamic understanding. Some examples of therapist intervention and management of free-association are suggestive:

PATIENT: 'I went to a meeting this morning — it wasn't important — the car needs greasing — I'll have to take it in — I don't seem to be able to think of any dreams though I'm sure I've had some the last couple of nights. You looked sort of annoyed when I came in — I wonder what I've done that makes you seem so unfriendly. It's beautiful weather these days — I'd sure like to take a day off and go to the beach — it's ——'

ANALYST: 'What have you thought about me lately?'

PATIENT: 'Nothing especially — oh, I guess I've wondered why you put up with me when I'm sure you could find more interesting patients. Then when you sort of glower when I come in, I'm afraid you're displeased and that you'll decide to cut me off. But it really doesn't concern me. I know you don't have any feelings about me one way or the other — so why should I care about what you think?'

ANALYST: 'What do you mean — you're afraid that I'll cut you off?'

PATIENT: 'I know what you mean — but all I was talking about is that I think I need help some way — and I'm afraid that you won't be willing to give it to me.'

It will be seen in this excerpt that the analyst interrupted a series of apparently free but meaningless associations to focus upon one aspect, which then directed the patient's thoughts and feelings toward an essential problem. Seen in the light of the subsequent productions, the first series of associations were not meaningless at all — that is, they might be rephrased at a latent content level as follows:

Manifest Content	Latent Content
'I went to a meeting this morning — it wasn't important.'	'I failed at a meeting this morning.'
'The car needs greasing — I'll have to take it in.'	'I'm sexually inadequate and need help.'
'I don't seem to be able to think of any dreams ——'	'I don't understand myself.'
'You looked sort of annoyed when I came in.'	'Are you displeased with my failures?'
'It's beautiful weather these days.'	'I deny that I've said anything aggressive.'
'I'd sure like to take a day off and go to the beach.'	'I'll go home to mother — she loves me.'

The analyst's focus upon 'thoughts about me lately' interrupted the patient's production and shifted associations in two directions: (a) toward concern about inadequacy and affectional deprivation in general, and (b) toward a suspicion that the analyst was fishing for castration fears.

While this example suggests that associations are controlled by the analyst upon occasion, it also suggests that the analyst's control may lead associations into theoretically valuable channels, and that the analyst's control may be essential to facilitate theoretically valuable production. Whether this kind of value direction is of worth to the patient depends of course on the pragmatic adequacy of the therapist's operations rather than the theory itself.

It will also be recognized that the analyst could have focused upon many other aspects of the patient's production. He could have said: 'The meeting didn't go well?'

'How are you getting along with your wife?'
'You're distressed about not remembering dreams?'
'You feel that you're falling down in your work?'
'What are you afraid of?'
'You feel as though no one cares about you?'
'What have you thought about mother?'
'You don't want me to think you're criticizing me.'

These are also potentially valuable interruptions, but they would probably have changed the course of association in different directions.

RESISTANCE AND EGO-DEFENSE ANALYSIS: *. . . whatever interrupts the progress of analytic work* has been defined as resistance (29). Thus, for example, unwillingness to release repressive energy, refusal to give up the economic value of symptoms, and re-enactment of infantile experiences in the transference in order to avoid recognition of repressed memories are forms of resistance. Even the desire to be in treatment may express resistance, since it can sometimes satisfy an unconscious fantasy of being mothered.

Ego-defenses are commonly mobilized in the service of resistance. Thus repression is the major ego-defense against conscious awareness of id impulses. Symptoms are forms of ego-defense which implement repression by translating the repressed wish into a symbolic and disguised expression. Re-enactment of infantile experiences in the transference is an implementation of repression in that the ego asserts to the analyst, 'See, this is something you are making me do, and I deny that it ever happened before.'

In our example of an analyst's interruption of free-association the intent was apparently to reduce resistance and facilitate more productive associations. The analyst noticed that much of the associative content was coming close to feelings of fear and anger, but that the patient was skillfully sliding past these feelings. The therapist's focus on 'thoughts about me' was intended to be an invitation for the patient to think about his fear and anger without danger from the analyst. Perhaps, the patient was experiencing an irrealistic fear in his eleventh month of analysis and it was repressed hostility and fear about father that he was latently expressing. Hence the analyst's interruption was to circumvent the transference re-enactment and to loosen the repression about the infantile experience.

Another example illustrates the use of symptoms as resistance. This patient has intermittently reveled in feelings of depression, talked about the meaninglessness of life, a half-way wished-for and expected death, fear of graveyards, and the futility of everything that he does. As his analysis is nearing termination these symptoms are exacerbated into physical complaints including occasional attacks of tachycardia, stomach distresses which he thinks probably suggest an ulcer, and a chronic elevation of blood pressure. Even though physical examinations are consistently negative he retains the physical disabilities and the expectation of death. At the same time he is ostensibly comfortable and even happy about the approaching termination of his otherwise successful analysis. A brief excerpt from a late stage in the analysis will illustrate the resistance and ego-defense analysis of such symptoms:

PATIENT: 'There must be something wrong with that X ray department — they can't seem to find anything that's causing all this pain and weakness. I wish they'd get the lead out. It's amazing how stupid a bunch of medical technicians can be. The way that woman doctor let my father die because she didn't have enough guts to call in a specialist — seems to be the same sort of thing. It seems to me that you're willing to let me die too. You don't seem to care one way or another about my health. You just wonder if there isn't some psychological cause for it.'

ANALYST: 'What have you thought about ending the analysis?'

PATIENT: 'Oh, that — I'm pretty pleased about it — I almost cried after I left here the day you first mentioned it. It seemed to me that you were being very good — saying that you thought I was ready to quit.'

ANALYST: 'But you seem to be in worse physical health than you've been since we started.'

PATIENT: 'That's true, but I guess I can take care of that somehow — at least you've done all you can for me — I do wish, though, that they could find out what's wrong. I don't want to die like my father did.'

ANALYST: 'I wonder if all these troubles you're having could be a bid to keep from terminating analysis?'

PATIENT: 'Certainly not — I'm really pleased at the prospect — and grateful to you for what we've accomplished together — but there's nothing you're willing to do about my illness. Oh — I guess I do feel bad about leaving — and since you're a doctor you should be able to do something besides listening and making bright comments.'

ANALYST: 'You're pretty angry at me for letting you die like your father.'

PATIENT: I guess I am at that — I've said a lot of hostile things to you lately — maybe that's why you want to have me stop. And when it comes right down to it — I hate to give this up. It may be all right to be a responsible person — but I don't know if I can go it alone.'

In this sample it will be seen that the analyst raises questions about the possible meanings of the physical symptoms — leaving the patient to fill in the gaps as to emotional reactions that might be served by physical illness. The sample suggests that the symptoms are partly symbolic in quality — tachycardia as a symbolic equivalent of identifying with his father's death, gastric distress in reaction to the withdrawal of affectional supplies; and partly tensional — elevated blood pressure in reaction to repressed rage at the analyst and the father for deserting him. The value of the symptoms in the psychotherapeutic transaction was apparently as a plea for further attention from the analyst and a bid for postponing termination. These meanings were brought to the patient's awareness when the analyst inquired about such possibilities.

It will be observed then that analyses of resistance and of ego-defenses are essentially about the same aspects of the client. What techniques or maneuvers does the ego marshal to avoid awareness of the unconscious? What maladjustive methods does the ego employ in coping with reality and maintaining its self-deception?

DREAM ANALYSIS: 'The kernel of the dream is wish-fulfillment, imaginary gratification of repressed wishes' (53). As such it is *the royal road to the unconscious*. The dream, then, is of special importance to the psychoanalyst because it provides a more complete expression of unconscious strivings than does any other form of behavior. Dreams are not directly interpretable, however, since their manifest content — that is, what they express directly — is not their important meaning. 'A dream is the disguised fulfillment of a repressed wish; it is a compromise between the demands of a repressed impulse and the resistance of a censoring force in the Ego' (Freud, 53). Thus, it is the latent meaning of the dream — the wishes which it symbolizes — rather than the manifest or apparent meaning, which is of consequence. The dream is rarely interpreted directly. The various elements of a dream are taken as starting points for free-association — and the meanings to which such associations lead become the basis for dream interpretation. Thus, the essential therapist operations in dream analysis are the same as those in other therapeutic maneuvers. For this reason no special examples will be given.

TRANSFERENCE ANALYSIS: The transference is considered to be the most therapeutically valuable aspect of the psychoanalytic process. In transference the patient responds to the analyst as he has earlier to significant people in his development. That is, he transfers to the analytic relationship feelings, behavior, and perceptions that were appropriate to, or experienced in relation to, parents or other important figures in his life. E. Glover (43, 44) has distinguished three phases of the transference process.

The opening phase may be characterized as *transference development;* it is the experiencing of positive or negative reactions to the analyst, or an alternation of positive and negative reactions. In a sense the patient experiences that he is in the old parent-child relationship. This provides a readiness for experiencing intense emotion. In this phase, the analyst does not respond overtly to transference expressions, except to allay anxiety and promote transference development.

The second phase is described as *transference neurosis.* At this point the transference attitudes are expressed in an acting out of the Oedipus experience. The analyst comes to represent the parent as a love object. Associated with this affectional attachment are all of the old ego-defenses, anxieties, and incest taboos that were resolved at an earlier period. These disturbances are revived with intense feeling, and the analyst is target, or object, of the feelings.

The final stage is a *dissolution of the transference.* The 'artificial neurosis' is cured by demonstrating to the patient that his feelings are not relevant to the current circumstances but are a repetition of what has happened in earlier relationships. Thus the repetition of earlier reactions is recognized for what it is, the re-enactment of a memory; and the necessity for such re-enactment is resolved by putting the memory in proper perspective.

In other words the patient brings his old attitudes and feelings into analysis, experiences that the analyst is a lovable or hateable person, then re-enacts and experiences the same struggle with his picture of the analyst that he has gone through with his parents. This transference neurosis is a heroic struggle of the ego to maintain repression of the childhood memories themselves. As the analyst is able to point out that the transference neurosis enactment really has no excuse in the present situation, the ego is trapped into admitting its self-deception and allowing the repressed memories into consciousness. Thus the patient begins to differentiate the aspects of his behavior that were attributable to the infantile re-enactment and to recognize other aspects of his behavior in every-day life that are a result of irrealistic expectations rather than validily pertinent to present experiences. As a consequence he is able to work toward the development of more objective perceptions and reality-valid behaviors.

A sample from analytic interpretation and dissolution of the transference is as follows: The patient had gone through an original stage of very positive transference toward the analyst, thinking in general that his therapist is a very wonderful person. There had been occasional covert expressions of hostility — usually in an apologetic, self-abnegating form. As the patient developed a sense of acceptance in analysis he reveled in the experience, sometimes preferring to lie on the couch silent and blissful in what he experienced as a protectively mothering atmosphere. This was interpreted as resistance and gradually became supplanted by fears of rejection and desertion. His associations began to revolve around memories of an extremely harsh father who had made him do all of the crumby, unpleasant chores at home and who had beaten him into submission at the slightest signs of rebellion. He remembered only the unpleasant relations to father and managed to change even positive gestures from father into further evidence of meanness. At the same time he kept a fairly affectionate attitude toward the analyst — expressing only occasional gripes. On the other hand he brought in several memories of the bloopers and stupidities that physicians had pulled, including his accusation that one physician had allowed his father to die unnecessarily. These were interpreted by the analyst as indirect aggressions toward the therapist himself. An excerpt from a point at which some transference dissolution began is illustrative:

PATIENT: 'I can't see why I'm unable to think of anything good about Dad. It sure would be helpful if I could. It seems to me that my worst problem is this hatred I have toward him. I don't want to be like him in any way — he's a cruel, sadistic person. He never did anything for my interest. If he ever did anything that seemed to be for me — it was really to advertise himself — he wanted to show me off — but he didn't love me. If I hurt his vanity — which was often — he beat hell out of me. But you've always been good to me — I don't trust your motives. I'm sure you don't care about me one way or the other — but you act as though you care — and that will do for now. You've never required anything of me — and have listened to my inanities hour after hour. I don't see that you're a father symbol at all — maybe a mother symbol — you give me milk — but you're not like my father in any way.'

ANALYST: 'I ask you to pay me.'

PATIENT: 'Yes — but you have to make a living — and I don't feel that's punishment.

ANALYST: 'Isn't my requiring you to bring me money a little like your father's making you clean up the trash from his carpenter work?'

PATIENT: 'It doesn't seem like it to me.'

At the next session the patient was more openly hostile, noticing that the analyst looked a little sadistic and commenting on the apparently angry tone of voice. This led into some further associations about father, with a reappraisal of the meaning of some of the screen (distorted) memories about his father. The patient gradually reconstructed a more favorable picture of father as he was able to express more hostility toward the analyst. The ogreish figure of father was changed into a man with some unfortunate proclivities for temper outbursts and a moderately Simon Legree character, but it included an acceptance that many of father's reactions had at least been intended for the patient's growth. At the same time the analyst became reduced in his benevolent abundance and recognized as more of a reality. An excerpt from this later development is suggestive:

PATIENT: 'As I came up the stairs I thought what a bastard you are — my smiling at you was embarrassment over a thought like that — you're really a nice guy even though I don't act like it at times. That reminds me of that time I've mentioned so often when my father sent me to bed without supper. It seemed hideous then — I've always thought he was just being mean. But there's a different way of looking at it. You know — his cutting off my hair when I was four seemed such an attack — I guess you'd call it castration. I guess mother was trying to make me her little girl. Well — I've always resented his cutting off my hair — but I suppose he intended it as an attempt to help me be a real boy. The supper incident though — it always irked me when he started telling stories about "When Daddy was a little girl" — I don't remember what started it — but I'd been in trouble about something — and was crying at dinner. He said "Did I ever tell you what happened when Daddy was a little girl ——" I interrupted angrily, "Yes, and I don't want to hear it again." Well — he got mad and sent me to bed supperless. The whole thing was ridiculous — here I was having nerve enough to tell him off — and bang — I got clipped. That business of "When Daddy was a little girl" — you know — that must have been hard for him to say — I've always pictured him as a man who was trying awfully hard to assert his manhood — and he couldn't have said "When Daddy was a little girl" on his own account — he must have been trying to help me — and he got angry because I wouldn't accept his help. Must be he was more interested in me than I've ever admitted — Oh — I don't mean that he was as generous as I've called him mean — but he probably had some of each — at least I can credit the old boy with that.'

ANALYST: 'Does that have something to do with your being angry at me?'

PATIENT: 'Sure does. I'm angry at you partly because you've said that my bringing you money is like carrying weeds for Dad — and partly because you've canceled a couple of interviews. Then too — you're cutting me off — deserting me — just like Dad did — when he died and I hated him so much. It's funny — but the thought occurs to me — I wish you would die — I don't really — but I guess I want to be able to mourn someone — rather than be glad that someone I hate has kicked off. I guess I want to be able to mourn the good things about Dad — and the love I felt for him. I was pleased about his dying. I guess that's part of why I've had to keep hating him so — to justify my pleasure in his death — maybe you won't need to die — maybe I can mourn about his goodness leaving me. [tears] If he'd lived I might have learned he was a good guy while he lived — and he died and left me with mother all to myself — that was his worst offense. He'd tried to keep me from being mother's little girl — then he died and left me in her gentle clutches.'

In this excerpt it will be seen that the transference interpretations have helped the patient to re-experience his old memories of relationships to parents — and his current relationship to the analyst — so that he begins to achieve a more differentiated picture of father, mother, and analyst, allowing him to react pertinently to all three rather than retain his irrealistic attachment to the therapist.

MOTIVATIONAL ANALYSIS: In a sense all of the foregoing analytical operations have involved analyses of motivations. In order to bring these together in an integrated way, it seems valuable to consider motivational analysis as a separate topic. What the essentials of motivation are, and how these essentials are distributed in the first place or modified by the method of analytic therapy, are the questions. We have seen that free-association is intended to provide access to dynamically meaningful configurations of symbols, that resistance and ego-defense analyses are designed to facilitate free-association and to develop awareness of the reality inappropriateness of current ego inefficiencies. Dream analysis and transference analysis are also related to the core problem of loves, hates, and their derivatives in the patient. To illustrate motivational analyses, then, let us refer back to the examples already presented, focusing now upon their motivational aspects.

The patient sample under *free-association* (cf. p. 79) included a series of references to an unimportant meeting, the need for a grease job, inability to dream, the apparent annoyance of the analyst, a wondering about failure at something, a comment on beautiful weather, and a desire to go to the beach.

From this potpourri, the analyst elected to wonder, 'What have you thought about me lately?' This led the patient to express fears of rejection, dependency needs, inadequacy and castration fantasies, all of which appeared to revolve around his ambivalent loves and hatreds toward the analyst. Thus he seemed to fear rejection because he was feeling somewhat angry at the analyst. Later productions of the patient suggested that these ambivalences of love and hate related to a simultaneous investment of the analyst with qualities of the loving and erotically desired mother, and the hated and punishing father. Thus the analyst's focus upon 'thoughts about me' evoked movement toward understanding of the patient's pleasure and aggressive strivings, his fears in relation to the unacceptability of these wishes, and the transference meanings attributed to the analyst rather than to the more appropriate mother-father objects. 'What have you thought about me lately?' then, evoked further associations, opportunity for analyses of ego-defenses, transference analyses, and motivational integrations.

In the sample series of the use of symptoms as an ego-defense, the motivational analysis is fairly evident. It will be recalled that the patient developed a series of bodily complaints and fear of death in conjunction with the approaching termination of analysis. The protocol sample indicates that these symptoms served a threefold purpose: (a) they were an expression of hostility toward the analyst for 'rejecting' the patient; (b) they were a means of insisting to the analyst that therapy was incomplete, without at the same time recognizing the fear of inadequacy and aloneness; and (c) they were a partial acceptance of identification with a dying father. The analyst's recognition of these several facets is best summarized in his remark: 'You're pretty angry at me for letting you die like your father.' This comment suggests at once: awareness of the patient's identification with father; awareness of the 'death' symbolism of termination; and acceptance of the hostility toward the analyst together with the primitive reasons for this hostility. This kind of non-punitive understanding and integration of the patient's symbolic behavior made it possible for the patient to accept and understand his motives and techniques and to approach termination in a more maturely effective way.

In our sample excerpt from interpretation and dissolution of the transference neurosis, the motivational analysis is crucial. It will be recalled that the interchange centered around alternations between acting out blissful dependency upon the analyst as a mother-surrogate and hostility toward him as a cruel, depriving, and attacking father-surrogate. It appeared that the patient needed to protect a somewhat idyllic picture of mother and an extremely sadistic picture of father. One point at which these motivations were stripped nude was related to the analyst's inquiry, 'Isn't my requiring you to bring me money a little like your father's making you clean up the trash from his carpenter work?' Operations of this kind helped to focus father transferences upon the analyst and make it necessary for the patient to reappraise his combination of loving and hating attitudes in the transference. His need to protect the idyllic image of mother and the gradual acceptance of imperfections in this image are recognized. His need to maintain a cruel and sadistic image of father, in order to justify his pleasure at father's death, is modified to include the many good qualities that father had shown. The motivational analysis in terms of the erotic-aggressive urges, the repressive and ego-defense maneuvers, and the investment of love and hate upon the analyst to avoid changing his defensive memories are brought out in this interpretation and dissolution of the transference.

The discussion of the psychoanalytic therapist's operations to this point has been concerned with the relatively traditional, orthodox methods of the nebulous, impassive analyst who sits quietly at the head of a couch while the patient verbalizes his associations. In such an approach, the irreality of the transference is gradually worked through by the patient so that he recognizes that the many roles and attitudes he has imposed upon the analyst are products of his own unconscious. Applying the transference principle, however, it is possible for the therapist to use it more actively and become a more realistic representative of the patient's past. This possibility will be considered under the topic, transference *role-taking* operations where active participation as a parental surrogate has been found to be another effective use of the transference principle.

Role-taking Operations

In relatively traditional psychoanalytic therapy, the analyst's expressive behavior is reduced to a minimum. In orthodox analysis the room and seating arrangements are such that the analyst will be as nebulous and remote a figure as possible. The analyst reduces personal contacts to a minimum and is not visible during the therapy hour. The patient lies on a couch with the analyst seated in a place where he cannot be seen. These arrangements are designed to maximize the patient's freedom to enter a near-reverie state where his thoughts are provoked internally and are primarily expressions of himself rather than of his relationship to any present reality. As a part function of these arrangements (Freud, 30) 'the patient sees in his analyst the return — the reincarnation — of some important figure out of his childhood or past, and consequently transfers onto him feelings and reactions that undoubtedly applied to his model . . .' The expressive role of the traditional analyst then is to be as nebulous and impassive as possible, and to be expressively minimal in his contact with the patient. The patient's opportunity to project or transfer meanings that properly pertain to other significant figures is maximized by this nebulousness and impassivity.

TRANSFERENCE ROLE-TAKING: Some recent innovations in psychoanalytic method have included the transference theory, but have maximized transference utilization by what might be called *transference role-taking*. Rather than reviewing the many developments in this direction, Rosen's (86) direct analysis with schizophrenic patients and Levy's (62) transference relationship [1] therapy with neurotics will serve to illustrate transference role-taking approaches.[2]

Rosen's special psychoanalytic theory of schizophrenia proposes that schizophrenia is a defensive reaction to malevolent mothering. It is a personality maneuver to resolve the distress of having been deprived actually or symbolically of 'good' milk. Thus the schizophrenic is encapsulating himself from the poisonous, treacherous, and depriving mother-world. According to Rosen (86) then the patient is '. . . a sick baby who must not be left alone until it is well . . .' In other words the schizophrenic is a deprived child who must be *taken care of and fed into trusting mother* so that he can then go on and develop back into maturity after his fixation at an oral sucking deprivation level is modified.

In order to accomplish such a modification the direct analysis therapist takes the role of a loving, benevolent, protective mother. He

[1] The term *transference relationship* is the author's coinage to differentiate from the Rankian *dynamic relationship*.
[2] See also Alexander and French (1) for a somewhat analogous method with neurotics.

communicates his affection and understanding to the patient by completely controlling and accepting the 'baby' and by interpreting directly the oral symbolic meaning of the patient's behavior and conversation. In general, he loves and cares for the schizophrenic as a 'good' mother might protect a sick baby who needs and gets complete, affectionate care. An unpublished excerpt from a demonstration interview illustrates this 'good' mothering role approach. Rosen's expressions which verbally emphasize his 'mothering' efforts are italicized. It will be recognized that the printed protocol is but a faded mimic of the affectional flow that Rosen himself provides.[1]

PATIENT: 'You were talking about my mother, I was not talking about my mother in relation to her, telling my relation to her — assuming that you were my mother, because you were saying that I could say that you were giving me words and another face was brought to mind that I think of as my mother.'

DR. R.: 'Uh, uh. *I didn't say anything about me being your mother, but I'd like to be.*'

PATIENT: 'Well, that's good of you, and then you'd be a grandmother to my three children.'

DR. R.: '*You know even when you are well you meet people and they look like somebody else. I think when you are insane it's easier to mix people up. That's why you thought of me as your mother. Think about it.*'

PATIENT: 'And you are giving words ——'

DR. R.: 'Well — damn — think about it. Think about what I said.'

PATIENT: 'Now — that's called your hands — ah — touching — ah ——'

DR. R.: 'Yours.'

PATIENT: (Laughs) 'No — this part of it ——'

DR. R.: '*The elbow, the arm, the forearm? Did you mind when I touched you?*'

PATIENT: 'Well, I don't know — the idea — you know that Eskimos rub noses — would that be elbow touching also?'

DR. R.: 'Would you like to rub noses with me?'

PATIENT: 'That should be asked of Eskimos, and that they would probably have to meet an Eskimo — and I don't suppose unless one is an Eskimo rubbing noses wouldn't be much fun.'

DR. R.: 'You don't love me very much.'

PATIENT: 'Possibly it's because I don't love what is happening to my nose.' (Laughs)

DR. R.: 'But I didn't do that.'

PATIENT: 'Well, I don't know who stood around and touched me, but

[1] Excerpts from a demonstration interview by John Rosen at Colorado Psychopathic Hospital, November 16, 1951.

it would be a very good idea for something or other to bump my nose —
here and there it looks like a — ? ——' (Laughs)

DR. R.: 'Don't hide your mouth — don't hide your mouth, *I love your
mouth.*'

PATIENT: 'Then why is it so dry?'

DR. R.: 'Because your mother never fed you — with love.'

DR. R.: 'No. Now a person desperately needs a mother — like a man
dying of thirst in the desert — the sand becomes water — and everybody
becomes mother ——'

PATIENT: 'I think it would be much more fun for him to be sitting
there with that little square of sand in front of him and a glass of water be-
side him — and he could make little water places here and there in the
sand.'

DR. R.: 'You missed the point.'

DR. R.: 'I think all you ever got from your own mother was words.'

PATIENT: 'Oh? Sadly enough — I think sadly enough' (sighs) 'I had
ice cream from a traveling ice cream.'

DR. R.: 'Did you get it from your mother?'

PATIENT: 'Oh, the bell rang and I went out to the traveling ice cream
— and surely enough a small dime could produce two — ice cream.'

DR. R.: 'Breasts.' (Laughs)

PATIENT: (Laughs)

DR. R.: 'I beat you to that, didn't I?'

PATIENT: 'Whereas a nickel is one.'

DR. R.: 'Football.'

PATIENT: 'Ice cream or something that was frozen water with color in
it — that later on someone decided to make father very unhappy with
by calling it a popsicle and then he gets called pop.'

In this excerpt it will be observed that Rosen assumes a mothering
approach. Rather than serving as a blank screen upon which mother
symbolisms may be projected, Rosen actively assumes a mothering
role. Such transference role-taking is entirely consistent with the
psychoanalytic transference theory, but involves an enactment of
the transference role which Rosen considers most crucial in schizophrenia — that of the mother. Levy's (62) transference relationship
therapy involves a very similar role-taking operation with children as
Durkin (15) has demonstrated: 'You're afraid I don't love you
enough, like your mother, but I won't let you get cold.' This transference relationship approach will be elucidated further in Chapter VI by
comparing it with the Rankian dynamic relationship approach.

EXPERIENCE OF THE PSYCHOANALYTIC PATIENT

In attempting to systematize the operations of the psychoanalyst and the aspects of client functioning upon which the analyst focuses, we are providing a means by which changes in the experience of the patient may be investigated. The functional impact of the psychotherapist upon the behavior and improvement processes in the patient is the crucial problem. One aspect of this process may be viewed through the eyes of the analysand. How does the analysand experience the process? How does he experience the psychoanalyst? What is his perception of what happens in analytic therapy? At the present time there are several reports in the literature from the point of view of analytic patients. One valuable approach to research in psychotherapy might be to collect a series of such reports and make a systematic analysis of the kinds of meanings and processes experienced by such analysands.

Unfortunately, these reports of analyzed patients tend to be critiques of the method rather than reviews of experiences. As a beginning look at the experience of the patient, however, a brief review of 'Another Psychologist Analyzed' (111) is suggestive.

The psychologist reporting his experience says that he undertook analysis for help in personal problems. He describes his experiences in a somewhat academic outline form under the topics of the process, reorganization, integration, and professional results.

The process included, for him, an exploration of immediate problems such as emotional interaction with friends and family and conflicts about work. Relationships to mother were explored in terms of affection, dependency, and hostility. Relationships to father and siblings involved jealousy, love, pride, fear, and hatred on both conscious and unconscious levels. Explorations were made by recall of fantasies, dreams and memories. The analyst would ask questions such as 'Does that remind you of anything?' or 'How did you feel about that?' The analyst would occasionally propose her understanding of the ways that the patient behaved in his life situation. She would frequently bring the patient back to the problem they were working on, but especially she would encourage the patient to propose questions to himself and answer them as fully and frankly as possible. He says that 'After a while, in fact, I learned to anticipate the questions . . . and to carry on the process of association with less prompting from the analyst.'

This patient experienced that a reorganization of personality was achieved. A broadened and deeper understanding of himself was gradually acquired, but the most important change seemed to involve a '. . . form of emotional reconditioning.' For example, the patient gradually changed the meaning of his father's attitudes. Father had been an undemonstrative, self-righteous and denying person who was royally disliked by the patient. By reviewing and reliving some of his experiences with father the patient gradually developed the attitude that father had been quite fond of him even though undemonstrative about it. When reviewing experiences touching the affectionate attitude of his father the patient says, '. . . his deep love for me, and his confidence in my manliness — struck me with such force that I lay for several minutes weeping. When the emotion had passed, I felt that I had a deep and intimate experience of the warmth and devotion between my father and myself . . .'

The personality reorganization resulted in liberation of feelings which had been held in check. Redirection and development of personally and socially acceptable forms of realizing satisfaction were also achieved.

In conclusion the patient says that he is better satisfied with the kind of person he has become, has a more realistic picture of himself, and believes that he has more understanding of human motivation and behavior than he had acquired in fourteen years of study and teaching in psychology.

Obviously this one case review is not scientifically valuable at the moment, but it is illustrative of the possibility of approaching and understanding psychoanalytic therapy process from the viewpoint of the experience of the patient.

SUMMARY

In summarizing concepts and operations in psychoanalytic therapy, we shall recapitulate the basic concepts, review the aspects of the patient upon which the analyst focuses attention, and enumerate the operations or techniques employed by the analyst.

MOTIVATION: The conception of ambitendent biological drives toward life and pleasure versus death and destruction leads to an emphasis upon developing self-understanding and acceptance in terms of recognition, integration, and socially acceptable expression of these antithetical drives. Thus the analyst focuses upon, or pays special attention to, the loving and hating aspects of the patient's motives, and to the conflicts provoked by such seemingly incompatible motivation.

PERSONALITY STRUCTURE: The conception of personality includes a dynamic configuration of energy in the service of gaining a maximum of pleasure; a minimum of pain; and efficient, or economical, transactions between internal motives and external reality. This structure involves constructs of the unconscious id, made up of primitive impulses; the relatively conscious ego, which is the broker between id and reality; and the largely unconscious super-ego, which is a valuing structure precipitated from a 'yielding to conquer' resolution of struggles between the child and parental authorities.

Operationally, this conception of personality leads to the therapist's focusing upon unconscious id processes and contents; techniques which the ego develops to avoid awareness of the unconscious; techniques which the ego employs in maneuvering with reality; and the sources and meanings of the super-ego valuing system. In terms of technique, the therapist facilitates associations in dynamically meaningful directions; interprets resistance to facilitate association, focuses upon and provokes associations to dreams; and interprets the relationships among associative contents, unconscious meanings, ego-defenses, and super-ego valuing processes.

DEVELOPMENTAL PROCESSES: Personality structure is developed as a result of important experiences and relationships from the oral stage of infancy through the development of psychosexual maturity at the level of genital love and socialization. The concept of libidinal cathexis — that drive energy can be attached to particular objects, people, and processes — is essential. Thus energy and interest can be overinvested in some stage of development in the form of libidinal fixation. Thus it becomes operationally important to explore childhood memories and provide an opportunity to relive malforming experiences which produced excessive cathexes or fixations. This reliving and relieving of developmental misfortunes is accomplished especially by the production and resolution of the transference neurosis. The analyst helps the patient to re-experience his developmental cathexes and to become aware that these can be recalled with comfort. Thus, the patient's repetition-compulsions no longer need to be repeated in living while being excluded from consciousness. Acceptance of memories is substituted for their re-enactment.

The analyst focuses upon the patient's (a) unconscious love and hate contents and motives, (b) inferred motives, (c) techniques of self-deception, (d) techniques of maneuvering with reality, (e) valuing attitudes and their sources, and (f) developmental processes and experiences.

The analyst employs operations or techniques of (a) facilitating association, (b) resistance and ego-defense interpretation, (c) dream analysis, (d) transference analysis, (e) interpretation of motivations, and (f) appropriate role-taking techniques.

Psychoanalytic patients who have reported how they experienced the process suggest an experience of a broadening in conscious awareness, mature acceptance of relationships to parents, and acceptance of themselves in parental roles.

O wad some Power
the giftie gie us
To see oursels as
ithers see us
It wad frae mony
a blunder free us,
An' foolish notion . . .
—Burns

V. Interpersonal Psychiatric Theory and Method

Operations of the interpersonal psychiatrist are systematically related to the interpersonal theory. The therapist assumes that security and anxiety are primarily interpersonal rather than internal processes, and his emphasis is on behavior which tends to disrupt and behavior which tends to facilitate interpersonal adequacy and acceptability. However, since behavior is largely in the service of avoiding awareness of anxiety, the therapist's goal is the pursuit and understanding of anxiety in relation to its interpersonal behavior consequences.

The conception of motivation in terms of security seeking and anxiety avoidance produces therapist operations focusing upon the client's techniques for avoiding awareness of anxiety. Furthermore, the therapist expresses an accepting, security-giving attitude toward the client.

The conception of personality as part of an interpersonal process considers development as a continuing process of socialization. Hence the interpersonal therapist focuses upon and attempts to modify the meaning of developmental experiences which have produced the client's distortions.

Anxiety and loneliness are considered to result from disapproved 'bad-me' and dissociated 'not-me' aspects of the self-system. Experiences with 'bad' mothering persons lead to expectations of malevolency from others and to malevolent attitudes in the self.

The interpersonal therapist focuses upon the anxiety and loneliness, the qualities of distortion in relating to others, and the socially crippling aspects of the client's behavior. The therapist presents *himself* as an alternative and plausible social reality against which the client's distortions may be compared and corrected. The therapist gives acceptance and respect in place of the rejection and derogation which the client has learned to anticipate.

AN OPERATIONAL PSYCHIATRY

The most operational approach to psychotherapy is the interpersonal theory and methods defined by Harry Stack Sullivan. In his own philosophy he has insisted upon an operational conception and has vigorously attacked the artistic maunderings of those who defend unscientific treatment. 'Psychiatry as it is — the preoccupation of extant psychiatric specialists — is not science nor art but confusion. In defining it as the study of interpersonal relations, I sought to segregate from everything else a disciplinary field in which operational methods could be applied with great practical benefits.' (102).

Sullivan developed his method and theory after Calvinistic and Victorian puritanism had somewhat ebbed. Thus, while he accepted the validity of psychoanalysis, he considered it to be a special theory of neurosis in a cultural era which looked askance at sexuality. Furthermore, Sullivan began his clinical investigations with schizophrenics and generalized from schizophrenic rather than neurotic reactions to psychotherapy. Heuristically, it will be helpful to compare interpersonal psychiatry with the traditional psychoanalytic point of view.

THE THERAPEUTIC ATTITUDE OF THE
INTERPERSONAL PSYCHIATRIST

The therapeutic attitude of the interpersonal psychiatrist includes some similarities and many contrasts to psychoanalysis. Fromm-Reichmann (33) has noted that any mood or expressive behavior suited to the occasion, except frivolity, is considered pertinent in interpersonal therapy. By contrast to the impassive, nebulous distance that the orthodox analyst employs, interpersonal therapy requires maximum role flexibility and versatility. While the analyst provides an opportunity for the patient to conduct his internal struggle with ir-reality, the interpersonal therapist presents himself as a real person for the patient to differentiate from parataxic, fictional people. The interpersonal therapist accepts the transference phenomenon as a special case of parataxic distortion. The interpersonal client reacts to his therapist as a fictional representative of any historically or cur-rently significant figure. He reacts not only to the person of the thera-pist, but to his fictional picture of the boss, husband, father, mother, etc. These reactions are not only produced by a re-enactment of in-fantile erotic and destructive cathexes, but by an attempt to avoid experiencing uncertainty or anxiety. Since he does not know what the therapist thinks of him, the client's self-esteem is threatened; he expe-riences interpersonal insecurity, and it is more security-giving to fill in the unknown from his collection of real or fictional experiences than it is to suffer the distress of not knowing what the therapist is like.

The production of social integration in the client's life is the goal of the therapist. The therapist promotes the client's awareness of self and others in a consensually valid form, thus leading the client to collabora-tion and security in his culture. This is accomplished by the disruption of those security-operations which obscure sources of anxiety, increase loneliness, interfere with satisfaction, and enhance responses to fic-tional rather than currently real pictures of the self and others. In con-structing an operational outline of interpersonal therapy, we shall first summarize those aspects of the general interpersonal theory that are necessary background to the therapist's operations and the client's functioning.

The interpersonal theory of motivation proposes a clearly social rather than biological nature of man: The interpersonal man is seek-ing security in relation to other people. The conception of adjustment is in terms of effective integration into one's culture: The interpersonal man is a part of his social process. The conception of maladjustment is defined by lack of security and by ineffective interpersonal opera-tions: The maladjusted interpersonal man is anxious about being re-jected and unskillful in getting acceptance from others. These concepts of motivation, adjustment, and maladjustment will be considered in sufficient detail to provide a background for examining the operations of the interpersonal therapist.

Motivation

The essentially human motivation postulated by interpersonal theory is a search for security in relation to others. That is, this kind of 'interpersonal man' is seeking to maintain his self-esteem by approval from others, by effectiveness in gaining biological satisfactions, and by general mastery in his interpersonal environment. The biological drives are considered to be of relatively secondary importance, except when the search for security is interfered with by inefficiency in achieving biological satisfaction. A sense of comfort and pleasure in interpersonal relations is the uniquely human quality of the 'interpersonal man.' In contrast to Freud's emphasis upon the primitive biological drives toward erotic satisfaction, Sullivan emphasizes the socialization drive for satisfying interpersonal relations. The Freudian personality is a relatively self-contained organization. Its relationship to the world is conducted through the foreign-policy decisions of the ego, which determine under what conditions which drive can achieve gratification. Sullivan subordinates such internal, biological drives to the interpersonal transactions involved in achieving a sense of affection from the world and esteem from the self. The 'interpersonal man,' far from being a self-contained organization, is a part function of the interpersonal process. He is in no way 'an island unto himself' unless an island is defined as a part function of the geophysical process of interaction with the waves, winds, sun and ocean floor. The interpersonal man is a substructure of socio-cultural processes in human living. To the degree that the interpersonal man experiences conjunctivity and participation in such socio-cultural processes, he is relatively secure, experiencing self-esteem and the acceptance of others. To the degree that he experiences disjunctivity and separateness from the socio-cultural processes of which he is a part, he suffers from anxiety and loneliness, engaging in self-deceiving and distorting security-operations. Such security-operations are designed to abort awareness of anxiety and to provoke acceptance from the interpersonal world.

The interpersonal theory postulates an avoidant drive and a seeking drive, but these are very different from Freudian instincts of love and hate. The security seeking is emphasized and provides the basis for understanding the negative or avoidant drive. Mullahy (71) describes this relation in terms of two ideal constructs, complete euphoria versus complete tension. Complete euphoria is a totally blissful state which might be approximated by a warm, well-fed, healthy baby in a deep sleep. Complete tension is a totally disorganized, utter distress which might be approximated by an exhausted, terror-stricken soldier in the target area of a dive bomber. Human experience rarely reaches such exquisite extremes, but the feelings of security and anxiety are on such a continuum.

Thus interpersonal security is in the direction of euphoria, while interpersonal anxiety is in the direction of utter tension. To contrast this construction further with the Freudian approach, the place of anxiety in personality dynamics may be examined. We noted in Chapter IV that anxiety is the sense of discomfort and malaise arising as a danger signal that alien or unacceptable impulses from the id are struggling for expression. That is, if an unconscious erotic impulse — say to embrace on the street a woman who reminds one of one's mother — occurs unconsciously, this impulse will come into awareness as an undifferentiated sense of uneasiness, and might produce, for example, a quick shift in attention to the clothes in the store window, or a sense of urinary urgency, but no acceptance of the oedipal wish itself. The anxiety would be a result of the conflict between the erotic wish and the repressive force. The symptomatic act would implement repression by displacement. In the Sullivanian theory, such an incident would be understood as a sense of insecurity or anxiety that the mother-fiction does not respond with acceptance and tenderness.[1] The unconscious erotic wish would not be involved in the explanation, since all that would be needed for understanding would be the postulate that a person is seeking acceptance and tenderness from mother-fictions and that one fears to be rebuffed in these circumstances. The symptomatic samples would also be understood differently in the two theories. Psychoanalytically, 'looking away at the clothes in the window' might symbolize 'I must cover up — or put clothes upon my naked wish.' Interpersonal theory would be more likely to suggest the interpretation, 'I must find a means of appearing more socially acceptable so that mothers and other significant people will love me.' It will be noted that these two explanations are not mutually exclusive, but differ in emphasis.

The sense of urinary urgency would also be interpreted differently in the two theories. Developing a sense of urinary urgency might sym-

[1] But note that such interpersonal anxiety is similar to Freudian separation anxiety.

bolize psychoanalytically, 'My penis is not a sexual apparatus, it is an excretory apparatus. Therefore I could not possibly be experiencing an erotic wish toward mother.' The interpersonal theory would be more likely to select another meaning that might be expressed in a combination of hostility and avoidance. 'Piss on you for not loving me — but I'd better go to the lavatory so I won't get into trouble.' It will be noted that the examples constructed for interpersonal theory would also 'fit' into a psychoanalytic interpretation. However, these examples are designed to illustrate emphases in the contrast of motivational constructs. The psychoanalytic symbols emphasize erotic motivations and an internal ego-process of repression, with a foreign-policy ego-mechanism of denial. The interpersonal examples emphasize desire for acceptance and tenderness from other people leading to a sense of anxiety in the absence of security. The symptomatic acts are construed in interpersonal theory as substitutes for tenderness or avoidance of rejection. Thus the psychoanalytic theory emphasizes control or disguise of internal impulses, while the interpersonal theory emphasizes the seeking of security or affection from other people and the techniques of aborting anxiety in the presence of interpersonal affront.

Developmental Processes

Growing up is considered to be a continuing process of acculturation rather than a series of separably significant stages in character genesis. Interpersonal security and effectiveness result from a series of fortunate experiences in relating to others. Interpersonal anxiety and loneliness result from a concatenation of difficulties in affectional relations.

In infancy there comes an awareness of separateness from the mothering one — the child begins to recognize an independent selfhood. This learning is partly a product of the infant's differentiation of sources from which his discomfort is relieved. At this stage, the infant learns primarily from the mothering one, so the nature of the mothering one will largely determine what he learns. If mothers treat him with tenderness and interest, he is likely to experience comfort and to develop reciprocal attitudes of tenderness. If mothers treat him harshly, gingerly, or in a rejecting way, he is likely to learn attitudes of rejection and to experience insecurity. Sullivan's notion of *empathy* suggests the considerable ability of the infant to experience and imitate the feelings and attitudes of those with whom he interacts. If the mother is anxious, this will be communicated by empathic linkage to the infant. If the mother is comfortable, such comfort and security will be communicated to the infant. Stavern (100) cites an hypothetical contrast of such infancy conditions.

A comfortable and mature mother ministers to her child with non-anxious tenderness. 'Under such circumstances the child is apt to lead an existence relatively free from anxiety — the child's empathic experience of the mother's emotional state will add to his state of relative euphoria.' In contrast to this, an anxious, unhappy mother produces a high degree of anxiety. 'Since anxiety and uncertainty constantly interfere with his mother's powers of observation, and even more with her need or wish to manifest tenderness — . . . the tensions aroused by tissue needs are apt to go unrelieved. . . . But worse, and more continuously, most contact with his mother is apt to be poisoned by empathically experienced anxiety.'

Such adequacies or misfortunes in the mothering one lead to a sense of security on the one hand and to a sense of anxiety or insecurity on the other. As language develops and the child progresses motorically to the level at which habits of cleanliness can be taught, his interest is drawn toward urinary and bowel control training. Fascination with feces and genitals is an essential focus of the learning experience at this time, and there is no necessity to construe this in anal erotic and fixation terms. The child is also more active in his relation to parents simply because of his motoric developments and learnings. Hence he is likely to gain increased awareness of parental appraisals. What parental appraisals the child meets become a basis for his developing a reflected appraisal picture of himself. That is, the child develops a self-awareness that is essentially a reflection of the picture that significant others — especially parents — have presented him with. If the parents are pleased and continually reflect a good picture, the child will develop a large amount of self-esteem, or 'good me.' If the parents are continually displeased and respond to the child as a 'nuisance,' a 'misfortune,' 'a pain in the neck,' he will develop an intense sense of disapproval of himself. His 'bad me' will become the major aspect of his self-system, and there will be many things about himself that he cannot face and must deny as 'not me' at all.

The self-system, or -dynamism, developed as a result of such appraisals is the supervisory pattern or organization of awareness of one's self. The self-system is the awareness of 'What kind of person am I?' Thus, by selectively attending to what others think of him, the child learns to seek approval and avoid disapproval by predicting in advance what reactions he will provoke. These predictions become the kind of person he considers himself to be. Such selective attention leads to loss of awareness of other aspects of the interpersonal process, so that some things are selectively inattended and some aspects are not available to awareness at all — are dissociated 'not me' aspects.

The interpersonal juvenile era is roughly the same period that psychoanalysts label 'latency.' The interpersonal juvenile learns to cooperate and compete with his peers. Sex, in anything like the adult meaning of the term, is not involved in this period.

The isophilic experience in preadolescence is a most significant process in the well-adjusted individual. An isophilic relation of closeness and understanding with the same-sexed peer or chum is developed. This relation to a chum is of profound personality consequence. It leads to a capacity for concern about the happiness of someone else; it develops consensually valid meanings — that is, learning to see things and communicate as others do; it produces an integration of one's needs into those of another, so that collaboration becomes possible. The *isophilic* relation is not necessarily choice of a chum on the basis of identity of interests, but rather upon the basis of integrative interests, involving mutual respect and affection. This is an equality relationship which permits complete sharing of intimate experiences and provides a basis for empathy and communication with others. It is at this period that failure to develop successful chumship may result in personality disaster. Stavern (100) describes his hypothetical misfit in preadolescence as in '. . . extreme isolation, which is not lessened by even frantic attempts to copy patterns of relatedness he can see his compeers have . . .' He lacks '. . . even the superficial rudiments of patterns which facilitate one's getting along in groups . . .'

'He will watch his compeers gradually pair off, and with envy he will notice the development of experiences between them which he knows he needs . . . He will long for it, the way any lonely person would, but without being in a position to make any active moves toward another individual . . .'

Interpersonal security — capacity for tenderness, collaboration and ability to empathize with and understand the interrelatedness of oneself and others — is developed from a sequence of fortunate experiences. Such valuable learnings depend upon: (a) tenderness from the mothering one; (b) positive appraisals from significant adults, with a consequent development of a 'good me' emphasis in self-esteem; (c) the development of an isophilic chumship, where an experience of intimacy with a respected peer produces consensually valid communication, empathy, and awareness of one's satisfying role in the interpersonal process.

The pattern of interpersonal insecurity is compounded from: (a) lack of tenderness from the mothering one; (b) experience of intense anxiety in the presence of rejection and neglect as a result of negative appraisals from significant adults; (c) development of a 'bad me' and 'not me' in self-appraisals; (d) failure to enter into effective intimacy experiences in chumship. Such interpersonal misfortunes result in malevolent expectations and attitudes, ineffectiveness in communication, lack of capacity to empathize with others, intense loneliness, and crippling kinds of security-operations as defenses against intolerable anxiety.

The client who comes for the help of an interpersonal therapist is viewed in terms of his difficulties in interpersonal relations. Maladjustment is a function of an interpersonal field rather than a function of internal personality organization. Anxiety is both a cause and a result of interpersonal difficulties. The presence of anxiety arouses disjunctive, avoidant attitudes and behaviors; the difficulties in interpersonal relations result in insecurity and anxiety. In the presence of insecurity about one's acceptability to another, anxiety operates to produce some kind of picture of the relationship — to make the real person over into a fiction that will fill the informational gap.

Security-Adjustment and Anxiety-Maladjustment

Adjustment and maladjustment in the interpersonal theory can be summarized in terms of the degree and quality of socio-cultural integration, the balance between *anxiety* and *security*, and the characteristics of the self-system.

Socio-cultural integration expresses the central personality process in adjustment. The degree to which the personality is a comfortable part of the socio-cultural process is a measure of his effective security. If he is happily a part of his culture, he experiences security in interpersonal relations and acquires socially effective forms of satisfaction. Such conjunctivity requires providing as well as receiving approval and satisfaction. The well-adjusted interpersonal man, then, is conjunctive in attitudes and behavior; he integrates into and collaborates with other subsystems of the culture. He contributes to harmonious functioning of the generalized interpersonal process. The capacity for such integration is a function of a valid feeling of self-approval and approval from others. A person who is primarily 'good me' can function constructively rather than defensively.

The maladjusted interpersonal man is a tensional node in the sociocultural process. He responds with anxiety to interpersonal relations and applies his maladaptive security-operations for the exclusion of anxiety from awareness. He expects disapproval and he generates disapproval. He is relatively inflexible in behavior since his anxiety prevents him from awareness of much of himself and others. He avoids seeing much of what goes on — and is therefore maladroit in responding. Since interpersonal relations are painful, he reduces valid communication and is therefore disjunctive and disintegrative in his attitudes and behaviors. He provokes further insecurity in himself and others. Since he is largely 'bad me' and 'not me,' he functions defensively and is unconstructive in his behavior.

Anxiety or interpersonal insecurity can be contrasted with interpersonal affection or security. To the extent that the personality has experienced an excess of disapproval, he is likely to be anxious and to feel that he is not an accepted part of the interpersonal process. To reduce this sense of unbelonging, he develops various techniques of deception called security-operations. He masks anxiety by turning quickly to other things, refusing to notice the rising tension. Since such maneuvers are defensive rather than constructive, they are likely to be inflexible and rigid in performance. They are unconstructive and unlikely to transform energy into collaborative activity. They fail to reduce the tension-producing attitudes, but only restrict awareness of the tension itself. By contrast, the well-adjusted interpersonal man experiences and gives approval and security to himself and others, is aware of himself as 'good,' and experiences comfort in his self-awareness. He needs few techniques for avoiding anxiety experiences and is able to observe most of his interpersonal processes with comfort. He transforms tissue needs into socially acceptable patterns of behavioral expression. He facilitates the satisfaction of other people's needs.

The self-system incorporates the patterns of valuing and expressing one's interrelatedness in the culture. A self-system made up of primarily positive self-evaluations is able to accept awareness of most of the interpersonal behavior that goes on. A self-system which includes considerable 'bad me' awareness is continually on the alert for affront and intrusion and must operate in such a way as to exclude anxiety-provoking indications. Such a protective system reduces valid observation and limits opportunity for constructive energy transformations. The capacity for flexibly adaptive interaction is impaired and the defensive self-system protects and maintains its dynamic stupidity.

Personality Concepts Basic to Psychotherapy Operations

Interpersonal concepts which are essential to a cogent discussion of operations in psychotherapy may be summarized from the foregoing discussion.

The *motivation* that makes man essentially human is the pursuit of security in interpersonal relations. From infancy onward, the interpersonal man is a function of his integration in socio-cultural processes. An approved and constructive integration includes a sense of well-being and security. A disapproved and disintegrative involvement includes a sense of anxiety and loneliness. Needs for biological satisfaction are involved only to the extent that anxiety and security-operations interfere with acceptable methods for achieving biological sufficiency.

In his pursuit of security the interpersonal man learns a number of conjunctive — socially effective, or disjunctive — socially impairing, responses. He learns that some people who are important in his life approve of him while others reject him. For example, he differentiates a 'good mother' and a 'bad mother' from his experiences with mothering persons. Reflecting the attitudes of such significant others in his appraisal of himself, he develops 'good me' attitudes, 'bad me' attitudes, and disassociated, unrecognizable aspects which he cannot accept as himself, but disavows as 'not me' at all.

To maximize his sense of *security* and to minimize awareness of *anxiety*, he develops methods of selectively attending to those aspects of interpersonal situations which enhance self-esteem. He develops techniques of avoiding awareness of the anxiety-provoking behavior of himself or others which reduce feelings of security. Such security-operations protect him from recognizing anxiety without reducing the 'causes' of anxiety. He attempts to master his interpersonal environment by developing appropriate interpersonal skills for human living, or else he substitutes techniques of deception to produce an appearance of tensionless security to himself and others.

He selectively attends to those aspects of the interpersonal situation which increase his sense of well-being, and selectively disregards whatever increases tension and anxiety in himself. Thus, he has but an obscure picture of many interpersonal processes that produce difficulty in living. Thus also, his patterns of reaction are likely to be rigid and automatic, inasmuch as they are designed to avoid anxiety on the basis of a limited awareness of the total situation.

Entering a new situation, the anxious interpersonal man will experience a parataxic repetition of previous experiences. Such repetitive distortions are produced by expectations which were learned from significant people in the past. He will assume that people are treating him in the same old ways. He will also respond to the new situation in conformity with the anxiety-reducing operations he has found successful in earlier relationships. He will tend to perpetuate the old and ineffective patterns.

The motivation toward security — and the avoidance of anxiety experience — leads to social learnings about whether one is 'good' or 'bad,' and about what kinds of attitudes one will meet in others. Tension-reducing operations are developed to maintain self-esteem in spite of the expectation of being disapproved. Since these operations are defensive rather than constructive, they tend to limit awareness of interpersonal processes and to enhance difficulties in the presence of tension-provoking experiences. In any new encounter, the interpersonal man responds on the basis of his eidetic (fictional or parataxic) people rather than on the basis of the new people themselves. He avoids recognizing anxiety by using his old distortions and self-deceptive maneuvers.

Thus, the problem in psychotherapy as posed by interpersonal theory is: By what means can the client learn to elicit legitimately security-giving reactions from others? By what means can the client reduce the projection of his eidetic distortions into the present? By what means can he become acquainted with his own operations in self-deception, so that he will be able to develop a flexible interpersonal awareness with conjunctive, integrative, and collaborative attitudes?

INTERPERSONAL THEORY AND PSYCHOTHERAPY METHOD

The interpersonal therapist is conceived differently from the nebulous, impersonal psychoanalyst, who 'must never respond in a human way.' While the interviewer is considered to be an expert in human relationships, he is not a distant deity who observes and intercedes from Olympian heights. He is a real, sophisticatedly personal node of organization in the interpersonal transaction between client and therapist. He is expertly aware of both the client's and his own involvement in the process. He is compassionately interested in the client's anxieties and skillfully manages to control tensions in tolerable doses. He sees where relevant information is obscured or hidden, yet is aware of his own limitations and is humble in assuming that the client's potentiality for creative reconstruction is essential to improvement. To the extent that the *expert* can produce a valid relationship, interpersonal therapy can progress in constructive directions.

A valid relationship is one wherein the client sees some prospect of constructive benefit to himself. Thus the therapist must fit into the client's preconceptions of an expert in interpersonal relations. The therapist attends primarily to the problems that the client brings; he works at this relationship for no personal gratification of his own, but to ameliorate the client's difficulties. The expert therapist inquires only into aspects that are deemed to be consequential; he says the things that are likely to be useful and clarifying. The expert therapist avoids sayings things that may add to misunderstanding and uncertainty — since the client has enough misunderstandings of his own. In a tactically humble way, however, the therapist generally proposes his own understandings as hypotheses for the client to examine, rather than as truths to be accepted. Since the therapist understands that much of the client's capacity to change depends upon emotional acceptance by another, the therapist provides whatever affective expressions seem necessary for the client's progress.

The therapist's participant function in the interview is to establish a situation where he can examine and aid in correcting the client's characteristic pattern of living. To accomplish this, he must be comprehensively aware of the current interpersonal processes and must inquire astutely into the socio-cultural learnings which produced the current pattern. In a sense, this is an examination of both faces of an old coin — the process by which the person was launched into the interpersonal economy, and the wear and tear of cultural economics that determine his value in contemporary markets. The coin analogy underlines a final aspect of the therapist's attitude — the patient has worth. He is a valued person whom the therapist respects and acknowledges as important, regardless of the helper-and-helped relation in psychotherapy.

Interpersonal and psychoanalytic techniques have some parallels and many differences (33, 71). The psychoanalytic emphasis upon recovery of childhood memories is paralleled by the interpersonal therapist's inquiry into significant developmental phases in interpersonal relations. What is expected from the two approaches and how the investigation is conducted are different. The interpersonal therapist is concerned with relationships to significant persons and how these may have influenced the client's self-appraisals and security-operations. The interpersonal inquiry is analogous to — and perhaps explanatory of — Freud's repetition-compulsion principle. The repetition of patterns of reaction in interpersonal living is dependent upon the parataxic — unorganized — expectation that people he meets will respond to him and treat him in the same ways as other important people he has known. That is, if mother made him feel that his nose was a monstrosity and his penis a misfortune, he will so regard them himself and will assume that others will view them in the same way. To protect himself from such expected disapproval, he will muster whatever anxiety-reducing techniques appeared to be effective in the earlier circumstances — protesting perhaps that he smashed his nose in a football game. In a sense, then, such repetitions become patterns of successful anxiety reduction and are perfectly meaningful in the client's security system. Thus the interpersonal inquiry is designed to elucidate the obscure past history of a pattern in order to modify it in an understandable present.

In order to clarify the current meanings of the interpersonal situation, such genetic inquiry is essential. The client enters therapy with all kinds of explicit or inattended expectations of the therapist. The explicit expectations are likely to be determined by the folklore of the culture about the role of a psychotherapist — especially the popularized role of a psychoanalyst. These current expectations must be met and handled expertly. If the client expects to have his sex life investigated, the therapist will need to satisfy this expectation or be considered unskilled. The oedipal meaning of such an expectation is hardly necessary to understand it in current cultural terms, however, and the client's expectation of help can be satisfied without denying his original conception of the therapist's role.

The concept of transference posited by psychoanalysts is not discarded but put into a different perspective in the interpersonal interview. It is considered to be a special case of parataxic distortion, i.e. all significant people in the experience of a person are retained as eidetic images and trotted out at appropriate times to characterize a situation which is lacking in clarity. If the client is obscurely anxious because he doesn't know what the therapist thinks of him, he will substitute one or more of his eidetic people for the area of uncertainty in his picture of the therapist. 'Mother loved me, so maybe this man loves me too,' or 'Dad was always criticizing me — that seems to fit here.' One of the therapist's necessary inquiries is, 'With what characteristics is the client endowing me — what kind of personification is he giving me?' The therapist might wonder aloud, 'You're acting as if I were your father dressing you down.' That the client will distort the therapist in several ways as an eidetic image of the same significant person should also be considered. In infancy, the mother is differentiated into 'good mother' and 'bad mother'; hence, the attribution of mothering qualities to the therapist does not limit the variety of meanings he might have. The same eidetic image attributed to the therapist may involve a number of relationships to the client: 'You want to help me all right, but you sure make me suffer for it.'

The therapist's function in parataxic distortions is to help the client correct them. This is accomplished by pointing out the client's inappropriate reactions and by behaving differently from the way in which the eidetic person is expected to behave. The therapist must come to be recognized as a real person and different from the fictional image. One client bristled about '. . . that day when you called me skinny.' Dr. Sullivan (106) bristled back, correcting the error, 'I distinctly recall what I said, namely, that you seemed to have suffered your mother's opinion that you were thin.' Such therapist operations are designed to produce consensually valid, syntactic thinking by pointing out discrepancies and by making the therapist a contemporary social reality who is not the same as the eidetic person projected upon him. It is obvious that the transference relation is handled and conceived in very different terms from psychoanalysis, where a re-enactment of erotic and destructive cathexes upon the analyst is resolved by the patient's recovery of the infantile memories that he is acting out in the transference. The interpersonal therapist's response to eidetic images in an unclear situation is a different approach — directed toward syntactic or socially realistic experiencing of contemporary reality.

The interpersonal therapist reacts to the anxiety-avoidance intention of security-operations. Security-operations are maneuvers to reduce awareness of tension and to increase a sense of self-esteem or euphoria. Since they do not effectively resolve the cause of the anxiety in the first place — that is, the sense of being unloved or unacceptable — they do nothing permanent about the anxiety. As the interpersonal therapist becomes aware of the characteristic patterns of anxiety-avoidance by security-operations, he helps the client to awareness of such connections. The therapist pays careful attention to all aspects of communication — vocal, gestural and verbal. If he notices an abrupt shift in the productivity of the client, he presumes this to be evidence of an attempt to avoid experiencing anxiety. The therapist is also likely to notice the language quality, and to attempt to make sense out of its intention to obscure. The following illustration [1] shows an interpersonal therapist interpreting such obscuring language to his client.

> PATIENT: '. . . My father and mother thought — my father did — that being a child was sort of a necessary evil that you have to go through to be a grown-up. He really was like ashamed of having been a child himself, wasn't he? He didn't think it was anything creditable to be a child — to be a baby — and why shouldn't it be? Everybody is. Why is being grown-up so — contemptuous of a child? (Pause) It's real harmful, because children feel that.'
>
> DOCTOR: 'Let me think now — it seems to me (pause) that one might theorize that language was for communication — was to make things clearer between people, huh? But that as we grow up we also learn something else — we learn to be somewhat afraid of some people, and we often use language to obscure what we feel. And so I would *think* that some of *your* way of talking . . . your special ways of talking serve to *obscure* something from people . . . So I would think that you are often in the very difficult position of having a message to *want* to give, and to have to use language to do it, but to use this *technique* of speaking which obscures the real message, often. In other words, you can get across something in words when, at the same time, you have to be pretty much afraid of getting it across . . .'

This sample was abbreviated from the original to focus upon an interpretation of the security-operation of *obscure language* to reduce anxiety and prevent retaliation. It will be seen in the therapist's discussion that he talks about a particular kind of behavior — obscure

[1] Personal communication from David McK. Rioch.

language — as an operation designed to protect oneself against loss of approval. Earlier in this interview it had become apparent that the client feared that the therapist disapproved — was contemptuous of her, as her father was of her as a child. The obscurity the therapist was referring to was the client's failure to make this point clear.

The primary objective of the therapist is to help the client recognize — and thereby correct — his perceptual or behavioral distortions in interpersonal relations. That is, the therapist is attempting to lead the client into a consensually valid, syntactic mode of experience; he is attempting to help the client see reality in the same way as other members of the culture do, and to express himself in such a way that he can gain affection and approval rather than in such a way that he deceives himself and alienates others. Since such capacity for syntactic organization is hardly a logical problem, however, many emotionally constructive experiences are essential to the client's development of effectively socialized skills. Appropriate emotional reactions on the part of the therapist are essential to such relearning.

Some expressive behavior samples in interpersonal therapy will illustrate the therapist's affectional and aggressive role. By contrast with psychoanalysis, it should be noted that expressive activity on the part of the therapist is alien to traditional analytic method. One patient (106) describes Sullivan's intense and kindly interest in what was going on: 'I would suddenly become aware of a change in him, like the alertness of a pointer who has spotted a bird. It was a certain wave of thoughtful, kindly alertness, totally non-verbal. That knowledge of his already being where I didn't know where I was going, made it possible for me successfully to go through a number of rough spots.' Earlier, Sullivan had said to this same patient, 'Somehow or other I feel that there is a great deal of chagrin ahead.' These excerpts show the empathic understanding attitude that interpersonal therapists provide as a means of making the emotional swamps and rocks less arduous, and making it possible for clients to feel that their intimate and horrible experiences are not as alien and intolerable as they seem. Another kind of security-giving expression is described by Sullivan (106) in the case of a client who is distressed about a socially unacceptable experience. The therapist might say, 'Well, you feel that's unusual?' The client responds, 'Well yes, doctor, I'm afraid I do.' The doctor might reply, 'Dear me, why, I never heard anybody talk honestly who didn't mention that.' In this interchange, it will be seen that the therapist acts as a vehicle for a cultural value. That is, he gives support and reassurance to the client by indicating that the unpleasant idea is a very common one, and that there is no need to feel unacceptable on account of it. This is entirely consistent with the avowed purpose to aid the client in becoming an acceptable and creative part of his culture.

The indirect approach of the therapist protects the client against a frontal attack and provides him with the opportunity to develop a point of view for himself. Sullivan typically used circumlocutions instead of direct statements, such as, 'Some of the things one does to advertise insecurity do not tend to raise the self-esteem,' or 'One might be curious about the meaning of this information for the relationship with the therapist.' Thus, while the interpersonal therapist may know where the client is going, he also attempts to walk as slowly through the swamps as the client needs to pick his way rather than drag him by the hair or flail him from behind.

Aggressive attitudes are used by the interpersonal therapist, if they seem useful for the client's progress. Strupp (101) found, in a study comparing therapists from the interpersonal psychiatric school with client-centered counselors, that the only aggressive reactions were expressed by the interpersonal therapists. This is quite in accord with Sullivan's position that any expressive behavior suited to the occasion should be applied. At times Sullivan (106) might appear to fall asleep at an obsessional patient's ruminations. The patient might protest, 'How do you expect me to talk to you?' Sullivan would retort with mild irritation, 'Have you been listening? Have you any idea what you were saying?' Such indifference is obviously an affectation for therapeutic purposes — *I will listen to you only if you will get on with the therapeutic work — then I will approve.* Thus, appropriate amounts of affectional and punishing attitudes are used by the therapist to promote the client's progress in examining and understanding himself and to provide him with socially facilitating feelings of approval and disapproval.

Interpersonal therapy proposes a versatile therapist role. Most of the varieties of expressive behavior described in Chapter IX are pertinent to the interpersonal approach.

We may now present an outline organization of the principal aspects of interpersonal therapy. This will be organized around: (a) the goals of therapy, (b) the emphasized aspects of client functioning, (c) characteristics of the therapist's role — expressive and integrative, and (d) the temporal process.

GOALS OF INTERPERSONAL THERAPY

A 'good-me' self-system includes a maximum of approval toward the self and others and a minimum of anxiety and self-deceiving security-operations. Such a self-system is the core of the adjusted interpersonal man. Good adjustment includes a primarily syntactic organization of experience — the ability to be aware of current interpersonal processes and to function in socially conjunctive, integrative ways. This syntactic mode includes a consensually valid awareness of reality, that is, the tendency to see things as others in one's culture see them, and to respond in culturally approved ways. Such behavior is likely to produce a maximum of security and a minimum of anxiety. Hence, the major goal of interpersonal therapy is to produce as much movement as possible toward this ideal adjustment.

Instrumental goals toward such interpersonal syntaxis are to provide a basis for consensually valid communication — that is, to correct the client's parataxic distortions and his self-deceiving security-operations. Since valid communication is highly dependent upon the client's awareness of anxiety and his security threats, an additional subgoal is to provide the client with an atmosphere of respect and acceptance, so that he may be able to expect benefit and derive a feeling of being approved.

EMPHASIZED ASPECTS OF CLIENT FUNCTIONING

The aspects of interpersonal behavior emphasized include the client's typical patterns of living and responding to himself and others. This includes especially his self-system — the self-appraisals he has, the eidetic persons he includes, the primary sources of anxiety, and the typical patterns of security-operations. The interpersonal therapist attends to all aspects of communication, vocal, gestural, and verbal. He is likely to characterize such patterns of social interaction as Sullivan (102) has called: reserved, guarded, suspicious, hostile and contemptuous; supercilious, superior, conciliatory, deferential, and apologetically inferior; bored, irritated, angry, and actively obstructive; and finally an attitude of mutual respect, rarely encountered in clinical interviews. These several aspects of the client which the therapist emphasizes may be summarized as (a) his perceptions and distortions of perception, (b) his expressive behavior and its interpersonal meanings, and (c) his feelings, especially the feeling of anxiety. These emphasized aspects of the client require more specific illustration.

PERCEPTIONS AND PERCEPTUAL DISTORTIONS: These are responded to for the purpose of correcting them or leading to consensual validity. One patient in group therapy said, 'I know you don't like me as much as you do Mr. M. You always talk to him — but the only time you say anything to me is when you can find something to criticize.' The therapist responded, 'I like you very much. I wonder if you've noticed that I'm not really criticizing you at all — I've pointed out some mistakes — such as when you thought I was blaming you for being angry at Mr. M., but this was to help you recognize your anger rather than to blame you.' In this example the therapist has focused primarily upon the patient's perceptual distortion, saying, 'Let's try to get this straight as to what really happened.' The therapist has also expressed affection and an awareness of the patient's feelings.

EXPRESSIVE BEHAVIOR AND ITS INTERPERSONAL MEANINGS: The therapist emphasizes expressive behavior and its interpersonal meanings. Again from group therapy, the interpersonal leader has been noticing the competitive relation that Mr. M. has taken to him. Mr. M. has disagreed, contradicted, and disparaged the therapist at every opportunity. The therapist remarks, 'It seems to me that you are a very critical person, Mr. M. You seem to be trying to show the group that I don't know how to help them.' Mr. M. replies — agreeing for the first time — 'You're right — I am critical — why shouldn't I be — no one has ever been nice to me the way they are to you.' In this interchange the leader has summarized Mr. M.'s expressive behavior — 'You are critical toward me.'

FEELINGS, ESPECIALLY THE FEELING OF ANXIETY: The interpersonal therapist focuses upon feelings, especially that of anxiety. Anxiety is generally considered to be relatively hidden by security-operations, so that the patient does not experience it directly but engages in various interpersonal operations which divert awareness of anxiety. Thus the interpersonal therapist is likely to infer that the patient is disturbed rather than to observe the tension directly. Another patient in group therapy has constantly complained about his ubiquitous ailments. One day his head is aching, another day he suffers a pain in his chest, finally he expresses concern about a burning sensation in his rectum. The group leader says to Mr. S., 'You have so many pains, I wonder if you're afraid that we don't care about you and that the only way you can get our interest is by showing how helpless you are.' Here the therapist has emphasized the patient's feelings of anxiety in terms of his need for interest and affection from other people. 'You suffer these pains because you are anxious about being unloved.' This example happens to be an exact statement of the general conception of anxiety in interpersonal theory.

The threefold emphasis upon perceptual distortions, expressive interpersonal behavior, and feelings of interpersonal tension is most characteristic of the interpersonal psychiatric response to the current functioning of the client. The developmental inquiry of the interpersonal therapist is directed toward similar dimensions of the client's life history.

The elucidation of developmental history is effected by the interpersonal therapist's focus upon significant persons in the client's development (mother, father, bosses, friends) and their interactions with the client. He also focuses upon the pattern of change in development. For example, the job history and its meaning is considered to be especially significant (102). The intention of the focus upon historical development is to examine significant figures and their contributions to the client's present adjustment. These emphases are well summarized in Sullivan's (102) characterization of questions which the interviewer must ask:

'What does the interviewee esteem and what does he disparage about himself?'

'To what experiences is the patient's self-esteem particularly vulnerable?'

'What are the characteristic "righting movements" — security-operations — which appear after the patient has been discomposed?'

'How great are the interviewee's reserves of security? . . . How well is the person's life justified? Can he express estimable things about himself? Has he tried actively to accomplish worthwhile purposes? Does he have secret shames and regrets?'

Thus the interpersonal therapist focuses upon a multifaceted interpersonal man and his developmental history. That the therapist does not focus upon the kind of unconscious meanings as are found in psychoanalysis is a function of the difference in theoretical construction. Theoretically, such psychoanalytic symbols are not there. For example, the therapist does not look for the hostility that may have provoked a feeling of anxiety in the client. He looks for the anxiety that has been avoided by an outburst of hostility. The aspects of client functioning upon which the therapist will focus are largely a result of theoretical expectations. The analyst will look for and find characteristic material which is different from the material seen in the interpersonal scope.

CHARACTERISTICS OF THE THERAPIST'S ROLE

The therapist's role may be summarized in terms of his *expressive* and his *integrative* activities. Expressively, the interpersonal therapist uses any kind of expressive behavior or emotional reaction that seems to fit the client's treatment needs in the interpersonal framework. Integratively, the therapist does whatever is necessary to aid the client to become a syntactic, socially skillful, and interpersonally sensitive individual.

EXPRESSIVE ASPECTS OF THE THERAPIST'S ROLE: Expressive operations of the therapist may be subsumed in relation to the degree to which they fit along a management-participation axis, and the degree to which they fit along an affection-aggression axis (cf. Chapters VIII and IX). Such expressive operations will be examined informally here.

The expertness quality of the therapist includes the concepts that he is regarded by society as having special knowledge and skill in interpersonal relations, and that the patient has such expectations of him. He must *manage* the interview in such a way that he fits the cultural accreditation. As the culture's representative, he provides aid to the patient in developing consensually valid syntactic skills. He is and serves as a representative of the constructive culture. *Approval* and *respect* for the client are necessary aspects of the therapist's role. Since the client is suffering largely from insecurity arising out of real and imagined disapprovals, the therapist must help to correct the effects of eidetically maintained developmental experiences in being disapproved. Since the self-system is a reaction to losses in euphoria associated with reflected appraisals, the therapist provides respect for the client and approval of him as a person. This does not mean the therapist accepts him at face value, but that he provides respect and approval for the client's potentialities and understands the cultural disfigurements upon the interpersonal visage. He approves of the client and provides him with some security by this affectionate attitude.

Even in his *aggressive* reactions, the therapist maintains a basic respect. The example of Sullivan falling asleep and then saying irritably, 'Have you been listening?' is suggestive. The attitude, 'I expect you can do better than that' was implicit rather than 'I detest you for being obscure.' Thus, the interpersonal therapist provides aggression as a stimulus toward growth rather than as a rejection of the client's worth.

Respect and affection for the client are especially conveyed by the *empathic, understanding,* and *humility* operations of the interpersonal therapist. Sullivan (106) has described his reaction to an overflow of gratitude from the client, 'Can this patient afford to appreciate me so much?' The answer is, 'No!' Typical of Sullivan's reply to such a question is, 'When one overcomes a major fiction in the presence of another, one is apt to feel warm toward that person.' In other words, the therapist does not take personal gratification in warmth from the client, but respects the client's needs and progress in relation to it.

The circumlocution and indirection of the interpersonal therapist is characteristically humble, understanding, and nonconfronting: 'I have a vague feeling that some people might doubt the utility to you of the care with which your parents, and particularly your mother, saw to it that you didn't learn how to dance, or play games, or otherwise engage in the frivolous social life of people your age . . .' Such a round the mulberry-bush approach to 'Your mother really loused you up' conveys both an understanding acceptance of the client's need for regard for parents, and some humility about the possible incorrectness of the statement. That is, the circumlocution is designed to allow the client to grapple with the question without having to defend himself from the affront.

The role of the therapist as a participant in an interpersonal process is maximized. That is, the client is expected to learn interpersonal skills by engaging in a two-person group process with the therapist. Even though the therapist expertly *manages* the relation, he provides a therapeutic foil against which the client can practice his developing interpersonal skills. The therapist *participates,* however, not as necessarily himself but as the kind of person the client needs. While it is quite in order for the therapist to express irritation, he certainly should not feel it personally. The attitudes and expressions that he provides should be therapeutically rather than personally valid.

INTEGRATIVE ASPECTS OF THE THERAPIST'S ROLE: Integrative operations of the therapist are those in which he helps the client to understand how his ways of seeing the world are distortions; how his behavior, which is intended to reduce anxiety, fails in this intent and only provokes rejection from others. He helps the client to understand how past experience has produced ineptness, and how new and more effective integrations can be accomplished. In other words, the therapist focuses upon and elucidates characteristic patterns of ineffectiveness in living so that such patterns may be modified in constructive ways.

The therapist focuses upon those aspects of the client's past and present living which are important to his becoming integrated in the interpersonal process. He inquires into developmental experiences that may have been important to the present mode of behavior; he observes and comments upon the way that the client escapes the awareness of anxiety; he encourages the patient to notice his own peripheral thoughts and ways of behaving, which he usually does not notice.

Integrations of the client's processes are accomplished in several ways. The therapist remembers what he has said and firmly corrects any distortions that the client may develop. This encourages consensually valid, syntactic communication. The patient is taught to perceive and remember in a socially valid way. The therapist reasons with the patient, helps him to accept culturally logical ways of thinking. He summarizes his impressions of the important things the client has said and done, attempting to make a reasonable integration of the client's behavior and anxiety-reducing operations. When the client is obscure, he attempts to clarify the communication so that both client and therapist will understand. Finally, as the interview process reaches termination, he presents a complete summary of what has gone on in therapy and uses this as a basis for a prescription of action to improve future functioning.

TEMPORAL PROCESS IN THERAPY

It may be useful to take a brief look at the *temporal sequence* of therapist operations in interpersonal therapy. Sullivan (102) has divided this sequence into four phases in terms of the changing role of the therapist. These phases include the formal inception, the reconnaissance, the detailed inquiry, and the termination.

The formal inception answers the question, 'Why is this patient here?' Regardless of the client's source or manner of referral, it is necessary for the therapist and client to have some kind of mutual understanding as to why the client thinks he has presented himself or been presented at the therapist's office.

The reconnaissance may take anywhere from one to fifteen interviews and addresses itself to an outline sketch of the significant patterns of responding and to the primary contributors to these patterns. It asks such questions as 'What kind of a person was your father?' 'How did other people view your mother?' Such questions are not necessarily answered in the reconnaissance, but some light is thrown upon them. Following the reconnaissance, a summary sketch of the therapist's impressions up to this point is presented to the client for discussion and correction.

In the *detailed inquiry,* the developmental background of the client and its relation to his characteristic behavior is intensively investigated. The 'good-me,' 'bad-me' aspects, the sources of discomfort, the security-operations, the reserves of security and effectiveness are reviewed in detail. What kind of an interpersonal man is this? and How did he become himself? are the general questions.

In *termination,* the therapist makes a final statement that is intended to be correct and complete — he includes only those gross conclusions of which he is quite certain. From this assessment he derives a proscription for action. 'The interviewer indicates the course of events in which the interviewee might engage and which, in the interviewer's opinion, in view of the data accumulated, would improve his chances of success and satisfaction in life' (102). This is presumably not in the nature of advice, but is rather a summary integration of the compelling structure that the background suggests.

In the *final assessment,* the interviewer recapitulates what he has told the client up to this point and what the effects of this on the life course of the client are likely to be.

The temporal process in interpersonal therapy does not have the coherent relation to the developmental process that is characteristic of psychoanalytic theory and therapy. The interpersonal therapist is operating in a continuous interpersonal field and the temporal stages of the process are no more clear-cut than are the temporal stages of interpersonal learning; the entire interview process is a continuing experience in revising the pattern of living toward more constructive social integration.

SUMMARY

The interpersonal therapist's operations are a systematic expression of the interpersonal theory. Assuming that the sense of security and the reduction of anxiety are interpersonal rather than internal processes, the therapist provides those attitudes, behaviors, or interpretations which may be necessary to help the client become an effectively integrated part of the social process.

Interpersonal motivation is essentially toward acceptance by other people. Tension or anxiety is the threat that others will reject one. In growing up the interpersonal man learns that significant people — such as mothers or fathers — help him to build a picture of himself from 'good-me,' 'bad-me' or disowned 'not-me' aspects. Congruently, he develops expectations about how others will treat him, for example, the 'good-mother' or the 'bad-mother.' He brings such fictional expectations into every new situation and responds on the basis of his protective distortions (parataxes) rather than on the basis of social validity. His behavior, then, is designed to provide a sense of security in the face of anticipated rejection. He covers his anxiety by 'security-operations,' or behavior designed to keep him from experiencing interpersonal tension.

The therapist's method is designed to provide for the development of social integration and consensual validity. That is, the therapist intends to provide his client with those experiences which will help him to feel accepted and secure, to be skillful rather than defensive in his interpersonal operations, and to see things in a socially valid way — as other people see them. Thus the therapist is a sensitively social vehicle in therapy. He reacts to the patient with whatever expression of feelings the patient needs for improving his sense of security; he helps the patient to recognize sources of anxiety and distortion, to the end that the patient learns to see himself and others in socially valid ways and is able to modify himself into socially adequate behavior. Exploration of the past has the purpose of correcting distorted meanings in the present. Affectionate or aggressive attitudes expressed by the therapist are designed to help the client learn to experience and behave in socially valid and efficient ways.

                                    . . . as the swift
                                    seasons roll,
                                    Leave thy low-
                                    vaulted past!
                                    —LOWELL

VI. The Dynamic Relationship Therapy of Otto Rank

Otto Rank conceptualized neurosis as an ambivalent differentiation of the self from mother symbols. The neurotic recognizes his difference from others, but suffers fear and guilt from such awareness. The neurotic fears his individuality, but is caught in a conflict between desires to accept his creative differences and to be an accepting part of his society. He fears being different, yet resists the compulsion to conform. This conflict stems from a struggle for separation from the mother. The neurotic wishes to establish his creative individuality, but fears the loss of dependent unity with the mother and mother symbols.

In psychotherapy, then, the client is expected to be engaged in attempts both to unite with the therapist and to establish constructive independence. Therapist operations are congruent to this struggle. The therapist encourages both uniting and separating reactions. Since separation cannot be achieved without prior satisfaction of the need for unity with another, the client is encouraged to accept and verbalize his relation to the therapist. Since creative individuality is the therapeutic goal, the client is encouraged to express and accept his need to be different. Technically, both end-setting in therapy and a focus upon the immediately present relationships are designed to provide successful experiences in emotional unity and separation.

Since the neurotic's guilt and fear about creative independence are related to his resistance to coercion, the therapist accepts antagonistic reactions so long as these do not violate the selfhood of someone else.

Conscious acceptance of primitive impulses is considered to be the essence of constructive independence. The client is encouraged to accept his own uniqueness without guilt and without attack upon society.

CREATIVE INTEGRATION

In contrast to the *interpersonal* goal of security in human relations, Rankian philosophy prizes creative difference as the essence of personality integration. The creative man, *the man who* accepts and magnifies his constructive individuality, is the Rankian goal in therapy. 'Only insight into that which he is potentially, not the picture of what he should be normally, can form the foundation of dynamic therapy' (78).

Sullivan's interpersonal adjustment is somewhat analogous to Rank's conception of the normal, or average, person who has accepted the will of the majority. Such acquiescence in belonging to the group is a pale, anemic kind of social adequacy which is hardly to be imposed upon the potentially creative neurotic. The neurotic is a stage advanced from the normal — he should be helped to realize his unique potentiality rather than shoved back into the docile average. Acceptance and utilization of his creative self, not conformance with unconstructive mores, is the legitimate goal of treatment. Let the client find his own direction rather than showing him your way in therapy. Promote acceptance of individual ideals and goals rather than acquiescence to uninspired adequacy.

The role of the therapist in this conception of the client becomes quite distinctive. He cannot re-educate the child in the client — the client is already more than adult. Present ineffectiveness is the core problem — '. . . an emotional denial of the present' (Rank, 78). Any meandering away from the present, be it into the past or future, is a way of avoiding an active assault upon the now. Thus the *living present*, the immediacy of the therapy relationship, is the stuff from which the client can synthesize creative skills. As Taft (103) has said, 'I myself am the remedy at this moment. . . .'

Theoretically the client's creative potential is inhibited by his sense of guilt at being different from others, and by his fear of loss of unity with mother symbols. He yearns for both independence from and unity with another. He fears being himself, and he resents his lack of separateness. Thus the therapy experience becomes an opportunity for working with his struggle for separation and his need for wholeness with another. The value of the therapist is '. . . his ability to use consciously for the benefit of his client the insight and self-discipline which he has achieved in his own struggle to accept self, life and time, as limited, and to be experienced fully only at the cost of fear, pain and loss. . . .' (Taft, 103).

To assess therapeutic operations related to the Rankian theory we shall consider motivational constructs and adjustment and maladjustment as these are conceived in Rank's philosophy. Following this theoretical review, we shall construct an operational outline of dynamic relationship [1] therapy.

Motivational Constructs

Rank's conceptualization of motivation can be described as a struggle between drives for independent selfhood and social unity. That is, shall I be my separate, constructive self, or shall I be an integral part of the people to whom I relate? His answer to this question is threefold: (a) The normal or average person shall be only a part of his social world; (b) The antisocial person will continue his fight against society; and (c) The creative man, including potentially the neurotic, shall be a separate constructive individual contributing to and modifying society. These various ways of relating to society can all be conceived in terms of the *will* concept. In its most effective form, the will is '. . . a positive, guiding organization and integration of self, which utilizes creatively, as well as inhibits and controls the instinctual drives' (Rank, 78). As phrased by Karpf (58), it is '. . . the dynamic organization of the personality for the achievement of some objective.' Both of the statements represent the creatively effective will which is developed in the creative artist or forged into being by dynamic relationship therapy with the neurotic. Will in all its aspects is not necessarily so felicitous.

Creative will develops in response to the unyielding or ungiving quality of the environment. In his original paradisiacal state, the infant has no need to control, organize, or create anything. As a part of

---

[1] Since the term *relationship therapy* has been used for two somewhat different approaches in current literature, it will be necessary to designate them separately. *Dynamic relationship therapy* will refer to the Rankian approach. Levy's (62) relationship therapy appears to be more closely derived from the psychoanalytic conception of the transference. In this chapter, Levy's relationship therapy as represented in the protocols of Durkin (15) will be used heuristically to point up the distinctive aspects of Rank's position. The expression *transference relationship* therapy will refer to Levy's and Durkin's approach.

the organic wholeness of mother's body, he is blissfully dependent and complete. Suddenly, he is thrust out of paradise into an alien land wherein he has to find and masticate his own apples rather than having them flow into him. His needs are no longer automatically gratified and he becomes an organically separate individual. Awareness of individuality develops as the infant experiences demands upon himself. These demands are initially met with resistance — a *counter-will* that he opposes to the demands he experiences. He does not wish to be disturbed, so he resists either externally or internally imposed demands. This is the first step in the genesis of individuality and creative will. Later he may discover that his needs are best gratified by joining in the will of others. By wanting the same things that others have, he may find his needs more easily satisfied — thus, he joins in the group will, decides to will as others do, and is no longer compelled to belong since he has made the choice himself. This submergence in the group will is called *positive will*. A consummate development beyond positive will which occurs partly in the neurotic, and fully in the constructive individual, is called the *creative will*. This results from a recognition that one is *oneself*, a separate, unique phenomenon. The neurotic recognizes his difference from others, his *opposing will*, and suffers guilt and fear because of the difference. He yearns to be a part of the social organism but cannot accept such self-deception. At the same time, he yearns to be his separate self but believes this is 'bad' and punishable. The creative type, however, accepts his individuality with its attendant loneliness and guilt, becoming a constructive, creative individual who pays his debt to society by making useful contributions. He does not will in opposition to society. He accepts his own individuality, recognizes its value, and relieves his guilt in being different by enriching the social unit with contributions: 'I strove with none, for none was worth the strife.'

Having emphasized the constructive will and the positive evaluation of the neurotic conflict, we may examine the relation of this 'valuable' aspect of motivation to the more primitive drives of the individual. Rank contrasts his conceptual system to the psychoanalytic 'philosophy of despair' in which we are creatures of blind, instinctive forces which must be kept in leash. He prefers the term *impulse* to instinct, and proposes that the development of will achieves a creative synthesis of such primitive impulses as psychoanalysis describes. Primitive impulses are not in opposition to society, since the individual must satisfy his impulses in a symbiotic relationship to the group. Synthetically speaking, the will is the dynamic, conscious integration of impulse expression and inhibition to achieve a constructive end. The psychoanalytic concept of sublimation becomes unnecessary in this conception, since constructive behavior is a conscious transformation of primitive impulse into socially creative behavior. Rank proposes that 'the unconscious' be considered only as a negative construct, since whatever is 'unconscious' is merely a matter of what is irrelevant to the momentary reality. Anything relevant may be brought into consciousness by the constructive power of will. Karpf (58) says, for example, that 'Instinct lifted into the ego sphere by consciousness is the power of will, and at the same time a tame, directed, controlled instinct which manifests itself creatively.' Thus, the will is the functional integration of impulse and inhibition for the purpose of effective activity.

Relationship is the other emphasis in the motivational system postulated by Rank. We have noted the basic conflict between independent selfhood and dependent unity from which the theory stems. Creative will is the motivational principle associated with autonomy and independence. Such effective development of will is dependent upon the quality and meaning of relationships. The significance of relation ships to others is presumably to be found in birth symbolisms. Rank elaborated on Freud's discussion of the birth experience. Freud (28) said that '. . . the first condition of fear appeared during the first separation from the mother. . . .' Rank extended this notion to the position that all human experience is intensely determined by symbolic elaboration of the original birth trauma. In attempting to shorten psychotherapy, he explored the use of setting a time limit toward which the patient and therapist might work. Under these conditions he found that all of his patients responded with birth symbolisms in dreams and associations. From this, he reasoned that termination in psychotherapy is experienced as a recapitulation of the traumatic separation of the child from the mother at birth. The emphasis is not upon the physical assault of birth, but upon the psychological trauma of separation. He extended this principle as the basic problem in human relationships. The essential conflict in life is between wishes for psychological wholeness with mother versus psychological independence and individuality.

Thus the relationship between client and therapist leading to constructive separation and creative independence became the core of the therapeutic process. In end-setting experience, Rank also found that separation became an immediately present problem in therapy. In a sense, the future was brought into the present. The birth symbolisms evoked under these circumstances brought the remote past into the present as well, and it became plausible that the present meaning of the relationship in therapy was the core problem.

The structure of psychoanalytic theory is modified by Rank's emphasis upon the birth trauma as the primary source of anxiety. The relationship to mother becomes the significant problem on this basis, and the struggle for wholeness and separateness in relation to mother symbols is substituted for the oedipal problem as the nucleus of neurosis. Again, the meaning of transference is shifted from the repetition-compulsion defense against remembering traumatic oedipal meanings to a contemporary struggle between reunion with the mother-surrogate and acceptable selfhood. The prototype of all psychotherapy, and of every significant human experience, is seen in the mother-child relationship. Karpf (58) generalizes that 'Human development proceeds . . . in terms of relationship and separation by a succession of emotional attachments and dependencies on the one hand and independence-seeking separations and detachments on the other hand, with the creation of personality and the emergence of individuality as constantly evolving and expanding goals.' Allen (3) proposes the biological processes of individuation of part processes out of mass movements as a reasonable analogy. Applying the individuation concept to Rankian therapy, Allen suggests that 'Therapy emerges then, from an experience in living, not in isolation but within a relationship with another from whom the patient can eventually differentiate himself as he comes to perceive and accept his own self as separate and distinct.'

The process of separation and individuation is excruciatingly painful. The impulses to unity and separateness are both intense. Taft (103) says, for example, that '. . . fear is a necessary part of all experiencing, a consequence not so much of immediate external danger as of the inherent ambivalence of the human being who must always be pulled in two directions. . . . Fear is inherent in individuation and self-consciousness, in the necessity to be both part and whole. . . . The antidote for fear is successful experiencing. The fear of being caught in wholeness, in union with the other, can be reduced only when the impulse to unite completely is lived through deeply enough to convince the individual that since it has not, it need not destroy him. . . .' Thus the neurotic is hag-ridden by desires for and fears of independence in opposition to desires for and fears of social wholeness. The therapeutic experience provides him with means of experiencing that he can successfully separate himself, will creatively, and still retain some unity with the mother-group.

Adjustment and Maladjustment

In the Rankian theory adjustment and maladjustment are related quite simply to the concepts of will and relationship.

The *counter-will* (characteristic of early childhood resistance to internal or external demands) is maintained in the anti-social personality. Taft (103) presents the case of a destructively acting-out child who is brought for treatment because of incorrigibility in general and tearing her own clothes to pieces in particular. Taft summarizes the will development problem in Helen as follows: 'What Helen needs most, therapeutically, is to yield, to accept the defeat of her own will in a deeper need to submit to the claim of the love object after which she may be enabled to be herself more positively with less denial and defiance.' Maintenance of the counter-will is associated with anti-social, acting-out, aggressive behavior.

Positive will is associated with the development of the normal or average personality. This, in a sense, is an arrested development in personality growth. The normal individual denies much individuality, accepting the group will as his own. He wills positively and agreeably and thereby he retains his unity with society as a mother symbol. He yields his own will and accepts the will of others as his own in order to avoid rejection and separation. Even his fantasies are kept to himself because they are expressions of the bad, negative will which he has given up. He is uncreative, because he accepts things as they are and protects himself by being like the group of which he is a part. Such adjustment is an anemic compliance that is by no means a worthy objective in Rank's therapeutic philosophy.

The neurotic may be understood as an intermediate, dynamic, tensional state between the normal person and the creative artist.

Creative will is characteristic of the person who accepts his own individuality, prizes his uniqueness, and wills to produce what is characteristic of himself. Even though this highest adjustment appears to be out of harmony with society, it is not necessarily so conceived. The creative person is aware of his difference. He has suffered the pangs of separation and has achieved a unified selfhood. However, he does not will in opposition to the majority; he has simply accepted his own separateness and independence. He also finds it necessary to propitiate society for the guilt he feels in so separating himself. He brings the product of his separate creative fantasy back to society and enriches the world by his contribution. 'And yet when he has journeyed far into the lands beyond the dawn, lo, he becomes a guiding star to lead them whither he has gone.'

The neurotic is caught in the middle of his needs to be separate and unique versus his needs to be a part of a united whole. His childhood experiences have taught him that his will is bad and punishable. Therefore he acts to restrain and inhibit his separate fantasies and unique expressions. At the same time he cannot allow himself to accept the gross deception of 'normal.' He says in effect, 'I am myself, but this is dangerous, and I am like other people, but this is deceitful.' He fights against submerging himself into the majority, and fights against emerging as an individual. Taft (103) describes the will problem of a neurotic child as follows: 'Jack . . . has the task of learning to affirm his own will despite the pull of the love object or the temptation to assert himself indirectly through possession and domination of the other . . .'

Thus the problem of adjustment in the Rankian philosophy is concerned primarily with the transformation of the negative will of the conflicted neurotic into a creative, constructive acceptance of individuality. Rank does not concern himself about 'dumb driven cattle' of normal adequacy, but about the 'hero in the strife' of creative adjustment. We now turn to how this creative therapy is accomplished.

AN OPERATIONAL ANALYSIS OF DYNAMIC RELATIONSHIP THERAPY

The therapy process may be conceived in terms of (a) the goals and nature of the therapeutic process, (b) the therapist's role, and (c) the client's experience.

THE GOALS OF DYNAMIC RELATIONSHIP THERAPY: These goals can be considered from the point of view of anticipated outcomes. In this respect Rankian therapy is distinctively concerned with the transformation of neurotic will conflicts into creative will productivity. The neurotic represses his fantasies because he feels guilty about being different, the creative elaborates and affirms his fantasies to the rest of the world — '. . . a newly created whole, the strongest personality with its autonomous will' (58). The neurotic, however, compares himself unfavorably with the rest of the world. He suffers from his individuality. Recognizing his difference from others, he feels guilty and unacceptable. His awareness is focused upon his individuality, which appears to be a transgression rather than a potential value. He cannot accept the self-deception which the normal person achieves, nor can he accept the valuableness of his uniqueness as the creative individual does. The goal of therapy, then, is to strengthen the neurotic's acceptance of his individuality by modifying his fear of separateness and his guilt in opposing others. As a child, the neurotic has learned that certain will expressions are bad, while conforming will is good. He suffers from such 'reminiscence' and is unable to accept an emotional experiencing of the present. Thus, therapy provides '. . . an opportunity to feel in the present and gradually begin to accept responsibility for one's own feelings and impulses in all their ambivalences, with as little denial, rationalization and justification as may be' (Taft, 103).

No goal of social conformity can be imposed upon dynamic relationship therapy. The therapeutic goal is clearly an individual matter. This individualized goal is in sharp contrast to both the psychoanalytic goal of conscious *control* over biological instincts, and the interpersonal psychiatric goal of syntactic, consensual validity. Rank's therapy is not concerned about socially acceptable behavior. 'It is a purely individual affair and can be measured only in terms of its meaning to the person' (Taft, 103). 'Will people ever learn that there is no other equality possible than the equal right of every individual to become and to be himself, which actually means to accept his own difference and have it accepted by others?' (Rank, 79).

THE THERAPIST'S ROLE: *Unity* and *differentiation* are the two personality goals of any client. The struggle to separate oneself and become an autonomous individual is in opposition to the desire to be a part of the mother and secure in a wholeness with mother symbols. The value of the therapist in promoting selfhood and independence lies in the fact that therapy provides a *living present* in which it is possible to develop a separate integration. On this basis Taft (103) criticizes psychoanalysis as '. . . a practical denial of the reality of the present. . . .' The psychoanalytic therapist is '. . . hidden behind the screen of father, mother, brother, sister, while all the time [the therapist's] value for the client is that she is none of these and [the client] knows it. He may be using patterns which were developed by him in birth, nursing, weaning, toilet training, Edipus situation and what not, but he is using them now, with all the changes wrought by years of living, using them afresh as they are in the present hour. . . . He does not want a father or a mother, but he does want someone who will permit him ultimately to find himself apart from parent identifications without interference or domination; someone who will not be fooled, someone strong enough not to retaliate.'

Comparison with the psychoanalytic conception of the transference may clarify the Rankian conception of the meaning and utilization of the therapist-client relationship. A sample comparison from Levy's (15) transference-oriented interpretation of the present relationship with a Rankian-oriented interpretation will provide a basis for discussing this contrast.

> THE THERAPIST (Durkin, 15) comments: 'You don't like me because I'm like [your sister] T——.'
> PAULA: (Pouring out her feelings) 'Yes, I hate T——.'
> THERAPIST: 'I understand. It's all right not to want me.' Then, seeing that Paula was very anxious, the therapist verbalized the child's feelings more directly, 'You're very angry at me.'
> PAULA: 'Yes, I hate you. I'll kill you.'
> THERAPIST: 'I understand, I'm like T——. You hate me. It's all right, children often feel that way. I like you just the same.'

In this sample the therapist has treated the anger as though it is determined by a displacement of a feeling appropriately directed toward someone else. This might be called a *contemporary transference interpretation*. The therapist assumes that the feeling is properly directed toward a contemporary in the child's life.

By contrast the Rankian approach would treat the feeling as though it appropriately belongs to the immediate experience. A sample from Taft (103) in a similar situation illustrates this difference.

Helen, a child of seven, plays roughly with a doll. The therapist says, 'Are you mad, Helen? Do you feel like hitting something?' Helen will not admit that she is angry. The therapist continues, 'I think you are mad at me because you didn't come last time.'

HELEN: 'Some day I am going to miss you.'
THERAPIST: 'You mean you are not coming some time, Helen?'

In this exchange it will be seen that the therapist interprets the child's anger as appropriately directed at the therapist herself, and relates it to the problem of separation. This might be labeled a *present relationship interpretation.* Taft does not propose that the transference meanings are irrelevant, but that only the experience in the immediate relationship is of primary consequence. She uses the immediate experience to promote the client's ability to differentiate himself and establish his own will. 'Transference, like resistance, is accepted for what it is, a stage in the growth process, in taking over of the own will into the self' (Taft, 103).

A need that must be satisfied before individuality can be accepted comfortably is the need to fully experience unity with another. Taft (103) says that the client must '. . . yield himself once more to the feared love forces in order to separate more completely than he had been able to do at first.' Another illustration from the case of Helen suggests this process. Helen goes to the window and daringly poises herself in a precarious, half-way-out position. The therapist says, 'Helen, if you fall out on your head, it's not my fault.' 'Whose fault is it?' Helen asks. 'It's going to be yours. There's nothing I can do about it; just fall if you want to.' Helen responds by being very careful. She sits by the window and talks under her breath. The therapist catches the words 'I love,' and asks, 'What's that you are saying, Helen?' Helen says somewhat ashamedly, 'I love you and you love me.' 'Is that the way you feel?' the therapist asks. Helen assents.

In this exchange the therapist has been completely non-coercive — has allowed the child freedom of will; and the child responds with both greater self-control and acceptance of unity with the therapist. She finds it unnecessary to assert her will against the therapist and can therefore accept both a sense of unity and a sense of separateness. It will also be seen that the therapist's handling of the situation was not by assurance of affection but by the permission of complete freedom so long as the child was not violating the rights of anyone else. Such intense *permissiveness* can be contrasted with the *affectionate giving* characteristic of the transference relationship therapy of Levy (62), which is more psychoanalytic in flavor. Levy proposes that the relationship between therapist and client should be one in which the therapist does everything he can to promote strong positive feelings from the client. In Levy's therapy the therapist assumes an essentially affectionate attitude, reassuring the client at every opportunity that he loves the client no matter how the client feels or what he does. For example, Durkin (15) tells of an incident when Paula washed all the drinking cups, but conspicuously left the therapist's unwashed. The therapist commented, 'You don't like me today.' Paula looked doubtful, and the therapist continued, 'It's all right not to like me. I like you just the same.' While Taft's and Durkin's examples are similar in many ways, there is an essential operational difference with a theoretical justification in each case. Taft's intention is to allow the client freedom from coercion so that he may relinquish his negative will, experience unity with the therapist, and therefrom move toward a constructive individuation. Durkin's examples of Levy's transference relationship therapy illustrate the therapist as a surrogate for other people. The client's feelings are displaced upon the therapist in pretty much the way that the psychoanalytic theory of transference proposes that they should be. The client finds affectionate understanding rather than thwarting and retaliation.

THE CLIENT'S EXPERIENCE: In the struggle between unity and differentiation, feelings of guilt and fear are uppermost. The client feels guilty about accepting his difference; he fears the loss of belongingness and unity with another. He also fears the coercion and domination that ordinarily go with accepting a close relationship. In a sense both fear and guilt are essential parts of all experiencing. They cannot be eliminated, but they can be modified: 'The antidote for fear is successful experiencing' (103). In the illustrations from Taft, we noted that Helen was allowed complete freedom so long as she did not infringe on the rights of others. She found that she could be herself in a positive way without having to resist coercion. Thus the fear of separateness was reduced by her finding that even in individuality she was a comfortably accepted part of the therapist. Her suddenly desisting from the daring position at the window was followed by an expression of love for the therapist. We construed this expression as a verbalization of a sense of unity with the therapist. Equally likely is its meaning as an expression of guilt — a denial that she was really challenging the therapist. Such guilt can be reduced but never completely allayed. According to Taft (103), guilt '. . . is an inevitable by-product of self-conscious living, not a symptom of which one may be cured.' Thus, the expression of love and unity is partly an expression of guilt over having dared to be different, and partly a denial of the impulse to resist coercion.

Rank's relationship therapy could appropriately be called a therapy of *the living present*. The client can do only one thing; accept whatever new experience that the living present provides and utilize this experience in the exciting *now* as a basis for freedom in dealing with every new situation. Rank (78) says that the only therapeutic value for the client is '. . . to understand himself in an immediate experience which permits living and understanding to become one . . . an immediate understanding of experience, consciously, in the very act of experiencing.' Technically this emphasis upon the *living present* introduces three considerations: (a) the therapist's focus upon the present relationship; (b) the setting of realistic limits upon the client's behavior, including physical and time controls; and (c) the emphasis upon setting and working toward a fairly definite termination.

THE THERAPIST'S FOCUS: We have elaborated somewhat upon the therapist's focus upon the immediate present. Briefly, the therapist maximizes what is happening *now*, as the essence of the therapy problem. How this makes conceptual sense in relation to the historical source of personality formation in the birth trauma is plausibly understood if life is conceptualized as a series of relationships and struggles for independence. Each successful experiencing of separate selfhood leads to a greater freedom to accept individuality as well as unity.

LIMITS SETTING: That self, life, and time are limited is a reality of the therapy relationship. While the client is helped to become himself, this is not a swaggering self, insensitive to human and physical limitations and prerogatives. Rankian protocols are replete with limits-setting operations of the therapist. Allen (3) cites an incident where the therapist tells the child it is all right for him to feel any way he wants, but he must respect the legitimacy of physical and personal limits:

'In the midst of making considerable noise [George, a small boy] said to the therapist: "You are scared. You are a bad boy." The aggressiveness continued and the therapist had to limit its concrete expression: "George, you feel as bad as you want, but there are some things you can't do." George was both angry and anxious and said, "You shut up. I am not bad. I don't want to be bad." But it was important for him to discover he could feel angry and want to be bad, yet accept some limits as to what he did with that feeling.'

In this sample the therapist is not coercing the child. He is pointing out coercions from reality which have to be considered.

Similarly, Taft (103) objectively defines the limits of Helen's free movement. Helen can fall out of the window if she decides to, but when she threatened to cut some clay with the clinic's scissors, the therapist said, 'Helen, it will be your job to clean it off, for I won't have time. It's very hard to get off.' Then Helen made threatening movements toward the furniture, also she acted as though she were about to drop a dish. The therapist said, 'Helen, all you want is to have me say you can't do it, isn't it?'

In each of these samples the therapist is recognizing, and verbalizing for the client, the reality considerations which limit movement. Recognition of such reality is apparently essential to effectiveness in living. Equal emphasis is placed upon time limits in Taft's protocols. For example, Helen says, 'I am coming down Tuesday.' The therapist replies firmly, 'But I shall not be here then. I cannot come until Thursday.' The quality of firmness in this material is evident. The therapist is not imposing a coercive will upon the client, but is being quite clear in defining reality considerations.

Wanton destruction or greediness is also limited. In one episode Helen was making marks on several sheets of paper since she had learned that she was allowed to take home her drawings. The therapist said firmly, 'Helen, that is a mean trick. It isn't fair. You don't really draw a picture. You just put a mark on it. You can take only the ones you really draw.'

Thus the emphasis upon both individual and physical realities of the living present is intended to provide an opportunity to experience fully in the present relationship. This emphasis can be pointed up more clearly by another contrast with Levy's transference relationship therapy. Durkin (15) proposes that the children in her group should be allowed unlimited freedom, but is then concerned about the practicality of anarchy. She notes somewhat apologetically that 'I solved this problem by establishing a very few fundamental rules which were so universal and automatic that they were, I feel, dissociated from me.' These three rules were: 'We don't use weapons to hit people. We don't destroy property. We don't go out on the road.' No apology would be necessary for such rules from the Rankian approach, since the acceptance of limits is an integral proposition.

TERMINATION: *Planned termination* in an effort to make psychotherapy more efficient was the experience that initially provoked Rank's conceptual system. An important aspect of the Rankin therapy then is to keep the termination of therapy constantly in awareness. We have noted before that therapy of *the living present* does not 'look before and after.' Planning for life outside of therapy is not encouraged, but awareness that the therapy experience is limited in time and will eventually be resolved is insistently maintained. In a sense this brings termination forward in time, so that the problem of separation can be consciously worked through. In her third hour with Helen, Taft (103) raised the question of termination, which would occur thirteen interviews later: 'Perhaps you will want to come until your school is out, until you have vacation.' Helen said, 'Then can I come back again?' 'If you want to, but perhaps you will get tired.' 'I like to come.' 'Yes, I know you do, but you may feel differently someday.' End-setting brings the separation problem into the immediate present so that it may be worked with in the relationship. It will be seen in this example that the conflict between union and independence is precipitated immediately by raising the termination question. Again, however, the therapist does not say it must be so, but it will probably be so. That is, the therapist does not coerce, but raises the question whether *You may want to quit and it will be all right. You needn't be afraid of separation.*

Some poignant examples of the final separation are provided by both Taft (103) and Allen (3). Helen's final leavetaking started out with her being fifteen minutes late. As the hour is ending she says, 'Can't I stay until eleven?' 'No, Helen, you know I have to go the same as usual today.' 'But I have to see the doctor.' 'I don't think you have to this morning.' 'Can't I stay up here alone after you are gone?'

When the therapist finally says good-by to her, Helen holds out her doll and says, 'Kiss the baby.'

One of Allen's (3) cases: Grace brought two cents with her in her final hour. 'Would you give these back if I gave them to you?'

'What do you think I should do?'

'If I give them to you, I wouldn't have anything left — I'll keep them.'

In another of Allen's (3) cases, Bob set up a store toward the end of therapy and was selling everything indiscriminately. The therapist remarked, 'Bob, you are certainly through with those things, maybe you are through with this place.' 'Why?' Bob asked. 'You don't usually sell things you need.' Bob agreed and proceeded with the sale.

In each of these examples of termination, a sense of semi-completion and a willingness to separate, even though it is painful, are expressed by the child. The apparent growth toward individuation and acceptance of a separate selfhood is related theoretically to the separation of the self from the mother symbol, and technically to the bringing of termination into the early stages of the process. 'The patient goes on to a new world which needs him as he needs it. It is the therapist who is abandoned . . .' (Taft, 103).

THEORETICAL NATURE OF THE THERAPEUTIC PROCESS

A *constructive taking over of will* and assuming responsibility for one's own individuality is the essence of the client's personality process in Rankian psychotherapy. This is well illustrated by the Rankian attitude toward *resistance, inhibition, consciousness,* and the *verbalization of feelings.*

Resistance in Rankian therapy is conceived as an active striving against the coercive will of another. In therapy, resistance is never handled by interpretation or any attempt to break it down. Even though resistance is an expression of counter-will, it provides a basis for constructive striving toward independence. Hence, resistance is supported and strengthened by the therapist as an active expression of potentially creative will. Resistance is responded to '. . . frankly and without denial or counter-resistance in feeling . . .' (Taft, 103), even when it must be checked in a reality sense.

Helen is talking about what time she should leave, even though she knows very well. The therapist says, 'Very well, you can go any time you want to, Helen.'

'Did you expect me this morning?'

'Yes, I did. Why?'

'Well, maybe I might not come.'

'I think you want to make me feel bad, Helen, by making me think you are not going to come. . . .'

In this interchange, Taft accepts the resistance and allows Helen to do whatever she wants with it. At the same time, however, she points up the negative will expression involved — 'You want to make me feel bad.' The handling of resistance here assumes that it can be a constructive striving toward independence if it is not met with counter-resistance.

Inhibition is conceived as an autonomous internal process which becomes *denial* at a conscious level. Both inhibition and denial are negative will expressions which can become part of a constructive will expression. These relationships may be illustrated by the same hypothetical situation that we used to contrast differences in symbolic meanings between psychoanalytic theory and interpersonal theory. It will be remembered that we described an incident in which a young man saw a woman on the street who interested him very much but who did not respond to his glance. A quick shift in attention to the clothes in a store window or a sense of urinary urgency necessitating a hurried trip to the lavatory were proposed as symbolic resolutions of the emotional difficulty. We proposed that the psychoanalytic interpretation of the two resolutions could be an almost hysterical denial (cf. p. 101), 'I must cover my naked sexual wish,' and 'My penis is a urinary, not a sexual apparatus.' The hypothesized interpersonal theory meanings could be selective inattention partly resolving the feeling of insecurity, by (cf. p. 102) 'I will substitute warm clothes for mother's lack of warmth,' or an angry counter-reaction against anxiety, expressed symbolically, as 'PO'd, but in private so it won't get me into trouble.'

The same situation in the Rankian theory might be conceived as 'I want to submerge myself in this mother symbol, but that would put me under her control — instead I will buy some clothes like other people wear — but I'll get a distinctive pattern that suits me best.' Or, considering the urinary urgency result, 'Unity with this mother symbol would relieve me of all needs for self-control — but this is dangerous. I must manage my own physiological processes and be a separate individual.'

Here the impulse to unite is in conflict with the impulse to separate, so at the conscious level both are denied and either the clothes or the physiological mechanism are used as a counter-will expression against the coercion to relate. It might also be supposed that some guilt feeling would arise in connection with either resolution.

Related to the therapy situation, the Rankian might be expected to help the client verbalize such impulses to unite and separate and to accept these in such a way that the guilt would be reduced.

In his concept of *consciousness,* Rank disregards the antithesis of conscious and unconscious, assuming that all experiences are available to the present moment if they have relevance and value. The unconscious is primarily a *denial* of will 'in order to evade the conscious responsibility following of necessity . . .' from the recognition of impulses. The development of constructive will, then, involves an acceptance of all impulses and the conscious utilization of these in creative living.

Verbalization of emotions is the means by which the client develops an acceptance of responsibility for his feelings. Such verbal awareness provides a basis for recognition and responsibility. Constructive decisions are dependent upon effective awareness and utilization of one's feelings in the service of controlled self-guidance. Ordinarily, a person tries to deny his feelings in order to evade responsibility. By verbally recognizing impulses, he develops conscious control and effective use of feelings in constructive *willing.*

Verbalization to achieve conscious control may be illustrated by an incident in Helen's therapy (Taft, 103). Helen was daring the therapist to keep her from the open window. The therapist responded with, 'It's your fault if you fall out the window.' Then Dr. Taft encouraged the verbal expression of feelings — 'What's that you are saying, Helen?' 'I love you and you love me.' 'Is that the way you feel?' Dr. Taft asks. In this sample, Helen verbalizes her feelings; they are accepted and she presumably assumes responsibility for them since the therapist does not accept any — the therapist says, in essence, *'I accept your right to feel that way. It is your own responsibility.'*

Therapist and client roles in dynamic relationship therapy will be examined briefly as separate topics. Though the respective roles have been implicit in the discussion of therapy process, a brief review of the role of the therapist, followed by a discussion of the focus upon the client, may help to emphasize operations in the process.

The therapist's operations and role derive primarily from the assumption that the therapist is a current representation of mother-surrogates from whom the client has failed to differentiate himself. In the *living present,* the client will struggle with his needs for unity with the mother and his needs for separation from the mother. A rubric *mother-surrogate* must be defined in its Rankian meaning in order to be distinctive for the dynamic relationship therapy process. A contrast with the Sullivan *mother-fiction,* the Rosen *mother-role* and the Levy *contemporary transference* may help to specify the dynamic relationship mother-symbol quality of the therapist. The *mother-fiction* in Sullivan's interpersonal psychiatry is the present representation of the client's experiences in interpersonal security and anxiety with the mothering one. The successful resolution of such mother-fictions is accomplished by differentiating the therapist as a separate, present individual who is not legitimately a consensually valid mother. By contrast the phenomenology of Rank proposes that the therapist is in some sense a true representation of the mother, from whom the client really needs to differentiate himself by experiencing that he can safely be a part of the mother-symbol and yet comfortably separate himself from the mother. Thus, while the *interpersonal* therapist *corrects* the client's misperceptions about the mother-fiction, the *dynamic relationship* therapist *allows* the client both to submerge himself in the mother and to separate himself from the mother. This is accomplished by the mother-symbol therapist's refraining from coercion and encouraging constructive will expressions.

Rosen's *direct analysis* mother-role assumes that the patient is suffering from the real mother's refusal to provide good milk — that is, tender affection in infancy. The mother-role assumed by a direct analyst, then, is designed to provide the patient with an experience in being symbolically nursed by a loving mother who will provide 'good milk' and tender affection, so that the affectionally malnourished infant can revise his experiences in malevolent mothering and begin his psychosexual development afresh. This position emphasizes the psychological effects of symbolic poisoning which requires an antidote of symbolic mothering for a sick child. The Rankian position differs by its emphasis upon the problem of symbolic union with, versus symbolic separation from, the mother.

The Levy relationship therapy, which we have called transference relationship, is somewhat similar to Rosen's direct analysis except that mother's importance is not focal. Here, feelings and attitudes appropriate to any contemporary figure are interpretable as displacements upon the therapist. The difference between this and the Rankian viewpoint lies in the idea of displacements of reactions to other figures, as compared to the Rankian assumption that the present, living relationship can be considered as the immediate source of whatever happens. Thus, in dynamic relationship therapy it is the immediate-present meaning which is consequential. Even though the present meaning is derived from the relationship to the mother and the anticipated termination, it is to be understood as it is experienced *now* in the vital moment in which it is lived.

The symbolic mother in Rankian therapy is a theoretical foundation which contributes to the nature of the therapist's operations, but is not introduced operationally into the therapy transaction. The mother-unity, separation problem is *assumed* to be there and contributes to the quality of the therapy process and to the nature of the therapist operations. The therapist, therefore, *focuses* upon the *living present*. That is, he is responsive to what is going on in the right now. Furthermore, he is especially responsive to the *immediate relationship* between the client and himself. The client's impulses and movements toward unity and submergence in the therapist are accepted without clinging. The client's impulses and movements toward separation and expression of his own will are accepted and encouraged. In being non-coercive, the therapist is likely to present his understandings of the client in the form of *inquiries* rather than assertions. 'Is that the way you feel, Helen?' He is likely to encourage the client's own expression when possible, rather than take considerable responsibility for expressing the client's feelings for him. 'What is that you are saying, Helen?'

In apparent contrast to this non-coercive attitude of the Rankian therapist, is the insistent focus upon *limits*. There is emphasis upon time limits and approaching termination, upon restriction of physical activity and upon the necessity to not violate the individuality and rights of others. In a sense this is an emphasis upon reality — that in order to be an individual, one must also allow for other individuals. Creative will is not in violation or opposition to the will of others, but is acceptance and use of one's separate differences. The therapist emphasizes the limits that exist in reality, in a sense, rather than imposing coercive limits. The therapist is not providing restrictive rules, but is verbalizing the reality limits within which constructive will must be exercised. Thus, the limits operations of the therapist consist essentially of the recognition and verbalization of the proposal that life, space, and time are limited; and responsibility can be achieved by recognizing the social, physical, and temporal restrictions within which freedom can be constructive.

SUMMARY

The major categories of therapist operations in dynamic relationship therapy may be summarized as verbalized focus, facilitations, and limits; and expressive permissiveness and firmness.

A. *Verbalized Operations*
1. The therapist's *focus* is upon:
    a. The immediate relationship between client and therapist.
    b. The client's feelings in this relationship.
    c. The client's movements toward unity and separation.
    d. The client's expression of will.
2. The therapist's *facilitating* operations include:
    a. Inquiry rather than assertion and coercion.
    b. Encouragement of expressions of feelings and will.
    c. Encouragement of client verbalizations of immediate experience.
3. The therapist's *limits* operations include:
    a. Firmness in verbalizing physical, social, and time limitations of reality.
    b. Setting and maintaining time limits in both present hours and termination prospects.
B. *Expressive Operations: Permissiveness and Firmness*
1. Permissive acceptance summarizes the non-coercive attitude toward expressions of will.
2. Firmness characterizes the attitude in the clarification or statement of reality limits.

The client's experience and behavior in dynamic relationship therapy can be inferred from the foregoing. But since no systematic studies have been made on this kind of therapy, we must depend primarily on inference. The proposition that the client is an ambivalently differentiated person would lead to the expectation that a struggle between unifying and separating drives would occur in the client's experience of the relationship. Helen's challenging and loving vacillations could be so construed. As she discovers that her negative expressions are not attacked, she is able to express a more positive attitude toward the therapist. As she discovers that she is not entrapped by the therapist as a result of her positive feelings, she is able to accept some sense of constructive independence. She is allowed to be herself, whatever that self may involve; hence she no longer finds it necessary to assert her separateness. She can both unite with the therapist without entanglement and express her individuality without fear of reprisal.

The client finds that he is able to experience success in expressing his own will. Expression of either good or bad feelings is acceptable, so he discovers that he has less need to use these in a struggle for independence. He learns to accept independence and to use his will constructively rather than for conforming or attacking purposes. He finds in the relationship to the therapist that it is reality to which he must adapt himself, not the compulsion of a stronger person. He begins to accept a conscious awareness and acceptance of himself because he, as a person, is a valuable individuality so long as he operates within the reality limits of time, space, and the rights of other individuals.

Rank conceptualized neurosis as an ambivalent differentiation of the self from mother symbols. That is, the neurotic recognizes his difference, but suffers fear and guilt because of it. At the same time, the neurotic resists the compulsion from society to be merely a part of the docile herd. A twofold emphasis upon (a) constructive difference and (b) dependent unity as the essential motivational conflict in the neurotic leads to the dynamic relationship therapist's focus upon the client's struggle for independent selfhood and his seeking for dependent unity with the therapist. Congruent operations include the encouragement of both uniting and separating reactions of the client. Since separation cannot be achieved without a satisfying experience of wholeness, the client is encouraged to accept and verbalize his relationship to the therapist. Since creative self-expression cannot occur without acceptance of some pain and guilt, the client is helped to struggle with his independence, difference, and separation from the therapist. Technically, end-setting and focus upon the immediately present relationship are designed to provide successful experiences in both emotional unity and separation.

Since the neurotic's guilt and fear about creative independence are related to his resistance to coercion, the therapist accepts in a noncoercive way any antagonistic reactions so long as these do not violate the independence and selfhood of someone else. The therapist represents reality in the sense of helping to define and limit interference or assault upon the rights of other people. The client is encouraged to accept his own uniqueness without guilt and without attack upon society.

Conscious acceptance of primitive impulses is considered to be the essence of constructive independence. Thus the therapist facilitates the patient's verbalization of his feelings and reactions, so that these can be accepted and effectively utilized.

In general, the dynamic relationship therapist attempts to provide an immediate experience in living which allows the client to experience and accept both dependent unity and independent separateness.

> . . . Every clod feels
> a stir of might,
> An instinct within it
> that reaches and
> towers. . . .
> —LOWELL

VII. Phenomenological Theory and Client-centered Therapy

Client-centered therapy is best understood in its phenomenological background. The behavior and experience of the client are considered to be meaningful only from the point of view of the client himself. The client has the capacity to modify his experience and to actualize himself if he is accepted and understood by another individual. Thus, the essential role of the client-centered therapist is to provide empathic understanding and respect for the client. The essential equipment of the therapist is a basic philosophy of respect for the client's individual worth. Implementation of this philosophy is the core operation in client-centered counseling. This implementation is carried out by assuming the *internal frame of reference*. The therapist attempts to see events and experiences in the same way as the client perceives them, and to communicate this perception to the client.

Examination of client-centered protocols suggests that the internal frame of reference and the philosophy of respect for the client are communicated by techniques of: (a) simple acceptance; (b) restatement of the content or problem expressed by the client; (c) recognition or clarification of feeling; and (d) expressions of respect for the client's adequacy or independence. These techniques relate to the theory in terms of the presumption that a client is able to examine and revise any experience when he is in a situation completely devoid of threat. By providing such non-threatening conditions, the therapist promotes the reorganization of the client's self in personally and socially constructive directions.

Client-centered therapy developed originally from the creative-will aspect of Rank's method of dynamic relationship (see 81). Since this beginning Rogers (82 and 83) has increased the Rankian emphasis upon phenomenological philosophy and has developed a consistent account of the principal concepts in both psychoanalytic and interpersonal theory. Rogers's most complete statement (83) proposes an integration of psychodynamic and interpersonal processes as they may be accounted for from 'the *internal frame* of reference' (Porter, 73). To represent the phenomenology expressed in client-centered therapy, it may be helpful to review it first from its European background.[1]

PHENOMENOLOGY IN PSYCHOTHERAPY

The position that the behavior and world of the individual can be usefully understood only from the point of view of the individual himself is the essential premise of phenomenology. For example, Von Weizacher (in Van den Berg, 105) represents the experience of a woman suffering from *diabetes insipidus*. 'Of course her complaint consists in the subjective state of continual thirst. But it would be a mistake to think that this thirst shows itself to her solely or even principally as a state subjectively perceptible. She expresses her disturbance as follows: "I feel akin to water. I swim whenever and wherever I find an opportunity. I often think that it is definitely beautiful when a powerful jet of water is made to flow in at the neck. I love brooks, that is why I always go to the Black Forest. When I am there, I look for the paths skirting a brook. Water is purity." '

This patient's expression may be summarized conceptually by Rogers's (83) proposition that: '*The organism reacts to the field as it is experienced and perceived. This perceptual field is, for the individual, reality.*'

Private Reality Determines Behavior

The reality to which the individual responds is the world as *he* perceives it. Van den Berg (105) illustrates this point of view by re-

---

[1] The European sources cited are variously considered as phenomenological or existential psychology and psychiatry (105). However, there is sufficient correspondence to client-centered theory to justify the integration presented here.

porting the experiencing of an apparently schizophrenic patient. In spite of consistently negative medical findings, this patient knows that he is physically ill. '. . . he has only . . . to walk a few steps down the street to feel in his chest how ill he is . . . does not he feel his heart hurting all day? His heart is ill; that is the reality of his life.' Whether other people are basically friendly and accepting or not, this patient's experience does not reveal them so. 'The people in the streets remain at a curious distance. . . . Even when they brush against him on the pavement the distance remains . . . they make him feel uneasy, lonely, frightened and angry. He would like to destroy these hostile figures. . . .' Whether the world is bright and cheerful in an 'objective' or 'consensually valid' way, the inner experience of this patient is the unpleasantness he sees. It is this vile private world to which this patient will respond: '. . . the street appeared very wide . . . and the houses . . . so old and tumble-down, that he could not but expect to see them collapse at any moment.' These excerpts represent the world as seen by the patient himself. To the phenomenologist such inner experience is the only stuff to which an individual can react. To help another, the inner experience must be seen from the vantage point of the client. The therapist must experience and enter into the client's private world. The approach to therapy from the *internal frame of reference of the client* is the client-centered expression of the phenomenological viewpoint.

Other Theoretical Realities Contrasted with Phenomenology

Comparison of this emphasis upon the importance of internal reality with the psychoanalytic, interpersonal, and relationship approaches to the reality question may elucidate all four. In a sense *psychoanalysis emphasizes an objective reality.* The world is validly represented in physical, social, and biological terms. The psychoanalytic organism and psyche are expected to adjust to an objectively real world. Inner experience, in this psychoanalytic sense, varies from a relatively distorted to a relatively valid representation of the objective world. The process of becoming adjusted consists of modifying inner experience to conform with the objectively real, and in increasing skill in manipulating reality situations for erotic satisfaction. The *interpersonal theory proposes consensual validity* as the nature of reality. That is, the way that members of a culture agree in responding to the world is the nexus of reality. The interpersonality becomes effective and secure as it participates in and accepts such social consensus. The *dynamic relationship theory tends to agree with interpersonal theory* on consensual validity as the reality of the normal, average man. But Rank's theory disparages this reality as a deception and an imposture which the neurotic cannot accept and the creative individual must modify. Rank's conception of a valuable reality is *creative* inner experience as this is translated into constructive modification of the consensually valid. The unique, inner experience of the creative person can be expressed in the form of artistic, scientific, and literary productivity which will modify social reality. Oscar Wilde's assertion that 'nature copies art' is one way of epitomizing this viewpoint. The reality which Rankian theory espouses is essentially the creative aspect of phenomenology. We have already noted that client-centered therapy derived initially from the creative-will aspect of Rank's theory. The essential modification that Rogers has introduced is the generalization of Rank's valuing of potentially creative people to the valuing of everyone's individuality. The client-centered viewpoint prizes the uniqueness and selfhood value of everyone's inner experience. In a sense it represents a democratization of Thomas Carlyle's hero-principle by proposing a Hero in Everyman. Rephrased in one of Rogers's (83) postulates, we have '*Every individual exists in a continually changing world of experience of which he is the center.*' Client-centered counseling is a psychotherapy based upon the recognition and utilization of the personally meaningful private experience.

THE THERAPIST'S ATTITUDE IN PHENOMENOLOGY

The client-centered therapist's philosophy is insistently dependent upon concepts of (a) empathic respect for the client's individuality and capacity for adjustment; (b) motivation in terms of growth and self-enhancement; (c) personality organization in terms of the conception of the self; (d) personality adjustment in terms of the integrative scope of the self-concept; (e) personality maladjustment in terms of exclusions or distortions in the self-concept; and (f) the therapist's operations and the therapeutic process in terms of increasing the scope of self-acceptance and self-awareness. Since these characteristics of client-centered therapy are interrelated with the three other theories, some integration will be made in the present chapter.

Empathic Respect for the Client

That the client is an essentially valuable individual in his own uniqueness is a metaphysical premise. Kant's *categorical imperative* that any person is valuable as an end in himself rather than as a means to an end is represented in the client-centered approach. In *Client-centered Therapy* (83), Rogers is emphatic about this metaphysic as a central premise in the counselor's attitude: 'How do we look upon others? Do we see each person as having worth and dignity in his own right? . . . Do we tend to treat individuals as persons of worth, or do we subtly devaluate them by our attitudes and behavior? . . . Do we respect his capacity and his right to self-direction, or do we basically believe that his life would be best guided by us?' Rogers presents his belief that '. . . the person whose operational philosophy has already moved in the direction of *feeling* a deep respect for the significance and worth of each person is more readily able to assimilate the client-centered techniques which help him to express this feeling.'

Respect for the individuality of the other is a crucial concept in client-centered therapy. By comparison, psychoanalysis tends to derogate the patient by putting him somewhat helplessly in the hands of a distant and austere parent-surrogate who more or less *knows* the answers. Interpersonal psychiatry *proposes* respect for the client as a potentially effective personality, but *emphasizes* the culturally valuable role of the *expert* who can direct the client's movement toward social integration. Dynamic relationship therapy *prizes* creative potential, but despises the ordinary person. Client-centered therapy alone proposes a basic respect for *any* individuality. '. . . The counselor chooses to act consistently upon the hypothesis that the individual has a sufficient capacity to deal constructively with all those aspects of his life which can potentially come into conscious awareness.'

The hypothesis that the client is capable of solving his own problems is carried out operationally in the principal technique of client-centered therapists. The counselor assumes the *internal frame of reference* (Porter, 73). That is, he attempts to see events and experiences in the way that the client himself perceives them. Rogers (83) proposes that this *internal frame of reference* operation is *the crucial* implementation of the philosophy of respect for the client; '. . . to focus my whole attention and effort upon understanding and perceiving as the client perceives and understands, is a striking operational demonstration of the belief I have in the worth and significance of this individual client. . . .'

That client-centered therapy actually shifted in less than a decade of practice from the laissez faire non-directiveness originally espoused to the empathic internal reference frame heralded in later years is demonstrated by a comparison of Snyder's (96) analysis of cases treated from 1940 to 1942 with Seeman's (90) analysis of cases treated in 1947 and 1948. In the earlier cases, questioning, suggesting, interpreting, and encouraging were common counselor responses. In the later cases, 85 per cent of counselor responses were attempts to communicate understanding of the client's attitudes and feelings. "Understanding and acceptance have become the basic intention of the counselor' (Rogers, 83).

Self-enhancing Motivation

The actualization, enhancement and maintenance of the phenomenal self is the essential motive in client-centered theory (Snygg and Combs, 99, and Rogers, 83). This means simply that the organism struggles to maximize its effectiveness, achieve a satisfying self picture, and actively maintain this 'self-concept.' The organism develops a sense of selfhood which becomes the basis for the meaning it sees in later experience and for the ways in which it will respond to its perceived environment — e.g. 'I feel akin to water.' Hence, 'I swim whenever and wherever I find an opportunity.' Behavior, then, is '. . . the attempt of the organism to satisfy its needs . . .' as these are experienced in its picture of the world. Thus Van den Berg's patient (105) did everything he could to avoid going out into streets edged (as it seemed) by dilapidated houses and thronged with malevolent people.

Feelings or emotions both accompany and facilitate behavior toward self-actualization and enhancement. The intensity of emotion is related to the degree of *perceived* significance for self-maintenance and enhancement. Thus, the feeling of Van den Berg's patient that 'he would like to destroy these hostile figures' would relate to his perception that they refused to provide him with a sense of closeness and warmth.

Self-Structure Personality Organization

The Rogerian conception of personality organization is essentially identical with the interpersonal theory as outlined on pages 100 to 108. By reason of the phenomenological as opposed to the interpersonal emphasis, however, the Rogerian conception leads to different consequences.

For Sullivan's 'self-system' Rogers prefers the term 'self-structure,' which is formed (83) '. . . *as a result of evaluational interaction with others.*' The 'self-structure' is '. . . *an organized, fluid, but consistent conceptual pattern of perceptions of characteristics and relationships of the "I" or the "me," together with values attached to these concepts.*' This statement is a modified adoption of Sullivan's conception that the self-system, including 'good-me,' 'bad-me,' and 'not-me' evaluations, is developed on the basis of reflected appraisals. Like Sullivan, Rogers proposes that behavior is generally consistent with the self-concept. Like Sullivan's 'not-me' conception, certain aspects of one's experience may be '. . . *inconsistent with the organization or structure of the self . . .*' and may therefore be perceived as a threat, so that the self-structure must be more rigidly organized in order to maintain its integrity.

When experiences are inconsistent with or not accepted as part of the self-structure, they are *disowned* or '*denied symbolization.*' Thus, a person's experiences '. . . *are either* (a) *symbolized, perceived, and organized into some relationship to the self,* (b) *ignored because there is no perceived relationship to the self-structure,* (c) *denied symbolization or given a distorted symbolization because the experience is inconsistent with the structure of the self.*' This statement of the *self-structure* is almost identical with the Sullivanian conception of the self-system, including: (a) 'good-me,' 'bad-me' symbolizations; (b) 'selectively inattended' behaviors and situations, and (c) 'not-me' dissociations or fictional, parataxic distortions.

The context in which these parallel conceptions become operationally and consequentially different is in the frame of reference from which each is approached. *The interpersonal theory emphasizes the importance of seeing and accepting oneself as others see one* — that is, security is achieved in the acceptance of consensually valid reality and in interpersonal skill. The interpersonal criterion of adjustment is social adequacy and effectiveness. *The client-centered theory emphasizes the importance of accepting and valuing oneself in all aspects.* The phenomenological criterion of adjustment cannot consistently be social effectiveness, but personal self-acceptance. Thus, to emphasize the difference, the interpersonal concept might be restated as an 'interpersonal self-system' and the client-centered concept as an 'organismic self-structure.' Sullivan's frame of reference emphasizes the interpersonal, social nucleus of self-organization. Rogers's emphasis is placed upon the organism-personality nucleus.

Integrative Personality Adjustment

Personal adjustment is conceived primarily in terms of the scope and flexibility of the self-structure. To what degree is the individual able to accept and integrate all *sensory* and *visceral* experiences in some symbolized form? In the well-adjusted phenomenological self there are minimal distortions and exclusions of potential experience. Rogers's (83) postulate is definitive: '*Psychological adjustment exists when the concept of the self is such that all sensory and visceral experiences of the organism are, or may be assimilated on a symbolic level into a consistent relationship with the concept of self.*' [1] When a person is able to accept himself as he is without shame, embarrassment, or guilt, he has achieved adjustment. In this sense, Cyrano de Bergerac's rejection and Jimmy Durante's acceptance of noses relate to adjustment. More broadly, the degree to which any individual accepts comfortably all aspects of his organismic functioning constitutes a measure of his psychological integration and adequacy.

To gain some specificity in this self-structure definition of adjustment, we may contrast it briefly with the other approaches. In contrast to psychoanalysis, the emphasis is upon self-acceptance rather than upon control or sublimation of impulses. In contrast to interpersonal theory, the emphasis is upon the separate selfhood of the individual — an organismic rather than an interpersonal self. In contrast to Rank's theory, the emphasis is upon the valuableness of any individual rather than upon the exaltation of the creative and the derogation of the normal. Thus the client-centered theory of adjustment emphasizes the separate individual with his self-accepting, organismic integration, his valuable normalcy rather than mediocrity, and his self-actualizing motivation rather than his dangerously raw and asocial impulses.

Personality Maladjustment

Maladjustment results from failure, refusal, or distortion in symbolizing significant sensory or visceral experiences. If certain aspects of the organism are inconsistent with the self-structure, they are not in-

---

[1] The terms 'self-structure' and 'self-concept' appear to be used synonymously in Rogers's later work. The self-concept appears to have been introduced into client-centered theory by Raimy (75).

cluded in awareness or they may be included in some distorted form. Porter (73) quotes a client who said, 'I have the queerest feeling. Whenever anything good happens to me — I just can't believe it. I act as though it never happened. And it worries me. I wanted a date with Myrtle — and I stood around for weeks before I got up enough courage to ask her for a date and she said "yes" — and I couldn't believe it. I couldn't believe it so much that I didn't keep the date!' This example epitomizes the exclusion and distortion of significant experiences. The self-concept expressed by this client appears to include strong attitudes of self-derogation in relation to women. The client expects to be rejected and is unable to symbolize accepting reactions: 'I act as though it never happened.'

'Psychological maladjustment exists when the organism denies to awareness significant sensory and visceral experiences, which consequently are not symbolized and organized into the gestalt of the self-structure. When this situation exists, there is a basic or potential psychological tension' (Rogers, 83).

The sample quoted from Porter exemplifies Rogers's postulate and emphasizes the client-centered approach to understanding of personality processes. It is the difficulty in accepting evidence which is contradictory to the self-structure that this client is struggling with. It is the incompatibility of self-concept and experience which interferes with symbolization and behavior. Psychoanalysis might view this behavior in terms of masochistic gratification; interpersonal theory might see it as disjunctive attitudes involving 'bad-me' and a 'bad-mother' fiction. Client-centered theory sees it as significant experience which is not organized into the gestalt of the self-structure because it is contradictory to the self-concept.

It should be noted finally, that 'basic or potential psychological tension' attends such lack of integration. Freely translating, 'anxiety occurs when some experience is excluded from awareness.' In this conceptual setting, tension is a function of a lack of symbolic integration. In psychoanalysis, anxiety is somewhat similarly conceived, as the danger signal that certain drives are not integrated into the ego. The difference lies partly in the conception of drives involved. Psychoanalytic anxiety is a function of the inefficiency of the ego in assimilating repressed drives or in maintaining them in the unconscious. Self-structure tension is a function of lack of integration among drives which are all essentially positive and growth oriented. Psychoanalytic anxiety has

the quality of battle. Self-structure tension has the quality of admin-
istrative disorganization and confusion.

THE THERAPIST'S OPERATIONS

Empathic understanding is deemed to be the *sine qua non* of client-
centered therapy. The core operation of the therapist is to understand
the client and to communicate such understanding to him. The client-
centered counselor finds '. . . a point of view in human relationships
which tends to carry him further philosophically than he has hereto-
fore ventured, and to provide the possibility for an operational technique for putting into effect this respect for persons, to the full degree
that it exists in his own attitudes' (83). Rogers prizes as the most
promising client-centered counselor '. . . the person whose operational
philosophy has already moved in the direction of *feeling* a deep respect
for the significance and worth of each person. . . .' Thus, he supposes
that a phenomenological metaphysic is essential to the effective psychotherapist. Regardless of this insistence on a philosophy, it is possible to examine the operational implementation of empathic understanding of, and respect for, the client. The question becomes, 'How
does the therapist communicate his acceptance and understanding?'

Van den Berg (105) paraphrases Kierkegaard on how a phenomenological philosophy of helping can be implemented: 'The secret of all
helping . . . is before everything to put oneself in the other's place,
to make one's home in his existence, to learn to know the world in
which he lives. Undoubtedly to help is not: to dictate a way to the
person needing help without knowing or even wanting to know
whether the way dictated can join up with his existence. To help is: to
enter the existence that is the other's.'

To be operationally specific we may cite Rogers's (83) comparison
of the internal versus the external frame of reference. The client expresses, 'I don't feel very normal, but I want to feel that way. . . . I
thought I'd have something to talk about — then it all goes around in
circles. I was trying to think what I was going to say. Then coming in
here it doesn't work out. . . . I tell you, it seemed that it would be
much easier before I came. . . .'

Empathic, internal frame of reference thoughts that the counselor
might have to this could be:

1. 'It's really hard for you to get started.'

2. 'Decision making just seems impossible to you.'

Objective, external frame of reference thoughts about the same points might be:

1. 'I wonder if I should help him get started?'
2. 'Why this indecisiveness? What could be its cause?'

In a sense, the 'internal thoughts' express a part of the client's reactions. They are an acceptance of the client's frame of reference. The 'external thoughts' express a sympathetic attitude toward the client from *someone else's* point of view. They are descriptive rather than understanding; sympathetic rather than empathic.

Porter (73), who first elaborated the *internal/external* approaches, provides numerous examples. One comparison from this source will complete our illustration. A client says: 'What's the use of anything? No one plays fair and square with a guy. The fellows who stayed at home got all the plums. They all took advantage of us while we sweat it out at the front. I hate their guts — every one of them. They are all double crossers. And my wife —— '

Porter's example of an internal frame of reference response to this is: 'You feel they took advantage of you and it really makes you boil.' This response is a brief restatement of the feeling quality in the client's expression. That is, it summarizes the feeling quality in the client's expression. The counselor has taken the client's point of view and has tried to see clearly and cogently what the client sees.

We may compare this 'empathic' response with some external viewpoints which can be constructed from psychoanalytic, interpersonal, and dynamic relationship approaches.

Psychoanalytic: 'Does that remind you of your mother in any way?' Here, the inquiry is obviously directed toward a genetic-historical meaning of the hostility. The remark does not say, 'I understand how you feel,' but rather, 'I understand that your reaction is a result of your childhood relation to your mother.'

Interpersonal: 'I wonder what you're so anxious about that your anger covers up?' Here the emphasis is upon understanding what security value the hostility provides, rather than upon merely accepting and understanding the anger itself.

Dynamic relationship: 'I guess you're pretty angry about coming here. You doubt you'll find I can be trusted.' Here the assumption is made that the feelings are partly directed at the therapist, and that movement will come from experiencing the meaning of the feelings toward the therapist.

In no case, except the client-centered, is the point of view of the client himself accepted as the frame of reference from which the response should be made.

Porter (73) proposes the following categories of *internal frame of reference* responses:

1. *Simple acceptance:* Such responses as 'M — hmm,' 'I see,' and 'That's right,' are considered to be acceptance.

2. *Restatement of content or problem:* When the counselor rephrases the client's verbalization, it is intended to be an expression of understanding or appreciation of what the client has expressed:

'You say that upset you pretty badly.'

'If I follow you, you're really dreading this trip. Is that right?'

3. *Clarification or recognition of feeling:* The counselor may rephrase in such a way that the feeling tone is clarified or emphasized:

'That really leaves you all excited.'

'It's pretty hard to see such a good person do such mean things.'

'You're almost tired of life.'

Rogers is currently opposed to 'techniques' of empathy. He proposes that *implementation of the philosophy* of respect for, and understanding of the client is the essence of the counselor's role. For example, that the *counselor clarifies the client's feelings* connotes a subtle derogation of the client. *Empathic expression* is the one essential operation of the counselor in Rogers's recent statement. Some sample operations of empathic understanding are drawn from Rogers's protocols (83).

> COUNSELOR. 'It's really a tough struggle — digging into this like you are — and at times the shelter of your dream world looks more attractive and comfortable.'
>
> CLIENT: 'My dream world or suicide.'
>
> COUNSELOR: 'Your dream world or something more permanent than dreams ——'
>
> CLIENT: 'Yes. (A long pause. Complete change of voice) So I don't see why I should waste your time — coming in twice a week — I'm not worth it — What do you think?'
>
> COUNSELOR: 'It's up to you, Gil — it isn't wasting my time — I'd be glad to see you whenever you come — but it's how you feel about it — if you don't want to come twice a week? — once a week? — It's up to you.' (Long pause)

CLIENT: 'You're not going to suggest that I come in oftener? You're not alarmed and think I ought to come in — every day — until I get out of this?'

COUNSELOR: 'I believe you are able to make your own decision. I'll see you whenever you want to come.'

CLIENT: (Note of awe in her voice) 'I don't believe you are alarmed about — I see — I may be afraid of myself — but you aren't afraid for me —— ' (She stands up — a strange look on her face)

COUNSELOR: 'You say you may be afraid of yourself — and are wondering why I don't seem afraid for you?'

CLIENT: 'You have more confidence in me than I have. I'll see you next week — maybe.'

This excerpt is striking in its demonstration of the emphasis in client-centered therapy upon (a) respect for the client, and (b) empathic understanding as the implementation of such respect. In the protocol excerpt, the counselor expresses — undoubtedly more intensely than the printed words convey — his deep understanding and acceptance of the client's mortal struggle with herself. Somewhat paradoxical to this empathy is the refusal of the counselor to understand anything that abrogates his philosophy of respect. When the client is obviously expressing her anguish at not receiving sufficient dependency gratification from the counselor ('You're not going to suggest that I come in oftener?'), the counselor retreats from empathy to respect: 'I believe you are able to make your own decision.' Thus there appear to be at least the empathizing and respecting positions that the client-centered counselor can consistently take. While they are not mutually exclusive, neither are they necessarily cohesive. How empathy and respect could be expressed at once by the counselor is suggested by the following alternative to how Rogers handled the client's dependency plea:

CLIENT: 'You're not going to suggest that I come in oftener? You're not alarmed and think I ought to come in — every day — until I get out of this?'

ALTERNATIVE COUNSELOR RESPONSE: 'You desperately want more help and can't see why I don't offer it. I'll help by seeing you oftener if you think it's necessary — but it's up to you. Decide to do whatever you think best.'

The example as quoted from Rogers indicates that empathy can be considered as one kind of client-centered operation rather than simply as an implementation of respect for the client. The attitude of respect for the client requires other implementations which appear to be expressive or verbal implications that the client is able to accept responsibility for himself. Even in the alternative counselor response, designed to convey empathy and respect simultaneously, we found it necessary to make a separate statement for each. 'I understand' was expressed as 'You desperately want me to help . . .' 'You are capable of managing your own life' was expressed as, '. . . but it's up to you. Decide whatever you think best.'

Thus it appears that the therapist's operations can be defined and illustrated, whether they are called 'techniques' or 'implementations of a philosophy.' Perhaps the principal operations of the client-centered counselor can be summarized in terms of the empathic categories proposed by Porter (73): (a) Simple acceptance; (b) Restatement of content or problem; (c) Clarification or recognition of feeling; and an additional category derived from Rogers which might be labeled (d) Expressions of respect for the client.

THE THERAPEUTIC PROCESS

Reorganization of the self-structure to include previously disowned or distorted experiences can be achieved under conditions of minimal threat. Rogers's postulate about psychotherapy process is that '*Under certain conditions, involving primarily complete absence of any threat to the self-structure, experiences which are inconsistent with it may be perceived, and examined, and the structure of self revised to assimilate and include such experiences.*'

The conditions which presumably provide such absence of threat are the empathic understandings provided by the therapist's viewing with the client through his eyes. Rogers (83) interprets the experience of one client in this light. 'The attitudes which she could express but not accept as part of herself became acceptable when an alternate self, the counselor, looked upon them with acceptance and without emotion. It was only when another self looked upon her behavior without shame or emotion that she could look upon it in the same way.'

The process of client-centered therapy has been subjected to intensive research over several years. A summary of this research (Rogers, 83 and Rogers and Dymond, 84) suggests:

1. There is movement toward increased discussion of plans, steps to be taken, and the likely outcome of planning and action.

2. There is change from relatively immature to relatively mature behavior.

3. There is a reduction of verbally expressed psychological tension.

4. There is a reduction in defensive behavior and greater awareness of defensive behavior which is not eliminated.

5. There is an improved tolerance for frustration as measured physiologically.

6. There is improved adjustment to life in general as measured by performances in jobs, school, etc.

7. There is increased acceptance of others and of being 'like' others.

We called attention earlier to the fact that social adjustment cannot be a consistent criterion of success in client-centered counseling, since the unique selfhood of the client and his private experience are valued so centrally. However, research appears to demonstrate that improved competence in life and increased acceptance of other people actually may develop. Rogers's (83) postulate to this effect is as follows: 'When the individual perceives and accepts into one consistent and integrated system all his sensory and visceral experiences, then he is necessarily more understanding of others and is more accepting of others as separate individuals.' While improved understanding and competence in interpersonal relations are expected in client-centered therapy, they are indirect consequences. It will be noted that the process and the kind of outcome are avowedly different from the other theories considered. Acceptance of others as separate individuals is a different relation to other people, for example, than the interpersonal outcome of accepting oneself as part of a collaborative interpersonal process.

THE CLIENT'S EXPERIENCE

Several clients have made summaries of how the client-centered process looked to them (83). Generally these experiences have been that the counselor is a sort of second self who looks at the client's world through the client's eyes. 'We were mostly *me* working together on my situation as I found it.' Changes in behavior take place so spontaneously that they are hardly noticed, yet there is a 'raw, unsteady, "new-born" feeling . . .' as progress is made. While the emphasis in client-centered counseling is so patently upon the self, the result seems to be less, rather than more, self-concern. 'I'm not self-conscious like I used to be . . . I don't concentrate on being myself — I just am.'

SUMMARY

Client-centered therapy is based upon a philosophy of respect for the individuality and private world of the client. It assumes that personality adjustment can be best implemented by the counselor's assuming and expressing the client's point of view. Every individual has the capacity to maximize his own adequacy and to solve his own problems.

This philosophy of respect for the client leads to a criterion of adjustment in terms of the acceptance and valuing of oneself in all aspects. Maladjustment is a result of exclusion of significant experiences, a failure to value and integrate all of one's self. Anxiety and disorganization result from excluding experience from awareness.

The role and operations of the counselor become definable in terms of a consistent acceptance of the client from the client's point of view. By expressing the client's experience for him, the counselor provides an opportunity for the client to increase his respect for himself and to include all significant experiences in conscious awareness.

PART THREE

Operational and Theoretical Integration

An operational and theoretical integration of psychotherapy and leadership is the principal objective of this book. The many aspects of behavior in individual interview or group process can be organized in such a way that a relatively articulated picture of the psychotherapies is developed. Such an organization requires a synthesis of therapist and client functioning in the four theories so that the therapists' operations, the clients' behaviors, and the functional relationships among therapists and clients may be seen in their several forms. Part III will successively examine psychotherapy and group processes from six organizational frames of reference:

1. An over-all structure for synthesizing theoretical operations and behaviors of therapist and client;

2. An examination of the personal-theoretical expressive behavior (or personality) of the therapist;

3. An examination of the client's functioning (or personality) in terms of theoretical determinants of how therapists describe their clients;

4. An assessment of the joint contribution of theoretical interpretation and client personality to the processes by which behavior and values are modified (or improved) by psychotherapy;

5. A theoretical simplification designed to discover what common processes of change occur under theoretically diverse conditions; and

6. A programmatic conception of the clinical importance of an operational, cross-theoretical approach to the science and practice of psychotherapy.

The reader will remember that *successive frames* of reference (rather than legitimately separable parts of a total process) are to be described in the chapters to follow. We begin by a brief look at a total structure of the interview process, then examine some subparts of its occurrence.

With them the seed
of Wisdom did I sow—
And with mine own hand
labored it to grow . . .
—KHAYYAM

VIII. An Operational Outline [1]

The four theories of psychotherapy provide an adequate basis for
organizing a conceptual schema for understanding interviewer [2] operations, client functioning, and process of change in behaviors, values,
and effectiveness of the client. This organization will cut across theoretical boundaries in such a way that a therapist's operations may be
defined independently of their conceptual roots; the client will be
describable in terms of the many theoretically therapeutic aspects of
his functioning; and the process of change will be investigated in empirical terms as a joint function of interviewer operations and client
behaviors. Essentially this operational integration will present an
over-all structure of the many things that therapists or leaders do in
promoting processes of personality change. This will, of necessity,
include an analysis of the cardinal aspects of the interviewers' expressive behaviors (or personalities) and the principal kinds of things
that interviewers say about their clients. How do interviewers *express
themselves?* What kinds of word pictures do they paint, or how do

---

[1] Modified from the author's 'An Operational Conception of Psychotherapy,'
Psychiatry (1956), *19:* 371–82, by permission of the William Alanson White Psychiatric Foundation, Inc.

[2] The term *interviewer* will be used in this and succeeding chapters to cover
the miscellaneous colloquialisms of *counselor, doctor, therapist, analyst, teacher,
case worker, group leader,* and *pastor* which are used to distinguish the culturally
accredited forms of *interviewer* role. The term *client* has a similar intent; it will
include the meanings of *patient, analysand, counselee, interviewee, group member, parishioner,* etc.

they *represent their clients?* The general topics of *interviewers' expressive operations* and *interviewers' representational operations* provide a basis for examining in later chapters the functional interaction of interviewer and client in producing a process of change in the client's functioning.

The general outline of interviewer and client functioning will be presented in terms of the interviewer's theoretical-personality expressions, or *expressive operations,* and the interviewer's descriptions of the client, or *representative operations.* The interviewer's *expressive operations* will be organized in terms of the degree to which he expresses feelings of *affection, neutrality,* or *aggression,* and the degree to which he shows qualities of *management, passivity,* or *participation* in the interview process. The interviewer's *representative operations* will be organized in terms of *descriptive focus, inferential logic, values,* and *interpretations.* Which aspects of the client's functioning does the interviewer *focus* upon or describe? (Does the interviewer talk about the client's psychosexual symbolisms, his verbalized content, his social behavior, his feelings, his motives, or what?) What personality-theoretical *logic* does the interviewer use in deciding what he should talk about? What does the interviewer *value* or consider important in promoting the client's 'improvement?' How does the interviewer synthesize and integrate in arriving at an *interpretation* of the meanings of the client's behavior? The reader will observe that even though a cross-theoretical integration is intended in this chapter, it will be necessary to maintain considerable awareness of theoretical kinships in defining interviewer operations. Hence, it seems essential to summarize from the four theoretical chapters the kinds of emphases that must be accounted for in developing an integrated outline.

THEORETICAL-PERSONALITY EXPRESSIONS: The orthodox analyst assumes an expressively impassive, distant attitude; the interpersonal therapist assumes any expressive behavior or attitude suited to the occasion; the dynamic relationship therapist assumes an attitude of complete acceptance of uniting and separating strivings; the phenomenological therapist enters empathically into the client's frame of reference, attempting to see and understand from the client's point of view. These aspects of therapist activity can be characterized in terms of personality expression or role taking. All of these *expressive operations* may be assessed in terms of the degree to which they show management, passivity, participation, aggression, neutrality, or affection.

THEORETICAL REPRESENTATIONS OF THE CLIENT: The interviewer's representations of the client will include:

1. *The psychoanalytic-symbolic emphases* upon unconscious love and hate motives, object cathexes, techniques of self-deception, reality skills, and developmental experiences or processes.

2. *The interpersonal psychiatric social-validity focus* upon security seeking, social operations for reducing anxiety, the anxiety so obscured, and the client's fictional or parataxic people, together with the developmental sources of such distortions.

3. *The dynamic relationship concern about feelings and motives* in the immediately present meaning of the relationship of the client to the therapist. This will include feelings and motives related to the client's strivings toward dependent unity and creative selfhood.

4. *The phenomenological self-feeling emphasis* upon the inner experience or private reality of the client, which will include especially the client's experiencing of himself and the world as he sees it.

GENERAL ORGANIZATION OF A STRUCTURAL OUTLINE

Relationships among therapist operations and client modifications will not be treated specifically in the present chapter, since a structural rather than a functional account is intended here. The problem of functional interactions will be considered in later chapters.

THE INTERVIEWER'S PERSONALITY OR EXPRESSIVE BEHAVIOR: The interviewer can be conceptualized in terms of the *feelings* he expresses toward the client and the *status-control* relationships he introduces into the interview. These aspects of the interviewer's expressive operations will be structured as varying degrees of *affection, neutrality,* or *aggression,* and varying degrees of *management, passivity,* or *participation.*

THE INTERVIEWER'S REPRESENTATION OF THE CLIENT: The interviewer can be conceptualized in relation to what he talks about and how he describes the client's functioning. Such representations will be considered as:

1. *The referential focus.* What aspects of the client's behavior are emphasized? To what in the client does the interviewer address himself?

2. *The inferential logic.* What kind of theoretical reasoning does the interviewer use in understanding the client?

3. *The value emphasis.* What does the interviewer consider to be important about the client?

4. *The interpretive synthesis.* How does the interviewer organize his emphases, inferences, and values into interpretive remarks?

The interviewer's referential focus will include an organization of the aspects of client behavior to which the interviewer addresses himself; for example, the client's experience, his childhood, his ego-skills, his anxieties, his social operations, his relationship to the interviewer, or his phenomenal field. In other words, What does the interviewer talk about? or, To what about the client does he refer?

The interviewer's inferential logic will be concerned with what inferential reasoning is used by the therapist in arriving at 'an understanding' of the client; i.e. how the therapist's concepts or theoretical premises determine the inferential steps he will take in arriving at his explanation of the client's behavior. For example, the psychoanalyst will *see* love and hate conflicts; the interpersonal therapist will *see* security-operations and anxiety; the dynamic relationship therapist will *see* unity and separation seeking; the phenomenological therapist will *see* constructive actualization. The metaphysics of each system will determine such inferential observation.

The interviewer's valuing of the client's behavior and experience again has theoretical sources. The analyst is largely interested in the unconscious meanings and ego-defenses in the client's behavior since these are considered to be quintessential to the process of change. The interpersonal therapist values the social operations or interpersonal behavior and is hence most likely to emphasize such aspects. The dynamic relationship therapist values the unity seeking and creative separation qualities of the client and will respond primarily to these. The phenomenological therapist values the inner experience of the client and will respond to this private world to the relative exclusion of more objective and social aspects of behavior.

The interviewer's interpretations will cohere with his theoretical perspective. How he synthesizes meanings will be a part function of what the client produces and a major function of the conceptual system applied to understanding the client's behavior.

In this structural outline, we have attempted to organize interviewer operations with some degree of independence from theoretical sources so that likenesses among theories as well as differences between them can be conceived similarly. Hence, after first determining our *frame of reference for defining interviewer operations,* we shall examine samples of such operations without respect to the theoretical sources from which they were drawn. This will provide a basis for a generalized organization of interviewer operations. We shall then re-examine typical operations in the generalized structure in order to illustrate some relationships between such a general structure and the more specialized theories.

FRAME OF REFERENCE FOR DEFINING INTERVIEWER OPERATIONS

It is apparent that any event may be examined or described from several points of view or frames of reference. Glancing through the front window in search of an illustration, I am struck by red sky-stairs framed against a blue wall, and softened by the spring-finger reachings of green-tipped trees. From an impressionistic, esthetic point of view, I have said, 'There is a promise of spring.' But shadows clutch at the east, darkening, splattering mud on the white-day carpet. Still from an esthetic point of view, I have said, 'It is getting late.' Now, from a very practical point of view, my poetic maunderings force me to look at my watch and see in terms of precise timing that I have only a few minutes before an appointment. The white-day carpet becomes cold snow on the ground, and the shadow-splattered black becomes real muck which I have to skirt around to get to my car. I have used an esthetic, a temporal, a temperature, and a practical frame of reference for examining the meaning of a half-winter, half-spring afternoon.

In examining and defining interviewer operations, we may also assume different viewpoints. The theoretical perspectives outlined earlier indicate at least one approach to describing operations in psychotherapy. For present purposes, however, it seems useful to provide a non-theoretical frame of reference from which to examine interviewer operations. How does the interviewer operate regardless of theory? What kinds of things does he do?

Broadly, we have said that he *expresses himself* — including his theory, to the extent that he has assimilated or that he postures it — and that he *represents the client.* Without specific reference to theory, however, how the interviewer expresses himself can be described in terms of the degree to which he manages or participates with the client, and the degree to which he shows affectionate or aggressive attitudes. Also without specific reference to any one theory, how the interviewer represents the client can be conceptualized in terms of the aspects of the client's functioning upon which he focuses his attention, the inferential processes he uses in arriving at his 'observations' and 'understanding,' the importance or value he places upon various aspects of the interviewer-client transaction, and the form of interpretive synthesis he makes on the basis of his observational focus, his inferences, and his values.

It will be observed that the interviewer's expressive role constitutes one frame of reference, while his representation of the client constitutes another — one in which the structure of the client's functioning becomes the focus of attention.

An 'Objective' Observer's Vantage Point

It is essential that we assume some vantage point for looking at the psychotherapy transaction at all. Since several ways of looking at the behavior of the interviewer are possible, a further specification seems necessary. Classification could be attempted from the viewpoint of the interviewer — his self-awareness of his expression. Such an approach would maximize subjectivity. An approach from the client's viewpoint — how does the interviewer's behavior appear to and affect the client — seems desirable. Obviously, the client's viewpoint and progress are the principal considerations. Since clients are extremely diverse, however, it appears that such a client-perception-and-effects approach should derive from investigation of the behavior of the interviewer in relation to the personality and current condition of the client. That is, having established a framework for describing the kinds of things interviewers do, it may then become possible to investigate the ways in which a variety of clients perceive, respond to, and change as a function of such interviewer operations. To specify the frame of reference applied in this chapter, examination and definition of interviewer operations will be made from the point of view of an observer who is watching or attending to the behavior of the interviewer and is only secondarily concerned about the behavior of the client. In the next chapter, the interviewer's expressive operations will be considered from the viewpoints of the client and the interviewer as well.

Figure 9A represents the frame of reference of an outside *observer* describing the *expressive behavior* of an interviewer, rather than the way that the interview might be experienced by either the interviewer or the client. Figure 9B schematizes the reference frame of an *observer* who is watching or perceiving how the interviewer describes or *represents a client*.

A. The frame of reference of an observer who is describing an interviewer's expressive behavior towards a client.

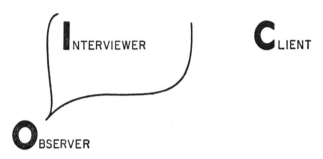

B. The frame of reference of an observer who is describing an Interviewer's representation or verbal picture of a client.

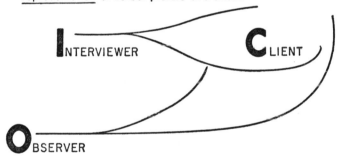

Fig. 9. Comparison of the Observer's Frame of Reference in Describing the *Expressive Behavior* of an Interviewer and the *Client Representational Behavior* of an Interviewer.

Discussion will focus first upon the expressive operations or personality role of the interviewer, and second upon the interviewer's representative operations. While essentially we are organizing response behaviors and activities of the interviewer, this becomes a process of defining *operations*. Hence the term *operation* will be systematically substituted as categories become defined.

THE INTERVIEWER'S EXPRESSIVE OPERATIONS

The interviewer's personality role or expressive behavior toward the client will include feelings, attitudes, preferences, and role-taking characteristics which may be expressed either verbally or non-verbally. The affectionate versus aggressive and the managing versus participating aspects will provide a schema for organizing the interviewer's expressive operations.

Behavior which primarily conveys the interviewer's personality — his affective and social involvement in the interview process — can be differentiated from those interviewer activities by which he represents the client's personality — the client's experience, doing, feeling, thinking, and motives.

Rogers's (83) intention '. . . to communicate . . . empathic understanding to the client . . .' appears to require expressive behavior from the interviewer whether such empathy is communicated by verbal or non-verbal means. Fromm-Reichmann (33) describes Sullivan's expressive behavior as giving '. . . evidence of understanding . . . by responding cautiously with gestures or actions appropriate to the patient's communication; for example by lighting his cigarette from the patient's cigarette instead of using a match when the patient seems to indicate a wish for closeness and friendship. . . .' Such expressive qualities may be communicated in either verbal or non-verbal form, and are essential aspects of both theoretical and personal contributions to interviewing.

Rogers (83) footnotes this point as follows: 'Just as it is impossible to convey on paper the venom and hatred in the client's voice, so it is utterly impossible to convey the depth of empathy in the counselor's response. . . .' It appears that part of the interviewer's expressive involvement is communicated in non-verbal form while other expressive aspects are communicated by verbal phrasing, punctuation, and grammatical syntax.

In examining the expressive behavior of interviewers in psychotherapy one is struck by the variety of attitudes, feelings, judgments, and role-taking techniques employed. Several attempts to reduce this complexity to some kind of simple structure have resulted in invidious and distorted descriptions of various psychotherapy methods. The separation of interviewer activities into those which are primarily expressive of the interviewer and those which are primarily representative of the client provides a basis for organizing this potpourri with some degree of credence for any approach. In the expressive activities of the interviewer we find that various kinds of structuring, assertiveness, understanding, uncertainty, role taking, empathy, and support are described or represented in the literature. Rather than attempting an exhaustive classification of such expressive behaviors, we shall present a schema which may include the variety in a simple outline.

The variety of the interviewer's expressive activities may be fitted into a two-way classification by using our two descriptive axes, management-participation and affection-aggression, as follows: [1]

	Managing		Passive		Participating	
Strongly	Moderately	Mildly		Mildly	Moderately	Strongly
3	2	1	0	1	2	3

This series of categories [2] will account for the degree to which the interviewer assumes responsibility for the client, expressing qualities of directing, leading, controlling, manipulating, or structuring the interview, or for the degree to which the interviewer enters into the client's world, participating in perceiving, examining, considering, and understanding the client's private experience.

	Affectionate		Neutral		Aggressive	
Strongly	Moderately	Mildly		Mildly	Moderately	Strongly
3	2	1	0	1	2	3

The affection-aggression dimension will account for the degree of warm, accepting versus attacking, rejecting expressions of feelings, attitudes, and value judgments on the part of the interviewer.

By presenting the above axes on one grid, it is possible to classify or describe expressive operations simultaneously on both dimensions. A brief illustration of this schema will introduce the approach here.

[1] Strupp (personal communication) has applied essentially similar dimensions for the analysis of responses of 237 therapists to a motion picture of an initial interview. He apparently arrived at this schema independently of my publication in *Psychiatry*, November, 1956 (36).

[2] These descriptive dimensions are not intended to represent scales in any strict measurement sense; i.e. the basic intention at this point is qualitative rather than quantitative description. The arabic numerals, 1, 2, and 3 will be used subsequently as code numbers representing the adjectives and adverbs of degree. Mild and mildly will be coded as a 1; moderate and moderately, as a 2; and strong and strongly, as a 3. The absence of managing or participating expressive operations will be coded as a 0.

Five sample assignments are presented in Figure 10 and discussed below. More detailed analysis is presented in Chapter IX.

A. *Moderately Participating—Moderately Affectionate*

DOCTOR: 'I won't punish you. You can scratch your head. In fact, I'll scratch mine.' (Rosen, 86).

It will be seen in this excerpt that the therapist is joining in with the patient, showing an affectionate acceptance of her behavior and

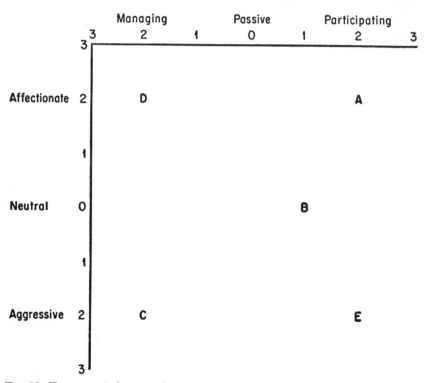

Fig. 10. Expressive Behaviors of Interviewers Judged on Management-Participation and Affection-Aggression Axes from the Viewpoint of an Outside Observer.

expressing warmth toward her. Participation and affection are both characteristic of this therapist expression.

B. *Mildly Participating—Neutral*

THERAPIST: 'Helen, if you fall on your head, it's not my fault.' (Indifferent tone of voice) (Taft, 103).

In this sample the therapist appears to be disengaging herself from involvement in the child's bravado. In a sense the therapist says,

'I am involved, but it's up to you what you do.' At the same time she attempts to express an attitude of unconcern — 'I am willing to let you do whatever you wish, but you should consider the consequences.'

C. *Moderately Managing—Moderately Aggressive*

> PATIENT: 'I always enjoy doing things for people.'
> THERAPIST: (Ironically) 'I guess you do.' (Wolberg, 109).

In this interchange the therapist critically suggests a different meaning from what the client has expressed: 'Yes, you enjoy doing things for people — and you're sure missing the point. What is the meaning of your enjoyment?'

D. *Moderately Managing—Moderately Affectionate*

> CLIENT: 'You're not going to suggest that I come in oftener?'
> COUNSELOR: 'I believe you're able to make your own decision.' (Rogers, 83).

In this sample, the client expresses concern that the therapist does not take more active responsibility for her welfare. The therapist expresses an attitude of affection toward the client's potentialities: 'I have confidence in your ability to handle things in your own way.' At the same time, it will be noted, the therapist is managing the interview by saying, 'I refuse to make decisions for you. How often you come is up to you. I insist on your making your own decision.'

E. *Moderately Participating—Moderately Aggressive*

> THERAPIST: 'I have a vague feeling that some people might doubt the utility to you of the care with which your parents, and particularly your mother, saw to it that you didn't learn how to dance, or play games, or otherwise engage in the frivolous social life of people your age' (Sullivan, 102).

In this example the therapist engages in the client's problem, 'I understand how difficult it was for you to be smothered by your mother's control — however, you're being pretty silly to assume that mother was really being good to you. You'd better re-examine what she was really doing.'

In these five samples, we have attempted to account for the principal expressive aspects in terms of the degree to which they include qualities of management, participation, affection, and aggression. It is of interest that a 'non-directive' therapist expression can be seen to have managing qualities, and that an analytic therapist expression has distinctly participating qualities. It is not supposed that all nuances of therapist expression can be simplified to a useful 'fit' in this schema, but a maximal amount of therapist expressive behavior can be so classified.

THE INTERVIEWER'S REPRESENTATIONAL OPERATIONS

Thus far, one frame of reference has been applied to the interviewer's role; we have examined the interviewer's expressive operations. How does he express himself as an individual and as a proponent of his theory? Equally important are the client-representative aspects of what the interviewer says. What kind of picture of the client does he portray? To what features of the client's functioning does he address himself? We have chosen to call this view of the interviewer's activity his *representational operations*. How does he represent the client? What does he emphasize about the client's functioning?

Those aspects of the interviewer's activity which refer to something about the client by selecting, phrasing, synthesizing, or making sense out of what the client is doing, experiencing, wanting, feeling, or thinking, may be described generally as representing the client. In this sense, what the interviewer refers to, what he selectively perceives and comments on, what he attributes to the client, inferentially or interpretively, are defined as the interviewer's *representation of the client*. By contrast, the interviewer's *expressive behavior* is more consistently a representation of the interviewer himself. An earlier example from Sullivan may illustrate the difference between the self-expressive and the client-representative features of the interviewer's behavior.

> INTERVIEWER: 'I have a vague feeling that some people might doubt the utility to you of the care with which your parents, and particularly your mother, saw to it that you didn't learn how to dance, or play games, or otherwise engage in the frivolous social life of people your age.'

The expressive aspects of this sample include the uncertainty and humility ('I have a vague feeling that . . .'); the sympathetic understanding ('I'm saying this indirectly so that it won't hurt too much'); and the moderate aggression ('Some people might doubt . . .'). A theoretically consistent representation of the client's development, however, is indicated by Sullivan's selection of a lack of affectionate mothering as a basis for the failure to develop socialization skills. The representative aspects of this communication are largely accounted for by the statement that 'Your mother injured you by preventing you from learning to socialize.'

It will be noticed immediately that there is an overlap between expressive and representative aspects of this sample. What the interviewer selects to talk about expresses his value judgment as to what is important for the client's progress. At the same time, the interviewer is representing certain aspects of the client's behavior or experience. This overlap illustrates that a functional taxonomy has no intention to delineate communication units which are purely expressive from those which are purely representative. The purpose is rather to provide *successive* frames of reference from which the therapist's communication may be examined. Thus it is assumed that any interviewer activity will be expressive *and* representative rather than expressive *or* representative.

To recapitulate the difference between expressive and representative aspects of the interviewer's behavior, then, the expressive aspects are those in which some attitude, feeling, point of view, role, or value judgment is communicated. The representative aspects are those in which the interviewer presents some impression of the client; he indicates that the client is doing, feeling, experiencing, or expressing something.

The observer's picture of the interviewer as a personality is included in the interviewer's expressive behavior. The interviewer's picture of the client as it is verbalized in the interview constitutes the representative aspect of the interviewer's behavior.

Having conceptualized such a difference between expressive and representative activities, it becomes feasible to examine four sub-aspects of representation. These are the interviewer's *referential, inferential, valuing,* and *interpretive* representations of the client. These four aspects of representation will be examined by contrasting illustrations of therapist representations which fit the four definitions.

REFERENTIAL OR FOCUSING OPERATIONS: The question 'What does the interviewer talk about?' is answered by the category of referential operations. In any sample of behavior it is possible for the interviewer to respond to a number of different facets of the client's activity. To emphasize a *reference* to the client in the following examples, the most important one is summarized before the quotation.

You interpret — 'Have you noticed that you tend to interpret everything you say?' (Colby, 12).

Your sickness — 'What was the sickness you had?' (Rosen, 86).

Tendency to complicate — 'Living is simple, are you not aware that you have a tendency to complicate it?' (Sullivan, 106).

Attached to me — 'You really feel very deeply attached to me' (Rogers, 83).

These are examples of the referential aspect of the interviewer's operations. They are sample answers to the question, 'To what does the interviewer refer?' The illustrations chosen are relatively simple, indicating only that the interviewer is likely to focus upon, or refer to, some particular aspect of the client's functioning.

In the inferential, valuing, and interpretive samples to follow, each has at least one or more referential aspect. The inferential, valuing, and interpretive representations go beyond the referents but of necessity depend upon them.

INFERENTIAL OPERATIONS: The question 'How obvious is the behavior quality that the interviewer talks about?' is answered by the category of inferential operations. Referential operations already presented were chosen to illustrate relatively observable or apparent aspects of the client's behavior. The interviewer commonly refers also to aspects of the client's functioning which are not so obvious. In such cases some kind of inference is involved in the interviewer's choice of what to talk about. He responds to things that are not evidently there. In the following illustrations the interviewer makes some inference about the client. In order to emphasize the inferential aspect, it will be summarized before the complete interviewer quotation.

> *You're trying to outdo me* — 'Why do you think it is you have to beat me to it, so to speak?' (Colby, 12).
> *You're hiding something* — CLIENT: 'I had another dream last night. I was storming a height. That suggests to me the return of vigour and energy.' INTERVIEWER: 'Yes, but what are you denying?' (Berg, 6).
> *You're being cautious* — 'You know, I thought I smelled something a a minute ago. I thought I smelled a bit of — what shall I say — caution." [1]

In these samples the interviewer refers to something he *infers* about the client, rather than something that is clearly observed.

VALUING OPERATIONS: Some kind of value judgment is implicit in each referential and inferential example cited. This value judgment is expressed partly by the interviewer's selection of what he will talk

[1] An example provided by David McK. Rioch in a personal communication.

about, and partly by other qualities of expressive behavior. The sample interview exchange to be presented here is the same one to be used in Chapter IX, as an example of expressive behavior, under *selection*. There, we shall emphasize the expressive quality of selection as *managing* the interview process by evidencing what the interviewer prefers to talk about. In the illustration here, the emphasis will be upon the *representation* of the client. This overlap of categories recapitulates the philosophy that interview operations must of necessity be defined from successive frames of reference rather than as unitary categories.

From the total client behavior the interviewer selects (and focuses the client's attention upon) parts of what is going on to the deemphasis or exclusion of other parts of the situation. This selective responsiveness is an implicit effect of the interviewer's theoretically or personally determined opinion as to what is important for the client's progress. When he *represents* the client, the interviewer says in effect, 'What I am responding to is the important part of all that is happening at this moment. The things I don't respond to are relatively less consequential.' An analysis of one sample interchange will illustrate such selective valuing:

> CLIENT: 'I had another dream last night. I was storming a height. That suggests to me the return of vigour and energy.'
> INTERVIEWER'S VALUE EMPHASIS UPON THE EGO-DEFENSE: 'Yes, but what are you denying?' (Berg, 6).

The interviewer — an analyst — selected the ego-defensive aspect of the behavior. It is apparent that other theories or other occasions could have justified different emphases in response to the same event. Some such alternative possibilities might have been:

Selection of expressed motivation: 'You're hoping to get more zest for life?'

Selection of expressed feeling: 'You're feeling somewhat better then?'

Selection of behavioral expression: 'You're showing more confidence.'

Selection of relationship to interviewer: 'Are you also, perhaps, attacking me?'

Selection of transference symbolism: 'I wonder if this dream represents an intention to conquer your fear of your father by attacking me?'

Selection of sexual symbolism: 'Does this dream suggest any sexual associations to you?'

These alternatives represent a variety of value judgments. They do not necessarily reflect differences of point of view as to what is really present in the client's behavior, since any of the samples may be observably or symbolically valid. The difference that they do reflect is the therapist's evaluation of the importance of one meaning or another. The defense, the feeling, the motivation, the relationship to the interviewer, the behavioral expression, the transference or the sexual symbolism are all potentially valid aspects of the behavior, if validity involves only the question, Is it really there? The selection of one aspect or another, however, proposes that there are differences in therapeutic movement validity — that the emphasis of certain aspects and the neglect of others is considered likely to affect the quality and speed of therapeutic change.

INTERPRETIVE OPERATIONS: The question 'How does the interviewer make sense out of the client's behavior?' is answered by the category of interpretive operations.

Interpretations may be conceived as elaborations and syntheses of inferences — putting together and logically relating the meanings of observations, inferences, and the interpretive frame of reference. It is in interpretations that the theoretical perspective of the interviewer becomes extremely important in determining the meaning that he will attribute to the data which he synthesizes. To illustrate generally, the Freudian interpretation of *snake* is likely to have something to do with masculine sexuality. A Jungian interpretation of *snake* is likely to have a relationship to healing. On the principle of condensation, either interpretation could be correct in the identical case, since a penis symbol may be simultaneously a healing symbol. To illustrate further, Rosen (86) provides the following patient material:

> A male patient felt compelled to discover a transmission which would be infinitely more powerful than all transmissions known to automotive engineering. . . . His problem was how to transmit . . . fluid.
>
> It was easy enough to understand this from a genital point of view as a transmission of semen, but the effect on the patient's psychosis was dramatic when we made an oral interpretation. 'How can you transmit mother's milk to your mouth?'

In contrast to Rosen's choices, it is also apparent that an anal interpretation would have been plausible: 'How can you control your hostility?' The interpersonal psychiatric frame of reference might have led to a security-operation interpretation: 'How can you communicate with others so that they will accept you?' A client-centered example might be: 'It's distressing not to be in control.' A dynamic-relationship interpretation might have been, 'How can you manage to accept and use your impulses in a creative way, without always having to have me take care of you?'

Theory Tends to Determine Representational Operations

Several different interpretations of the same symbol are plausible and theoretically valid from different viewpoints. Such theoretically probable interpretations of a single patient symbolization suggest that the theoretical value system applied will determine the interpretive meaning given. The effects upon the client of one interpretation rather than another may be different in degree, kind, and quality of usefulness to the patient's movement in therapy.

Two additional interviewer samples will be examined for relationships among referential, inferential, valuing, and interpretive aspects of the interviewer's operations.

INTERVIEWER: 'I think you are mad at me because you didn't come last time' (Taft, 103).

The primary *reference* to the client's behavior or experience is, 'You didn't come last time.'

The interviewer *infers* that the client is 'mad at me.'

The interviewer *values* — from a Rankian approach — the relationship of the client to the mother-surrogate, hence she *interprets* that the client is angry about being neglected by the therapist.

Starting from the same client behavior, the client-centered counselor might have tried to take the point of view of the client, saying:

'I guess it's a bit uncomfortable coming back after missing last time.'

The primary *reference* to the client's experience is the client's perception of discomfort or uncertainty.

The interviewer *infers* only how the client experiences the situation.

The interviewer *values* the client's point of view as the position he must take for the client's welfare.

The interviewer does not *interpret* except insofar as his statement of the client's position is inaccurate. An interpretation from the client-centered point of view would be a mistake rather than a valuable operation.

In the following sample the therapist has chosen to focus upon those aspects of the behavior that make sense in a transference interpretation (Colby, 12):

> THERAPIST: 'It's interesting that of the two things you've wanted to steal, the first involves your father and the second, me.'
>
> PATIENT: 'You mean I think you're a father to me?'
>
> THERAPIST: 'Maybe. At least we see that you want something I have, just as you wanted something your father had. You compete with me as you do with your father. Even in the interview here you struggle with me, like in holding back to see what I'll do about it.'

The principal *focus* of the analytic therapist in this interchange, is upon 'Compete with me as you do with your father.'

The interviewer *infers* that the meaning of the behavior in the interview can be best understood (for therapeutic purposes) as a transference expression. That is the therapist *values* the transference meaning, and hence *interprets* the inferred competition as transference.

Approaching the same client behavior from a client-centered approach, we might expect the therapist to respond differently. He might say:

'You wonder whether you feel the same way about me as you do about your father.'

Here the therapist *focuses* upon the client's perception. He *values* this perception as the most likely springboard to improvement. There is little *inferential* or *interpretive* logic involved in the therapist's representation. If he sees and expresses what the client has expressed, the empathic understanding will have been communicated.

From a dynamic relationship point of view, the therapist would be likely to say:

'You want me to do your thinking for you. You don't like to be yourself.'

In this illustration, the therapist *focuses* upon the dependent questioning, but points up the fear of independence. The therapist *infers* that a struggle between independent and dependent strivings is involved in the request for clarification. He *values* this unifying and separating conflict as the nuclear problem in psychotherapy and, hence, *interprets* the questioning as a dependency bid and a denial of independence.

From the interpersonal psychiatric approach, the therapist might be expected to wonder aloud:

'Do you suppose that you're asking me to tell you whether I'll treat you as your father does so that you'll know how to treat me? I'm not your father — I'm a different person than he is.'

In this illustration the interpersonal therapist *focuses* upon the security-gaining operation of substituting an eidetic person for the real person of the therapist. He corrects this fictional modification, emphasizing that the interpersonal reality of the interview is different from an interpersonal reality with father.

The interpersonal therapist *infers,* then, that the client is introducing a parataxic distortion which must be corrected. The therapist *values* consensual validity (that is, 'Let us notice and agree on what is really going on here') as therapeutic. Hence, the therapist *interprets* the client's misperception as an anxiety-reducing, but erroneous, security-operation which needs to be corrected.

These sample series indicate how each theoretical approach tends to produce somewhat characteristic representations of the client. What aspects of the client's functioning will occupy the interviewer's attention (what he will focus upon), what inferential structure he will use in observing and understanding the client's behavior, what aspects of the client's functioning he will consider most important, and how he will synthesize these observations and value emphases into an interpretation of what the client's behavior means are all theoretically determined to some degree. The client's personality expression and meaning are understood as a function of the interviewer's theory.

ILLUSTRATIVE SYNTHESIS OF THEORY AND OPERATION

Having outlined a generalized structure for defining interviewer operations, we now propose to illustrate the relation of theoretical approaches to this general outline. We may do this by comparing a psychoanalytic reaction with a client-centered reaction to the same client behavior.

It will be recalled that psychoanalytic therapy was summarized by emphasizing the ambitendent drives toward life and pleasure in conflict with the drives toward death and destruction. Thus, the analyst was seen to focus upon, or refer to, the loving and hating aspects of motivation together with the conflicts involved in this antithesis. The psychoanalytic conception of personality as a dynamic configuration of energy in the service of gaining a maximum of pleasure and a minimum of pain by efficient or economical transactions between internal motives and external reality leads to an operational focus upon ego-defenses — that is, the methods by which the personality achieves or fails in its pleasure seeking. The conception of the unconscious id and super-ego leads to an operational focus upon hidden, or covert, meanings and upon processes that must be inferred rather than observed directly.

Psychoanalytic operations may be examined and summarized as including expressive and representative aspects as follows. The *role taking*, or *expressive behavior*, of the orthodox analyst is usually considered to be emotionally neutral. The analyst maintains a relatively impassive, distant role. However, in certain ways this role is extremely expressive. The orthodoxly impassive analyst expresses by selective emphasis what he thinks is most important in the client's 'free' association. He does this by responding to those aspects of the client's production which seem theoretically valuable. Thus, by facilitating certain associations and interfering with others, the analyst is expressing his theoretical value system. Modifications in analytic therapy have introduced *transference role taking* as illustrated in Rosen's and Levy's approaches (cf. Chapters IV and VI). In these innovations the role of the therapist is modified to provide an enactment of expressive aspects that seem theoretically valuable. Generally, both the orthodox impassivity and the transference role-taking approaches are distinctively psychoanalytic in theoretical quality. The theory prescribes the therapist's expressive role. In either event, the expressive role is clearly managing in quality. The selective interest of the orthodox analyst determines the direction which the client's associations are encouraged to take. How such selective encouragement occurs will be discernible in the representative aspects of the analyst's verbalizations. In the case of transference role taking, the expressive role is defined in terms of the attitude the therapist should express in order to modify the client's experience of relationship to parents: 'I will be your mother — but a kind and loving mother who gives good milk,' or 'You are really angry at me — it's all right, children frequently get angry at their parents — I love you anyway.'

The representative operations of the psychoanalytic therapist can be considered in terms of (a) their referential or focusing aspects; (b) their inferential logic; (c) their selective value emphasis; and (d) their interpretive structure.

REFERENTIAL ASPECTS: The analytic therapist focuses upon, or consistently refers to, the loving and hating affects and motives, together with the anxiety aroused by this motivational antithesis; unconscious contents in general, including values and value sources in the super-ego; techniques of self-deception and techniques of maneuvering with reality — that is, the ego-defense system; developmental processes and experiences; and the transference relationship.

INFERENTIAL LOGIC: Inferential logic is involved in much of the analyst's focus upon the client's functioning. That is, the theoretical system provides *a priori* constructs as a basis for determining what is worth noting and attending to in the client's production. The conceptions of Eros and Thanatos provide an emphasis upon love and hate; the conception of the unconscious id and super-ego leads to the search for symbolic meanings rather than manifest meanings; the conception of the ego-defense system against unconscious strivings leads to an emphasis upon techniques of self-deception and techniques for maneuvering reality; the conception of psychosexual development in terms of erogenous zone fixations, repression, and regression leads to an emphasis upon forgotten (i.e. repressed) developmental experiences. Finally, the conception of the relationship of the client to the analyst in terms of a defensive re-enactment of patterns of relating to father and mother in childhood leads to an emphasis upon the substitutive, transference meaning of the client's experience in the therapy relationships.

SELECTIVE VALUE EMPHASIS: What the analyst selectively values, then, is determined by his inferential logic. The aspects of client functioning to which he attends are determined by his theory.

INTERPRETIVE STRUCTURE: Finally, how the analyst integrates, makes sense out of, or interprets the client will be a summation of his focus, inferences and values. For example, the interview excerpt reported from client-centered counseling in Chapter VII (cf. p. 158) showed the client's intense feelings of despair, thoughts of suicide, and her impression that the counseling process was completely futile. It will be recalled that Miss Gil was expressing her wish to die, her feeling that she was wasting the counselor's time, and her surprise that the counselor did not try to protect her more actively:

CLIENT: '. . . you're not alarmed and think I ought to come in — every day — until I get out of this?'

COUNSELOR: 'I believe you are able to make your own decision. I'll see you whenever you want to come.'

An analyst would undoubtedly have handled this differently. He might have said:

> 'What are your feelings about me?'
> CLIENT: (somewhat bitterly) 'I have no feelings about you — except I'm wasting your time. I can't really — think of anything — to say.'
> THERAPIST: 'You sound pretty disappointed in me — as though you were asking your mother for something you knew she wouldn't give you.'
> CLIENT: 'Well — you don't seem to care about me — here I'm ready to kill myself and you don't do a thing about it.'

By contrast with what the client-centered counselor actually did — i.e. express his confidence in the client's own responsibility, we have represented the analyst as being likely to respond to the psychoanalytic dynamics of the problem. It may be inferred psychoanalytically that the client's expressions of despair and hopelessness relate to a fear of abandonment by the parent-surrogate, partly because of the client's anger (oral-aggressive feelings) toward the therapist. The analytic illustration focuses upon the client's feelings toward the therapist, providing the client with an opportunity to express her anger at the therapist without objective threat of retaliation, and simultaneously to consider whether her angry and self-destructive thoughts are really pertinent to the present situation.

The analyst's *focus*, then, is upon the unconscious affective quality of the client's behavior, upon the oral-deprivation content of the production, and upon the transference relationship — 'You are expressing these feelings about me when they really pertain to your childhood relation to mother.' His *inferential logic* leads him to emphasize these latent affective meanings, their historical-genetic sources and their current expression as transference rather than as legitimately contemporary meanings. The aspects of the client's functioning which he *values* as having therapeutic consequence depend upon his theoretical system. He sees as important those features which make conceptual sense in the analytic theory.

His *interpretive synthesis* consists of pulling together and integrating the inferences he can draw on the basis of how the client behaves, how this behavior is likely to relate to the psychoanalytic conceptual system, and how these make sense in terms of modifying the client's difficulties. In the example given, the analyst has not made a verbalized interpretation. His thoughts might have been, briefly, 'It sounds as though she's threatening to commit suicide because she wants so desperately to have me assure her that I love her and will take care of her in spite of her angry, destructive feelings about me. She sounds like a little girl who bangs her head against the wall and screams in order to force her mother to show some interest in her. She's afraid to express her hatred toward me, for fear of retaliation or abandonment. But she already feels abandoned because she feels her hatred really justifies my rejecting her. Of course, I can't tell her all of this, but maybe she can tell me off a little if I give her a chance, and she'll find it's not so dangerous after all. She can also find out a little bit that I'm not really her mother. So I'll say, "What are your feelings about me?" '

SUMMARY

To reduce the complexity, subjectivity, and subtlety of psychotherapy to an operational level, a functional taxonomy of interviewer activities is proposed. Sample interviewer responses are examined from an 'objective observer's' viewpoint and fitted by *expressive* and *representative* descriptive dimensions. Expressive operations of the interviewer are considered (a) as expressing management, passivity, or participation, and (b) as affectionate, neutral, or aggressive in feeling tone. Operations by which the interviewer represents the client are classified on the basis of (a) the observable aspects of the client to which the interviewer refers, (b) what the interviewer infers to be present, (c) what he selectively values, and (d) what meaningful synthesis or interpretation he makes of the client's functioning. Consideration is given to the interaction between the interviewer's theory and his expressive and representational operations. That his expressive and representative operations may influence client perceptions and movement in psychotherapy is also considered. This general structure for summarizing interviewer operations is proposed as an integrative synthesis of theoretically derived interviewer operations and as an essential beginning for the research and clinical examination of functional interactions between interviewer and client in any process of therapeutic 'improvement.'

. . . like the alertness of a pointer
who has spotted a bird. . . . a
certain wave of thoughtful,
kindly alertness . . . Totally non-
verbal . . .[1]

IX. Expressive Operations in Psychotherapy

In this chapter, the expressive role of the interviewer is considered
in more detail. Expressive role examples are drawn from the several
theoretical sources and examined for their functional value. These examples of structuring, supporting, silence, selecting, asserting, uncertainty, reflecting, and clarifying are considered in terms of the degree
to which they express management, passivity, participation, aggression,
neutrality, and affection. An economical ordering of the expressive role
qualities of the interviewer may be achieved by such a behavioral
analysis. The chapter provides further organization of expressive operations derived from therapy concepts and protocols and illustrates the
relevance of these operations to problems in psychotherapy.

THEORY AND EXPRESSIVE OPERATIONS

How the interviewer or leader expresses himself depends upon his
theory, his personality, and the client or group. At this point, we shall
review the theoretical determinants of the interviewer's expressive
operations.

PSYCHOANALYSIS: Braatøy (11) describes the value of the couch in
psychoanalysis as an implement of impassivity. '. . . Sitting behind
the patient with his face out of sight, he may permit himself to ponder
a point without being concerned with . . . squinting. Face to face the
patient might observe the squinting and might react as if there were

[1] A description of Sullivan by one of his patients (106).

some specific importance to what he had just said. . . . He might even succeed in hiding or stifling a yawn, and a yawn does not always mean that the analyst is bored. . . .' Technically, then, the impassive, neutral distance of the analyst provides a *tabula rasa* upon which the patient's transferences are easily projected. One patient refrained from smoking for nearly sixty analytic hours because he assumed that his therapist disapproved. When the patient was finally able to express annoyance about his tobacco hunger, he found that the analyst had smoked cigars throughout the therapy sessions. The fantasy image of father in the analyst's chair had imposed the 'No Smoking' rule. A face-to-cigar relationship in interviewing would hardly have encouraged such a therapeutically useful distortion. Thus, expressive impassivity on the part of the analyst is theoretically crucial and empirically valuable in encouraging free-association and transference distortions. That such free-association is partly controlled by expressive attention from the analyst has already been noted. Responsiveness or unresponsiveness on the analyst's part, what he interprets as resistance and what he considers as free-association, become expressive communications to the patient. Braatøy (11) comments, '. . . By not inquiring about factors which are close to consciousness . . . the analyst informs the patient that he is not interested in those factors. . . .' Landis (60) has complained that his analyst permitted little associative freedom. When Landis talked about current perplexities the analyst treated this as resistance, since childhood associations were considered more valuable. Thus, even the impassivity of the orthodox analyst has expressive value to the patient. That orthodox impassivity may be more of an ideal than a reality, however, is suggested by Strupp,[1] who compared therapists of several persuasions in terms of their responses to the viewing of an initial interview. They were asked to tell how they would respond to the patient. A '. . . sub-sample of experienced orthodox Freudian therapists was contrasted with a neo-Freudian group of comparable experience. Freudians were significantly more "silent," they offered a larger number of interpretations, they showed greater initiative, and they were both "warmer" and "colder." ' Thus it appears that expressive versatility occurs in orthodox analysis as well as in other methods of interviewing.

INTERPERSONAL PSYCHIATRY: Interpersonal psychiatry actively applies expressive behavior as an implement for effective therapy. This

[1] Personal communication.

intentional, sophisticated use of human behavior is intended to provide the patient with a real, socially valid experience in living. Affectionate, punishing, and understanding expressions are used by the therapist to help the client examine and understand himself. The client is expected to learn the socially valid and socially ineffective qualities of his behavior as a result of such rewarding and punishing attitudes from the therapist.

DYNAMIC RELATIONSHIP THERAPY: The dynamic relationship therapist's expressive behavior has clear theoretical definition. The therapist is expected to be permissively accepting of all impulses toward unity and separation so long as these impulses do not violate the rights of others. Taft (103) reports severely reprimanding Helen, 'That is a mean, nasty trick,' when the child scribbled on several sheets of paper so that she could take these 'drawings' home. Here, Dr. Taft's hostility was directed against the greedy possessiveness of the child and her infringement upon the rights of others. Hence, the dynamic relationship therapist can be described as permissively accepting and realistically limiting in expressive behavior. Time limits and social reality limits are clearly set. Feelings toward the therapist are clearly accepted. It will be recalled that this permissive acceptance, characteristic of Rank's position, is less affectionate than the *transference role-taking* approaches of Levy (62) and Rosen (86), even though Rank first proposed that the essential importance of the therapist is in being a mother-symbol. Rank's approach is intended to provide experience in being accepted in both unity with and separation from the mother-symbol therapist; Levy and Rosen tend to share the Alexander and French (1) point of view that the transference role of the therapist provides a 'corrective emotional experience.' The patient needs to find out, for example, that mothers can be loving and accepting. The Rankian patient needs to learn that one can be accepted in both unity with and separation from the mother-symbol.

CLIENT-CENTERED COUNSELING: The client-centered empathy with the client seems generally less expressive than the other psychotherapies. It has been noted, however, that the manner of phrasing and the tonal quality are likely to be extremely crucial. Rogers (83) has commented on how impossible it is to convey on paper '. . . the depth of empathy in the counselor's responses. . . .' Nonetheless, client-centered therapists appear to be least likely to show expressive qualities in their communications to clients. Bortree and Glad (9) have shown this in a comparison of psychoanalytic, relationship, and client-centered protocols. They found that while psychoanalytic therapists were characterized by a questioning attitude, and relationship therapists included expressions of friendliness by the therapist, client-centered therapists were not describable in expressive terms. This meager expressive result may stem from the expressive impoverishment of printed protocols. Roosa (85) has shown that emotional expression is practically indiscernible in typed protocols, which indicated 15.8 per cent affective qualities, as compared to the same material coded from wire recordings, in which 64.7 per cent of the material could be classified as emotionally expressive. Perhaps the expressive qualities in client-centered empathy are lost in transcription. Strupp [1] reports a similar finding in his comparison of the reactions of 237 therapists to an initial interview. He found that the client-centered therapists were most likely to give expressively neutral responses. Be that as it may, we shall examine the expressive aspects of client-centered therapy in the same operational conception as the other approaches.

EXPRESSIVE OPERATIONS AND CLIENT PERCEPTIONS

The client's experience of the interviewer is likely to have some relation to the interviewer's actual behavior — but the relationship may be tenuous. A rather dour psychiatrist received a glowing letter from a discharged patient who said, in part, 'Were it not for your warm smile and blue eyes, I would never have been able to leave the hospital.' The usually unsmiling face of this psychiatrist emphasizes that the patient's fantasies about the therapist, rather than his real expressive behavior, prompted the patient's tribute. Similarly, the 'No Smoking' rule in an earlier illustration was expressed by the patient's fantasy rather than by his analyst. In Chapter VIII, it was suggested that an analysis of expressive operations might include consideration of (a) how the interviewer perceives himself expressively and (b) how the client experiences the interviewer's expressive behavior, as well as (c) how the interviewer 'actually' behaves from the point of view of an outside observer.[2]

[1] Personal communication.
[2] It is recognized that there is no such thing as 'actual' expressive behavior, nor a truly 'outside' observer. An approximate paradigm, however, might be a trained observer watching an interviewer-client interaction through a one-way vision screen.

In this chapter, we shall examine the interviewer's expressive behavior from each of these points of view. This can be accomplished by examining sample interchanges in the same way as was done earlier (cf. pp. 174–5). This time, however, we shall first look through the eyes of the client, then consider samples from the three viewpoints at once. Finally, we shall consider some exploratory research which illustrates relationships among interviewer, client, and observer judgments about the same expressive events.

VERBAL VERSUS NON-VERBAL EXPRESSION: The expressive qualities of grammatical form are most easily represented in a written document. The question 'Where shall we begin today?' seems to be a tentative, non-directive inquiry which might be expected to get the patient started on whatever he wants to talk about. Rephrased in this sense, it could mean 'We may begin wherever you wish.' By contrast, 'Tell me about your ninth mission,' seems to be a baldly authoritative directive which insists that 'This is what you will talk about.' In written form, the grammatical structure clarifies expressive qualities. Such clarity may be valid in some cases. However, the gestural and tonal qualities are likely to be lost, even though they are more expressive than the words themselves.

Consider some of the possible meanings of the question 'Well, where shall we begin today?' If the interviewer says this impatiently, he may communicate, 'Quit stalling — I have other things to do.' With a worried frown, the question could suggest, 'It may be that we're going to have a tough time today.' By a bored, tired look or voice, the interviewer might express, 'Do I have to listen to the same old stuff?' Expressed firmly and decisively, the question might communicate, 'Did you think about what I told you to?' In a very understanding, gentle tone, the question could convey, 'I know how hard it is to talk about these things.' 'Well, where shall we begin today?' presented in an overly friendly, near-seductive manner could imply, 'Gosh, I enjoy listening to your troubles.'

These few variations in the meaning of the identical written question emphasize the importance of non-verbal expression by the interviewer or leader. Personality as well as theoretical leanings of the interviewer will have potential bearing upon the interviewer's expressive interaction with the patient. Strupp [1] has shown that therapists

---

[1] Personal communication.

who expressed a positive attitude toward a patient seen in a motion picture interview were likely to recommend permissiveness, passivity and the encouragement of free-association. Conversely, therapists who expressed a negative attitude toward this patient were more likely to give 'cold' reactions to him in the interview responses, and '. . . to choose diagnostic labels such as psychopath, character-disorder, paranoid, and phobic . . .' Such relationships suggest that the therapist's personality and 'counter-transferences' modify his reactions in therapeutic interviews and may influence the course of therapy.

We have noted that the expressive role of the therapist is theoretically defined. Orthodox analysis is expected to provide an expressively impassive distance. One of the functions of the couch in analysis is to reduce the *real* impingement of the therapist's personality upon the patient, thus maximizing the degree to which the patient must struggle with his own fantasies, transferences, and irrealities. By contrast, neo-analytic approaches such as direct analysis and transference relationship maximize the transference role-taking behavior of the therapist to provide corrective emotional experiences. The client-centered approach provides empathic acceptance of the client as its major expressive variable, while the dynamic relationship approach encourages the client to accept both unifying and separating tendencies. Interpersonal psychiatry emphasizes the most varied expressive behavior in the service of providing a real person with whom the client can work toward consensually valid, syntactic experience. Some exploration of ways in which these theoretical premises may influence the client's perception of the interviewer's expressive operations seems in order.

An example from Sullivan (106) will serve as a point of departure for constructing illustrations of how various theoretical approaches may produce different expressive meanings. The patient had shown annoyance about '. . . that day when you called me skinny.' Sullivan bristled perceptibly and asked rather sternly, 'I beg your pardon?' The patient elaborated, sounding even more aggrieved, whereupon Sullivan corrected him, 'I distinctly recall what I said, namely, that you seemed to have suffered your mother's opinion that you were thin.' In this interchange the client's perception of the therapist's expression has been quite at variance with 'reality.' The therapist's theoretical goal is to implement consensual validity; i.e. the therapist wants the patient to see correctly. He implements this intention by being annoyed with the patient's mistake. Sullivan, self-consciously and intentionally, used expressive behavior as an implement of therapy. He 'bristled perceptibly' at the patient's error. Such an expressive operation should lead to the client's experiencing that the therapist is displeased with him. The more conventional psychoanalyst would presumably not bristle at all, or show any emotional involvement, but might say quietly, 'Perhaps you have me mixed up with your mother,' or, 'Your mother criticized you so much that you assume any reference to your thinness is an attack such as she used to make.'

By contrast, a therapist from Levy's transference relationship approach might be very expressive in a mothering way, warmly suggesting that 'You think your mother didn't like you because of your thinness, but I like you as you are.'

Practitioners of direct analysis might respond in the same mothering, accepting way with an oral interpretation: 'Your mother didn't give you enough milk and then made fun of your looking half starved. But I'm your mother now and I'll feed you with love.'

A client-centered counselor would try to understand and empathize with the client's distress, saying, 'You're pretty distressed about being skinny,' or, 'It's pretty obnoxious of anyone to comment on your thinness.'

The Rankian *will* emphasis might result in encouragement of the resistant belligerence and produce, 'You're pretty angry at me — I can see how you would be.'

Thus we have the possibility of the interviewer behaving in a variety of non-verbal and verbal ways as a result of his theoretical affiliation. Such differences in expression should produce differences in the client's perception. Sullivan's reaction of annoyance might be expected to modify the patient's misperception by punishing the error. The expressively impassive psychoanalytic examples convey that the analyst neither approves nor disapproves, but presumes that the patient will become aware of what he is doing, why he is doing it, and hence how he can modify it. The transference relationship and direct analysis examples provide affectionate mothering which may be expected to reduce the patient's expectation that he will always be derided and rejected. The client-centered examples provide understanding and clarification so that the client may more clearly understand and accept how he feels and perceives. The Rankian will-support example might be expected to allow the client to experience his angry separation with less guilt and fear, and encourage him to turn these feelings into creative channels.

Sullivan proposes that any mood whatever except frivolity may be effectively used by the therapist. For example, when chided by the patient for appearing half asleep and not knowing what was going on, he might reply, '. . . have you been listening? Have you any idea what you were saying?' (106). The apparent purpose of this reaction is to interrupt and punish a stream of apparently meaningless production. Sullivan seems to be saying essentially that the patient should be more organized or syntactic in his production. By contrast, an analyst who is unseen by the patient could hardly apply the same procedure. In a similar situation, he might attempt to reduce the 'snow job' resistance by inquiring, 'What is this all about?' or by suggesting, 'You're trying to avoid understanding anything today.'

Durkin (15) says in an affectionately accepting way to a child, 'You don't like me today.' The expressive role is likely to communicate, 'It's all right not to like me — I love you whether you expect me to or not.' If 'You don't like me today' had been expressed in a critical tone of voice, the child's perception would be unlikely to be 'She accepts and understands me,' but might be 'She dislikes me and is critical, even though she understands.' If a therapist were to say in a pleasantly warm tone of voice, 'You're bragging a bit,' the client's perception is unlikely to be 'He's criticizing me,' but rather, 'He accepts me even though I'm bragging.'

The theoretical background, then, influences the expressive participation of the therapist, and such theoretically determined expressive roles may plausibly make a difference in the patient's experience. They may also plausibly be expected to influence the kind of process of change that the psychotherapy produces.

Expressive operations may be used consciously and specifically as a precision instrument, or they may be an accidental fumble of one's own personality. Sullivan (106) describes himself in response to a patient's decision to rush into a precipitous marriage, '. . . I frown and I worry and I give the patient time to realize it. . . . According to all we know about personality, that means that the patient gets anxious about what I'm worried about. Then I say, "Look, I am not sure I know what is going on, and I am not sure you are right about what's going on. Is this an important relationship to you? Can't you let it rest awhile?"'

An understanding of what expressive effect one has as an interviewer and a sophisticated intention to provide the expressive role that one expects will produce the intended results seem desiderata in psychotherapy. While little is known at present about the contribution of the interviewer's expressive role to the psychotherapy process, it is at least possible to define expressive operations as a basis for research. So far, we have provided samples of the problem in operational definition with some suggestions about its importance and research potential. We now review our conceptual schema which may serve to organize expressive behaviors into functional groupings. Generally this schema is illustrative rather than exhaustive, but it does describe the major functional aspects of the interviewer's expressive role. Usually, the verbal–non-verbal dichotomy becomes irrelevant, since the expressive context is most consequential. For the same reason, grammatical structure also becomes of secondary importance.

The variables of expression that seem most relevant can be conceptualized in relation to the management-participation and affection-aggression classifications introduced in Chapter VIII. They were defined as follows:

Management-Participation

Management: To what degree does the interviewer assume responsibility for, direct, control, lead, or structure the interview process?

Passivity: To what degree does the interviewer maintain a hands-off policy, allowing the client a laissez-faire kind of freedom?

Participation: To what degree does the interviewer engage in the process in an active but following, rather than leading, way? Does he actively participate without directing?

Affection-Aggression

Affection: To what degree does the interviewer give evidence of warmth, friendliness, interest or accepting awareness of the client?

Neutrality: To what degree does the interviewer show lack of involvement, absence of emotional awareness, or commitment to the client?

Aggression: To what degree does the interviewer show annoyance, rejection, hostility, anger, or active disinterest?

How the client might perceive the interviewer's expressive behavior is illustrated by several examples located on the two-way classification matrix of Figure 11. The placement of these examples represents the author's judgment of the client's experience in the sample behavioral units which are described below. They are not intended to suggest that structuring, supporting, etc., in general, will be viewed in this way by all clients, but rather are designed to illustrate the feasibility of making such judgments from the client's frame of reference.

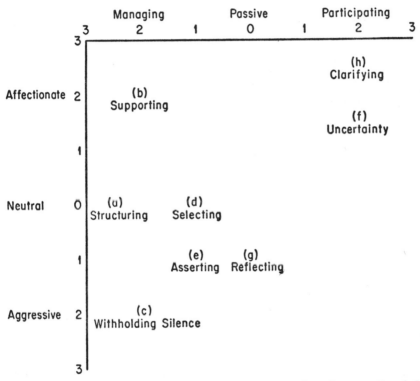

Fig. 11. Client Perception of Interviewer Expression: Sample Judgments Classified on Two-Way Conceptual Schema.

(*a*) STRUCTURING: The term *structuring* is used generally in psychotherapy to refer to interviewer expressions about the activities, processes, and interpersonal roles which constitute the interviewing process. In a sense, such structuring is essential to any kind of interview, in that the interviewer indicates what will be encouraged, what will be avoided, and what is expected of the client in the interview. We have used the word 'indicates' rather than 'tells the client,' since such communications are not necessarily at a verbal level. It will also be noted that the structuring example is presented first in this illustrative series, since everything that the interviewer does has some bearing upon the structure of the interview process. Certain aspects are most evidently structuring in quality, but the interviewer's implementation of his implicit or explicit plan may have results in the kind of processes developed in the interview. One sample of structuring (108) is as follows:

> DOCTOR: (Cough) 'You are asking how to grab hold of this thing, you know. . . .'
> PATIENT: 'Yes, how do we analyze it? How do we get better from that? How do we talk about it?'
> DOCTOR: 'One approach to it is to notice it when it happens here — in its detail, and what adjustment you have to make to me. . . .'

The structuring aspect of this sample says in effect, 'The way we will operate here is that we will notice and comment upon what you do in relation to me.' It will be noted that the interviewer assumes responsibility for the character of the interview — *this is how we will do it.* The management quality of structuring is apparent in the sample. The interviewer determines and expresses how the interviewing will be conducted.

(*b*) SUPPORTING: The term *supporting* is chosen to summarize those interviewer expressions which indicate sympathy, consideration, willingness to help, and all evidences that the interviewer is trying to make the patient or client more comfortable. An example (12) which emphasizes this vividly is as follows:

> DOCTOR: 'But why shouldn't you cry if something touches you? This is just the place for it.'

In this sample the interviewer expresses affection, acceptance, and understanding. At the same time he is telling the client what to do — 'Go ahead and cry — it will do you good.' Thus there is a combination of affection and management in this supportive role.

(*c*) WITHHOLDING SILENCE: Since silence can be enormously varied in expressive value, we have chosen to illustrate an interviewer's silence in the presence of the client's insistent bid for a response. This silence is judged to express a moderate degree of management — 2 — and a moderate degree of aggression — 2. The sample is drawn from an anonymous analytic hour:

PATIENT: (In obvious distress and after considerable blocking) 'It seems to me that you could say something about that. I'm all dried up.'

ANALYST: (Silence).

PATIENT: (Angrily) 'It isn't often I ask you directly to say something. What about it?'

ANALYST: (Silence).

PATIENT: (Resignedly) 'I see you're not going to give in, and even though I want you to reassure me that I'm all right — I can see that this is something I have to get from myself rather than from you. But it sure is disgusting to get up the nerve to ask something directly and get slapped in the face for it.'

ANALYST: (Silence).

It will be seen from this sample that the silence of the analyst could be experienced by a client as a combination of rejection and control. Rejection is expressed by refusing to respond, control is expressed by forcing the patient to stew in his own juice. Thus the analyst is expressing some aggression and some management in the situation.

(*d*) SELECTING: Some degree of preference is expressed by the interviewer every time he fails to respond, or responds to what he considers important. The direction that the interviewer's response takes indicates what he thinks is significant or valuable and thereby suggests what direction the interview should take. On this basis, while selecting may be affectively neutral, it certainly expresses some management of the interview process. Hence, it has been judged to be mildly managing in expressive quality. A sample of client behavior with a variety of possible interviewer responses will illustrate the expressive quality of selection.

PATIENT: 'I had another dream last night. I was storming a height. That suggests to me the return of vigour and energy.'

ANALYST: 'Yes, but what are you denying?' (6).

This response expresses 'I discredit your interpretation. Tell me what else it might be.' That the analyst is directing the patient to talk about some *other* meaning is indicative of the management quality of selecting.

An alternative interviewer response could have been, 'You're feeling somewhat better then?' This alternative, although it has none of the aggressive aspect, is still managing in quality. It says in essence, 'We'll talk about your improved feelings.'

Another alternative might be, 'You've been feeling pretty worn out.' Again the interviewer manages the process by selecting a particular aspect of the client's expression. In this case he has focused upon the negative rather than the positive aspects of the client's production.

These examples suggest that some element of management is present in every selection that the interviewer makes. Since selection is also likely to involve a representation of the client, it has been elaborated further under *valuing* representations of the client in Chapter VIII.

(*e*) ASSERTING *and* (*f*) UNCERTAINTY: The term *asserting* will refer to those interviewer expressions that are presented either by phrasing or non-verbal means as though they are matters of fact that the interviewer takes for granted. By contrast, the term *uncertainty* will summarize interviewer expressions which are presented in the 'I'm not sure about this but what do you think' fashion. Two examples illustrate this difference.

> CLIENT: 'I feel as though my mother is always watching me and criticizing what I do. It gets me all stirred up inside. I try not to let it happen, but you know, there are times when I feel her eagle eye on me that I just boil inwardly' (83).

Counselor's *assertive* response: 'You resent her criticism.'

Counselor's *uncertainty* response: 'If I understand you correctly, you feel resentful toward her criticism. Is that right?'

In this sample the manner of phrasing the response expresses an assertion in the first case, and uncertainty in the second. On the other hand, it will be realized that gestural, tonal and inflectional qualities might modify the impact of phrasing, even to the extent that the verbal assertion 'You resent her criticism' could express 'I wonder if that means you resent her criticizing you.'

Assuming that the *assertive* and *uncertainty* phrasing express what they are phrased to mean, there is an implicit value judgment difference in the two forms. The assertion says baldly and authoritatively, 'I see how it is and will tell you how it is with you.' There is a quality of *managing* the interview in this expression, i.e. 'I will tell you what is going on, and this will help you.' At the same time there is a quality of aggression in assertive expression, i.e. 'You are somewhat inferior and dependent.' By contrast, the *uncertainty* form may express humility, empathy and respect for the client: 'I would like to be able to understand this in the way it seems to you. Is this it?' Such an expression conveys a quality of affection and an attitude of participation with the client rather than a managing or directing attitude.

Sullivan's expressions were designed to convey understanding, acceptance, criticism, or affection, depending upon his momentary intention. The following example suggests his unwillingness to foist a particular point of view upon the patient, and his desire to have the patient feel understood:

> INTERVIEWER: 'I have a vague feeling that some people might doubt the utility to you of the care with which your parents, and particularly your mother, saw to it that you didn't learn how to dance, or play games, or otherwise engage in the frivolous social life of people your age' (102).

An assertive rephrasing of this meticulous uncertainty might go something like this:

> INTERVIEWER: 'It did you more harm than good for your mother to interfere with your socializing.'

The difference in phrasing conveys a difference in value judgment. Sullivan's phrasing suggests an interest in the patient's point of view and an awareness that the patient can reasonably assess the question raised. It suggests that the interviewer is participating with and expressing affection for the patient. The assertive rephrasing connotes, 'Here it is, take it or leave it.' The assertion, then, is both managing and aggressive in expressive quality.

(g) REFLECTING and (h) CLARIFYING: It may be useful to compare the expressive quality of interviewer responses in which the client's verbalization is reflected or repeated, with those in which the interviewer attempts to understand and clarify. Two possible responses to the same client expression will illustrate this difference.

> CLIENT: '. . . I had a dream that disturbed me. It was about this girl I ran around with in high school. I can't remember the exact circumstances. We were talking together, and I said, "I'd crawl on my belly if I thought it would do any good." Then she said, "Go away and leave me alone."'
>
> COUNSELOR: 'You said you felt somewhat disturbed by it.' (98).

In this example of *reflecting*, part of what the client has said is reworded, almost suggesting that the interviewer is unwilling or unable to understand. Such a response may be rated from the client's viewpoint as relatively passive so far as participation is concerned, and mildly aggressive so far as the affective quality can be judged. By contrast, a response in which the interviewer *clarifies* by empathizing and understanding may involve considerable participation with the client and a strong degree of affectionate expression. Such a response to the same client production might be expressed as follows:

> INTERVIEWER: 'It's pretty distressing to offer everything and be kicked in the teeth for it.'

In this example an attempt is made to understand and rephrase the client's affective experience. In contrast to *reflection's* aggressive passivity, *clarification* may express participation with and affection for the client.

The reader will have noticed that the expressive value judgments about these samples have all been made from the frame of reference of the client rather than from that of an outside observer. Earlier (cf. p. 170), we paid considerable attention to the fact that the client's experience of the interviewer's expression may be very different from the way in which that expression would appear to an impartial observer. We also noted in passing that the interviewer might have a viewpoint different from that of either observer or client.

COMPARISON OF INTERVIEWER, OBSERVER, AND CLIENT PERCEPTION OF EXPRESSIVE OPERATIONS

To clarify the difference which another frame of reference might produce, let us re-examine some of the samples by comparing their likely expressive value from three points of view. On the grid in Figure 12, we again locate four of the samples already examined:

(*b*) SUPPORTING: DOCTOR: 'But why shouldn't you cry if something touches you? This is just the place for it.' That the client, observer and interviewer may all have the same perception of the affection-management values of this interviewer expression is indicated by our locating all three judgments in the same place. That is, the frames of reference of the three may correspond.

(c) WITHHOLDING SILENCE: In the sample given from the patient's point of view, the silence of the analyst to repeated pleas for comment was judged to be both managing and aggressive. However, looking at it from an observer's point of view, the analyst has merely remained in his chair without responding. On this basis, the analyst has been emotionally neutral and passive. The observer's judgment would not correspond to the client's. The analyst is being technically competent in this silence, whatever emotional turmoil he might experience in the counter-transference; he has provided the patient with affective neutrality and role passivity for the client's own good. His judgment as to his role could very plausibly coincide with the observer's judgment — neutral and passive, rather than with the client's judgment — managing and aggressive.

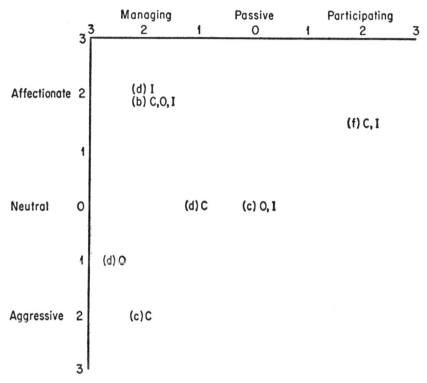

Fig. 12. Comparison of Interviewer Expression from Three Points of View.
The symbols C, O, and I following the letter designations refer respectively to Client, Observer, and Interviewer.

(*d*) SELECTING: We have shown the client's judgment that selecting is mildly managing and affectively neutral in the sample, 'Yes, but what are you denying?' From the viewpoint of an observer, this might be completely erroneous. It suggests the possibility at least that the analyst is criticizing or attacking the patient, forcing him to think of something else. This is shown in Figure 12, (d) O, as a relatively high degree of management and a mild degree of aggression. The interviewer is observed to be critical and controlling. From the analyst's point of view, however, he is interested in the patient's welfare, is

helping the patient to understand himself, and is beneficently prob-
ing by his question. This is shown in Figure 12, (d) I, as moderate
management and moderate affection. It will be seen then that the three
observers, client, observer, and interviewer, may all see different expressive values in the same transaction.

(f) UNCERTAINTY: COUNSELOR: 'If I understand you correctly, you
feel resentful toward her criticism. Is that right?' This client-centered
expression has been judged from the client's point of view to be moderately participating. An observer, however, might well wonder, 'Doesn't
that interviewer know his business? Could he really be that lacking
in understanding of what the client said?' Such a judgment as this
could well go off the grid since it lacks participation, empathy, and
skill. It does not fit a definition of psychotherapy from this point of
view. On the other hand, the interviewer is likely to have experienced
that he has expressed empathic understanding in an accepting way
(Figure 12, (f) C, I). He has understood and clarified the client's
point of view. His judgment would tend to correspond with the client's;
'we both see your problem in the same way.'

These sample judgments from three different frames of reference
indicate that the client's perception of the interviewer's expressive role
may be relatively valid, i.e. it corresponds with the observer's judgment; or it may be relatively autistic, i.e. observer and interviewer
agree with each other, but the client experiences it differently. Furthermore, both the interviewer and an independent observer may
experience the expressive role in different ways.

EXPLORATORY INVESTIGATIONS OF EXPRESSIVE ROLES

Studies conducted under the author's direction have explored some
aspects of the group leader's and interviewer's expressive roles. Smith
and Woodward (95) compared the effects of *unfriendly, neutral,* and
friendly behavior by the same interviewer. Six 'normal' subjects were
interviewed by Smith. In two interviews with each subject he was *unfriendly,* in two interviews he was *neutral,* and in two he was *friendly.*
To assure that the interviewer was actually behaving in the expressive ways intended, three judges watched through a one-way vision
screen and made ratings of Smith's expressive behavior on a scale
ranging from *friendly* to *unfriendly.* The interviewer was judged to be

expressing himself in the intended way 82 per cent of the time in the 36 interviews conducted.

Behavior observations were made and classified into Interpersonality Synopsis categories (37). Projective test reactions to the Emotional Projection Test (38, 40) were taken before and after each interview. Thus it became possible to assess both behavioral and projective test reactions to the interviewer's expressive role. Not all results were definitive, but they will be summarized for their suggestive value.[1]

When the interviewer was unfriendly, the subjects tended to become more directed toward others, more anxious, more likely to say favorable things about themselves and unfavorable things about others. Pleasant feelings were reduced in observable behavior. *The unfriendly interviewer role*, then, appeared to produce a tensional reaction in the subjects, critical attitudes toward others, and a favorable, perhaps defensive, self-justification. The psychodynamics of these reactions may be inferred from the differences in behavioral and projective test responses. In all instances the fantasy[2] changes were the reverse of the behavioral reactions. This may suggest that the subjects reacted defensively to the interviewer's unfriendliness and that while there was real disturbance in observed behavior, this defensive reaction reduced the need for fantasying disturbance since the interviewer's behavior justified their responses. It is of special interest that the subjects did not express feelings of annoyance or inadequacy, nor did they give any indication that they were aware of the interviewer's unfriendliness. Their reactions were disturbed and defensive, but they were not apparently sensitive to the unfriendliness which provoked the distress. Thus, it appears that the expressive behavior of the interviewer is likely to be reacted to in psychodynamically meaningful ways, but the subject does not necessarily understand the reasons for his reactions.

The neutral interviewer role provoked an increase in anxious feelings and a decrease in pleasant feelings. The subjects became less likely to talk about themselves and less likely to say unfavorable things when they did refer to themselves. In other words, the neutral inter-

---

[1] Differences at the .10 level of confidence or better are included since they may have suggestive value in an exploratory study.

[2] For simplicity I shall use the word *fantasy* to refer to projective test responses.

viewer role tended to increase tension but reduce self-criticism. Some explanation of the meaning of these reactions is suggested by the fantasy changes. The subjects tended to increase their fantasy of hostile feelings, suggesting that they may have felt rejected and angry in the neutral interview. Otherwise, their fantasy changes were consistent with their behavior, a reduction of self-consciousness and self-criticism in both fantasy and behavior. These relationships suggest that a minimum of expressive reaction on the interviewer's part is likely to be experienced as rejection by the client, but that self-consciousness is reduced while anxiety comes to the surface in the form of tensional, disturbed reactions. These tendencies seem altogether consistent with effects of the neutral expressive role in client-centered counseling.

The friendly interviewer role produced an increase in hostile feelings and a greater tendency to say that other people were critical and attacking. Tendencies to be self-critical were reduced. The subjects became less interested in others and showed less evidence of pleasant feelings in their behavior. Thus, we have a somewhat paradoxical situation in reaction to the interviewer's friendliness. The subjects became irritated or angry and expressed the idea that they were being criticized. These behavioral reactions make dynamic sense in relation to the fantasy changes in the friendly interviews. Hostile expressions decreased in fantasy as they increased in behavior. While self-criticism decreased in behavior, it increased in fantasy. In other words, the subjects apparently felt comfortable enough during the friendly interviews to be able to express their irritations with less threat, and thus reduce their fantasy annoyance. At the same time, however, some sense of guilt developed so that they fantasied unpleasant, derogatory things about themselves as a result of their attacking the friendly interviewer. Of special interest is the fact that the interviewer was most likely to be described as critical when he was being 'objectively' friendly. We have considered earlier that the 'actual' expressive quality of the interviewer is not necessarily consistent with the client's perception. Verbally, at least in this study, there is considerable discrepancy between the 'real' and 'perceived' qualities of the interviewer's expressive behavior.

This study suggests, then, that the interviewer's expressive behavior does have measurable and meaningful effects on the reactions of normal subjects. *Unfriendliness* produces disturbed, defensive reaction; *neutrality* tends to be experienced as rejection; and *friendli-*

ness is likely to encourage the expression of irritation and the fantasy of inadequacy.

Group Reactions to Leader 'Warmth' and 'Coldness'

Shearn and Thompson [1] investigated the influence of the personality warmth or coldness of a leader in influencing reactions of the members of a therapy-like discussion group. Six groups of college students, six members per group, were led in their therapy discussions by six different leaders. The leadership was systematically varied so that group members had an opportunity to become acquainted with two leaders over a period of eight meetings. To assess the leader's personality warmth and coldness, the members of the groups were asked to indicate which of a list of 22 warmth/coldness adjectives applied to each of their two leaders. This list included such terms as friendly, sociable, accepting, aloof, sarcastic, and critical. From these judgments each leader was described in warmth/coldness terms by two groups of six subjects each, thus making it possible to assess the influence of leader personality on group behavior. Group behavior reactions were classified directly by one observer in each group, who made a process recording of positive, or pleasant behavior; negative, or unpleasant behavior; neutral, or unemotional behavior; leader-oriented behavior; and group-oriented behavior.

Relationships between leader warmth and group reactions were as follows: Unemotional or neutral group reactions were produced by the 'cold' leader personality; negative or unpleasant reactions were produced by the 'warm' leader personality. This study provides evidence of an association between leader personality and the reactions of group members. Especially interesting is the fact that 'warmth' tends to produce unpleasant, aggressive behavior, while 'coldness' tends to produce unemotional, neutral, or perhaps overcontrolled, defensive reactions. These findings are in essential agreement with those reported from the Smith and Woodward study. It appears that warm, accepting, friendly leadership or interviewer behavior is likely to permit the expression of unpleasant, aggressive reactions; while cold, rejecting, unfriendly leadership is likely to provoke defensive, protective reactions in individual and group interviews.

[1] Unpublished study conducted under the author's direction by C. R. Shearn and E. F. Thompson, with the cooperation of H. W. Keely, R. T. Lewis, W. D. Roberts, and R. D. Hartley.

CLINICAL IMPLICATIONS OF THE INTERVIEWER'S PERSONALITY

I am reminded of two psychoanalytic therapists who hold very different views about how quickly transference develops in individual psychotherapy. One of these therapists, a warm, pleasant, accepting person, believes that transference reactions develop very quickly — in the first one or two weeks. The other therapist, an aloof, cold, reserved person, insists that transference reactions cannot develop before six or seven weeks of therapy at the earliest. It seems reasonable that both of these therapists may be right. The reactions of the patients are likely to depend on the personality expression of the therapist. Strupp's studies of therapist reactions to an initial filmed interview have shown that the therapists who report an unfavorable reaction to the patient are also more likely to give 'cold' responses, to be more controlling, to make a more negative prognosis for the patient, and to expect him to take longer to reach any satisfactory improvement. It seems altogether plausible that these data may be integrated into the reasonable picture that the interviewer who has a negative reaction to a client will provide conditions of therapy which are least likely to produce effective progress, while the therapist who has a favorable reaction to a client will provide conditions which are most likely to be helpful. The orthodox analytic proposition that the analyst must never respond in a human way can be countered by Sullivan's suggestion that 'we are all more human than otherwise.' How such antithetical expressive roles in psychotherapy and leadership influence processes of psychotherapy and group dynamics may well be a crucial problem.

SUMMARY

This chapter extends the analysis introduced in Chapter VIII. Consideration of the relation of psychotherapy theories to interviewer expressive operations provides a basis for examining the theoretical implications of these operations as well as the empirical effects of interviewer personality. Three of the four theories propose that the client's perception will have no necessary relation to the interviewer's 'actual' expressive behavior. Thus, a method for contrasting the 'objective' expressive behavior with the client's perceptions is introduced. The two-way classification schema, introduced earlier, is used to illustrate how Interviewer, Observer, and Client may agree or disagree in experiencing the expressive impact of interviewer operations. Exploratory research examples indicate how such perceptual agreement or disagreement may be empirically examined. Finally, it is hypothesized that the interviewer's acceptance or rejection of a client may have important implications for particular 'treatment' relationships.

... to talk of many
things ...
—CARROLL

X. What Interviewers Talk About

The referential or focusing aspect of interviewer operations will be examined in this chapter. It will be recalled that interviewer behavior was classified in Chapter VIII as *expressive* and *representational operations*. Representational operations were described as referential, valuing, inferential, and interpretive types. Furthermore, it was shown that a cogent presentation of valuing, inference, and interpretation is dependent upon a clearly defined structure of referential operations. Hence, this chapter will develop such a referential structure in detail. It will attempt to answer such questions as: To what aspects of the client does the interviewer address himself? What does he focus upon? To what does he refer? What aspects of the client's functioning does the interviewer emphasize? Or, more simply, perhaps, *What does he talk about?*

The *interpersonality* [1]*synopsis* model introduced in Chapter II will be presented and elaborated more completely as a basis for defining and clarifying the essentials of client behavior emphasized by the four theories. Such theoretical essentials may be summarized by means of the following conceptual outline:

Any interpersonality event may be characterized with relative completeness in terms of the following aspects:

    I. Its Modality of Communication. Is it expressed in

        A. Symbolic,

---

[1] The term *interpersonality* is intended to convey the breadth of interaction between people required by a synthesis of four theories. The term denotes that personality is a function of the organism in its humanized richness, of multiple interactions with other personalities, and of the theoretical value systems applied to the description of personalities relating to and being created by each other.

    B. Verbal, or

    C. Non-verbal mode?

  II. Its Dimensionality of Behavior. Does the interviewer describe the event as

    A. Perception,

    B. Activity,

    C. Feeling, or

    D. Motivation?

  III. Its Temporal Relationships. Does the interviewer respond to

    A. Past

    B. Present, or

    C. Future aspects of client functioning?

  IV. Its Attributed Qualities. Does the interviewer attribute

    A. Orientation,

    B. Tonus,

    C. Value,

    D. Status, or

    E. Control qualities to the behavior to which he refers?

It will be observed that this interpersonality synopsis model provides a framework in which the many aspects of the client emphasized by the four theories may be organized in a unified way. The model provides a structure for empirical categorization of interviewer operations; for theoretical specification of relationships between concepts and operations; and for a technical method of observing and analyzing interpersonality events in any setting.[1] In the present chapter, it will be used as an outline for specifying referential operations in psychotherapy. What does the interviewer talk about in responding to his client?

SOCIAL AND THERAPEUTIC TALK

In social intercourse people usually respond to direct, explicit meanings of conversation. Such directness may produce satisfying interstimulation. One person makes a remark or observation which stimulates (or bores, or angers) another, who then responds with more or less pertinent, verbally explicit reactions to the first person's thought.

---

[1] No attempt is made in this book to present interpersonality synopsis as a technical method. The intention herein is completely heuristic. A companion volume in preparation for publication provides the technical details of the method as an observational technique.

Social communication emphasizes such direct, explicit meanings. Therapeutic communication emphasizes more implicit, tangential meanings. Two socialized people attempt to converse in such a way that both will get information, stimulation, or a sense of satisfaction from talking. In psychotherapy a quite different intention and process occurs: the client is expected to express those things which will be most helpful in improving his ability to 'adjust'; the interviewer is expected to express those things which he considers most likely to facilitate the client's improved 'adjustment.' The content of therapeutic communication is emphatically the client's 'personality.' The content of social talking is usually not about either of the participants' personalities — except in courtship, seduction, politics, or vituperation. Since therapeutic talk is primarily about various facets of the client's 'personality' rather than about explicit, direct meanings of 'conversation,' the *client as a person* absorbs the interviewer's interest and determines much of the content of the interviewer's talking.

SOCIAL COMMUNICATION: Meeting a friend on the street, a socialized person might say, 'That's a good-looking suit you're wearing.' The friend might reply, 'Thanks. It caught my eye in a store window and I just had to have it. These new fabrics are really something.' This interchange might lead to a pleasant five minutes of chit-chat about clothes, weather conditions, high prices, and the miracles of modern living. Such a chat might be accompanied by a feeling of pleasure in having a friend to whom one enjoys talking.

That people mean what they say, and are talking about a good-looking suit when they mention one, is conventionally assumed in social living. However, many other things could have been implied from this conversation, e.g.:

'He's jealous of me.'

'He's trying to butter me up.'

'He's more interested in clothes than in me.'

'He really means this pattern is too loud.'

The author was chagrined when an old friend said, 'Haven't you gained a little weight?' Somewhat piqued, I replied, 'Well, I've lost ten pounds since I last saw you.' My friend's rejoinder was, 'I've lost sixty. Don't I look it?' Obviously, my friend had not meant 'I see you're gaining weight,' but rather, 'Why don't you notice my slenderness?'

THERAPEUTIC COMMUNICATION: While indirect meanings are commonly present in social interaction, they are rarely responded to explicitly, or even admitted into conscious awareness. Some form or degree of such indirect aspects of behavior become the basic stuff of group and individual interview processes. To illustrate again with the 'good-looking suit,' if this was a client's first remark in an interview, it would be likely to lead in very different directions than it did in the friendly conversation. Depending upon his own personality and his theoretical persuasion, as well as the stage of progress in psychotherapy, any of the following replies might be expected from the interviewer:

'You're anxious about your bill.'

'You're trying to be friendly.'

'You object to my clothes.'

'You're buttering me up as you do your mother.'

'You're feeling better today.'

'You want me to be a friend instead of a therapist.'

'What other thoughts have you had about me?'

'Thank you, but could we get on with the problems you're seeing me about.'

'You're pleased with my clothes.'

It will be observed that each of these possible interviewer replies involves a particular focus or emphasis in looking at the client's behavior; i.e. each assumes a somewhat different frame of reference toward the client.

REFERENTIAL OPERATIONS OF THE INTERVIEWER

In each of the hypothetical interviewer replies to the 'good-looking suit' remark, some aspect of the client's 'personality' was referred to, emphasized, or focused upon by the interviewer. To provide a way of organizing the several referents, the *interpersonality* model has been generated from our four theories of psychotherapy. This model is shown in Figures 13 and 14. Figure 13 provides a spatial diagram of communication modalities, behavior dimensions, and temporal relationships. Figure 14 provides a series of symbols which represent qualitative meanings which may be attributed to the client's functioning. The interpersonality synopsis [1] model will be used in this

[1] In addition to the obvious psychotherapy theoretical sources of the interpersonality synopsis model, I should like to acknowledge C. W. Morris' *Signs, Language and Behavior* (69), K. Lewin, see especially (63), R. White (107), and Joel and Shapiro (57) for technical concepts included in this model. I have also

chapter to organize the interviewer's referential operations. In Chapter XI, the inferential, valuing, and interpretive operations of the four theories will be analyzed and defined on the same basis.

The present chapter is intended to present an atheoretical synthesis of the referential or focusing operations of interviewers in general. Only minimal attention will be paid to theories here since the focusing problem can be treated in atheoretical terms. In the following chapter, in which questions of inferential logic, theoretical values and interpretations are considered, the referential or focusing organization will provide a basis for such theoretical integration.

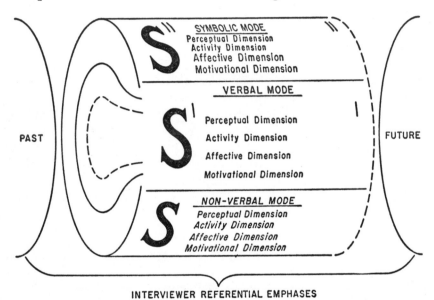

INTERVIEWER REFERENTIAL EMPHASES

Fig. 13. The Interpersonality Diagram [1] of Referential Operations in Psychotherapy Showing the Communication Modalities, the Behavior Dimensions, and the Temporal Relationships in the Interviewer's Representation of Client Functioning.

The Interpersonality Synopsis Model

The diagram in Figure 13 represents three principal concepts about interpersonality communication. They are: I. Communication Modalities; II. Behavior Dimensions; and III. Temporal Relations.

---

been impressed with the fact that K. Muenzinger's model for the analysis of behavior (70) and K. Menninger's model for the psychiatric case study (67) are relatively similar to the present approach. T. Leary has developed a similar conception, but has presented it technically in a different form (61).
[1] The *depth* of this cylindrical model is represented in the present diagram, but will be elaborated only in Chapter XI.

I. *The Communication Modalities* represent the proposition that communication between people may occur in at least three major ways. The interviewer may receive messages from his client in Symbolic, Verbal, and Non-verbal form, and may refer to these modalities.

A. *Symbolic mode* (S'' E'': Symbolic communications about the client or subject, S'', and the environment, E''): In responding to symbolic communications, the interviewer refers to latent or fantasy meanings of the client's behavior. One client was fascinated by the interviewer's cigarette smoking. The interviewer referred to the possible erotic meaning of this interest, saying, 'I wonder if that suggests any sexual thoughts to you?' Thus, the symbolic mode in the interpersonality diagram represents the possibility that the client's behavior may express latent or fantasy communication and that the interviewer may refer to such symbolic aspects of the client's functioning.

B. *Verbal mode* (S' E': Verbalizations about the client or subject, S', and about the environment, E'): In responding directly to the client's verbal communications, the interviewer may refer to some explicit meaning which the client has verbalized, e.g. 'You like the way I smoke cigarettes, but your husband's smoking offends you.' Thus, the verbal mode in the interpersonality diagram represents simply that the client may talk directly about something and that the interviewer may refer directly to what the client has said.

C. *Non-Verbal mode* (S E: Non-verbal communications about the client or subject, S, and the environment, E): In responding to the client's non-verbal communications, the interviewer may refer to some gestural or tonal quality which conveys discernible meaning. One client was huddled tightly in her chair while she talked about her father. The interviewer remarked, 'You're huddled there as though you expect me to beat you as your father did.' The client's reply: 'I've just got to get away from you.' Thus, the non-verbal mode in the diagram represents the eventuality that the client may communicate in tonal and gestural form and the interviewer may refer to such non-verbal meanings.

II. The four *Behavior Dimensions* located in the interpersonality diagram represent the concept that any behavioral event may be described in terms of its perceptual, actional, affective, or motivational aspects. These dimensions are repeated under each of the communication modalities to indicate that the interviewer may refer to any of these four behavior dimensions in any of the three modes. This will be illustrated by rephrasing the symbolic, verbal and non-verbal examples.

Each behavior dimension may be referred to by the interviewer in his response to symbolic communication:

Symbolic-Perceptual: 'Do you see any sexual meaning in my smoking?'
Symbolic-Actional: 'Are you flirting with me?'
Symbolic-Affective: 'Does that suggest that you feel sexually aroused?'
Symbolic-Motivational: 'You want more sexual satisfaction.'

Each behavior dimension may be referred to in the interviewer's response to verbal communication:

Verbal-Perceptual: 'You commented that my cigarette smoking is skillful.'
Verbal-Actional: 'You mentioned that you really sit up and take notice when I light a cigarette.'
Verbal-Affective: 'You feel very pleased with my smoking.'
Verbal-Motivational: 'You wish your husband could smoke as deftly as I do.'

Each behavior dimension may be referred to in the interviewer's response to the client's non-verbal communication:

Non-Verbal-Perceptual: 'You look as though you see your father beating on you.'
Non-Verbal-Actional: 'You're trembling and cowering in one corner of your chair.'
Non-Verbal-Affective: 'You look as though you're very frightened.'
Non-Verbal-Motivational: 'You look as though you want to run away.'

The behavior dimensions, then, are definable as the part-aspects of the client's functioning which the interviewer chooses to talk about, rather than as communication modalities through which the client's meaning is perceived by the interviewer.

III. The gross *Temporal Relationships* which are important in psychotherapy are also represented in the interpersonality diagram. The basic diagram of modalities and dimensions is shown as the *Present Time*. The same aspects of interpersonality events may be represented by the interviewer as in the *Past*, in the *Future*, and as relationships among the past, present and future, e.g. 'You admire the way I smoke a cigarette just as you used to enjoy being interested in your father and as you would like to be attracted to your husband.'

Thus, the interpersonality diagram of Figure 13 provides a *spatial* representation of three modes of communication, four behavior dimensions, and three temporal periods. It represents the major characteristics of the client which are referred to by the four psychotherapy theories.

The interpersonality diagram neglects the question of behavior quality, or the *attributed qualities of interpersonality*. In a sense, the diagram answers only two questions: How is a message communicated? and What is the message about? The particulars of the message require that qualitative as well as spatial concepts be included in the interpersonality synopsis model. Five categories of qualitative meanings which an interviewer may attribute to the client's behavior are summarized in Figure 14. These notations indicate that the interviewer may attribute *orientation, tonus, value, status,* and *control* qualities to the client's interpersonal behavior. Any of these qualities may be attributed to any mode and dimension of client functioning.

Orientation may be defined as 'with respect to.' It can be said that behavior is oriented toward something or away from something. A simple illustration is 'He is looking at her,' or 'She is looking away from him.' More complexly, the interviewer might say in relation to the

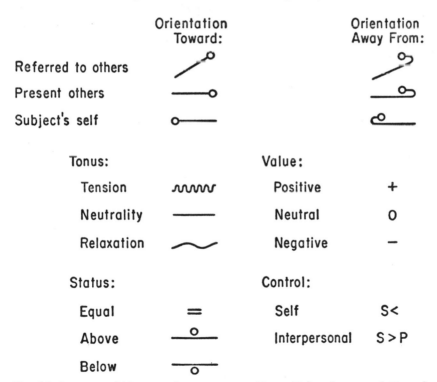

Fig. 14. Summary of Notations for Orientation, Tonus, Value, Status, and Control Qualities Which the Interviewer May Attribute to Client Behavior.

cigarette example, 'You really mean that you were very fond of your father.' The orientation in this sample is toward someone outside of the therapy situation. Alternatively, the interviewer might say, 'I suppose that means you like me.' In this case, the interviewer would be attributing an orientation toward himself rather than toward the smoking. Finally, the interviewer might say, 'You're feeling pretty pleased with yourself.' Here the attributed orientation would be toward the client herself. Similarly, orientations may be described as away from something, e.g. 'You're trying to avoid talking about your mother;' 'You don't want to criticize me;' or 'You find it easier not to talk about yourself.' Thus a quality of behavior which the interviewer attributes to the client may be defined as *orientation* [1] *toward or away from,* in relation to others who are not present in the interview, others who are present in the interview, or toward the client himself.

Tonus may be defined as a continuum ranging from *tension* [1] to *relaxation.* A client may be described as *tense, uninvolved,* or *relaxed.* In the 'cowering' example, the client was described as 'trembling' or tense. In the cigarette example, the client could have been described as 'not interested in talking about yourself.' This client actually was described as 'pretty comfortable when you're not thinking about yourself.' Thus, it is possible for the interviewer to attribute a variety of tensional, neutral, and relaxation qualities to the client's behavior.

Value [2] indicates whether the interviewer describes the client's behavior as positive (good), neutral (indifferent), or negative (bad). Thus, 'You like the way I smoke cigarettes' attributes a positive, pleasant value to the behavior. 'You mentioned that you really sit up and take notice when I light a cigarette,' is relatively neutral in value attribution. 'Your husband's smoking offends you' places a negative, unpleasant value quality on the behavior meaning. Thus the interviewer may attribute to any client behavior a positive, neutral, or negative value quality.

Status may be defined in terms of relative position. *Equal* would be partly expressed by, 'You are agreeing.' *Above* might be partly expressed by, 'You think you are better than he is.' *Below* might be expressed by, 'You're not as athletic as you used to be.' Returning to the cigarette illustration, the interviewer might have attributed *equality,* 'You think I smoke in the same way as your father did.' The inter-

---

[1] The orientation and tension notations are modified from Joel and Shapiro (57).
[2] The value concept and notation are taken directly from Lewin's (63) valence notation.

viewer did attribute an *above status* quality when he remarked, 'You like the way I smoke cigarettes, but your husband's smoking offends you.' In this example, the status which the interviewer attributes to the client's perception of the interviewer is *above*. The relative status which the interviewer attributes to the client's perception of her husband is *below*. Thus, the status qualities attributed by the interviewer can be conceptualized in terms of relative position between people or conditions.

Control [1] represents any quality of interpersonality in which force is applied. Self-control implies that management of one's feelings is accomplished by the application of some kind of force. Management of someone else implies that some element of force is applied in an interpersonal context. The interviewer's reference to 'flirting with me' suggests an element of interpersonal control. Conversely the interviewer could have said, 'You're trying to keep your sexual interest in me under wraps by talking about my smoking.'

Modes, Dimensions, and Attributed Qualities

We may now examine how any particular client behavior may be referred to by the interviewer and represented as a particular kind of interpersonality expression. These examples will be illustrative only.

Symbolic-Affective: 'Your dream of pushing that monster over a cliff suggests that you're angry at me,' refers to the client's *symbolic feelings* toward the interviewer. The attributed qualities include an *orientation toward the interviewer,* a *tensional* quality and a *negative* quality.

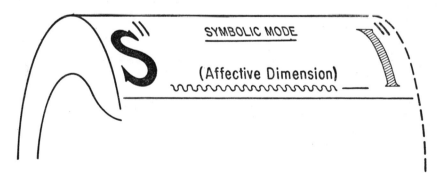

Fig. 15a. Symbolic Mode — Affective Dimension.

[1] The reader will observe that Lewin's (63) vector notation has been extended to interpersonal dynamics in this conception.

Verbal-Motivational: 'You mean you want me to be friendly,' refers to the client's *verbalized motives* or desires. In this case, the client is described as wanting the interviewer to take a *positively* valued relation to the client.

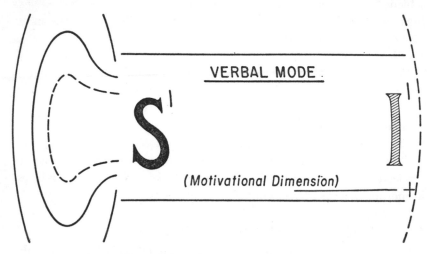

Fig. 15b. Verbal Mode — Motivational Dimension.

Non-Verbal-Activity: 'Are you perhaps flirting with me?' refers to the client's *non-verbal activity.* The attributed qualities include *orientation toward the interviewer,* a *positive* valuing of the interviewer, and an attempt to *control* the interviewer.

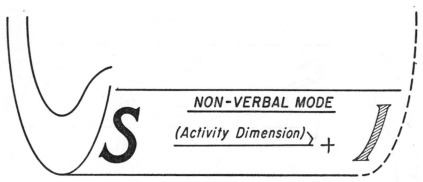

Fig. 15c. Non-Verbal Mode — Activity Dimension.

These three illustrations suggest how a combination of mode, dimension location, and attributed quality notations may provide a relatively complete synopsis of the possible referential operations in psychotherapy. With the addition of temporal relationships, it becomes possible to summarize more complex interviewer operations in this form.

THEORETICAL KINSHIPS OF INTERVIEWER REFERENCES

The interviewer's referential operations may be illustrated more clearly in their theoretical contexts. Several simplified examples from the theories will suggest such theoretical contrasts.

Client-centered therapists talk about what the client talks about. Essentially, the client-centered counselor is philosophically bound to empathize with, or perceive, and re-express what the client has verbalized. Diagrammatically, this emphasis is shown in the Verbal Mode of Figure 16. The client-centered therapist refers to the verbal mode with special emphasis upon the affective dimension. Subject- or self-orientation is a characteristic attributed quality. The client-centered therapist does not respond to what he observes the client to be doing, or to what he infers the client to be feeling, but to what he hears and understands the client to be saying. A criterion of validity in the client-centered approach is whether the client is able to agree and accept that what the therapist has said is essentially an understanding of what the client has said. Hence the client-centered therapist selects, focuses upon, and talks about the perceptual and feeling dimensions of the client's verbalizations. He attempts to perceive as the client perceives and to express this consensus of perception. An illustration that may seem absurd in any other context is essentially consistent here. It is specifically represented in Figure 16.

> CLIENT: '. . . I had a dream that disturbed me. It was about this girl I ran around with in high school. I can't remember the exact circumstances. We were talking together, and I said, "I'd crawl on my belly if I thought it would do any good." Then she said, "Go away and leave me alone." '
>
> COUNSELOR: 'You said you felt somewhat disturbed by it.' (Snyder, 98).

While the counselor's response in this instance could have properly included more of the feeling and attributed qualities of what the client said, his response is consistent with the client-centered emphasis upon the affective dimension of the client's verbalizations. This synopsis of emphasis in client-centered counseling is not intended to exhaust all of the aspects of the theory, but rather to provide part of a conceptual organization of relative emphases in psychotherapy operations.

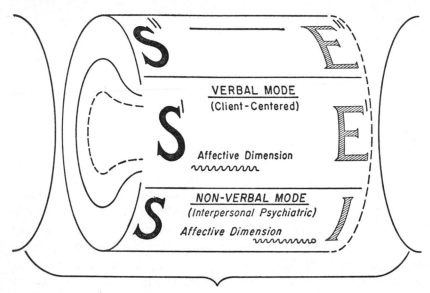

Fig. 16. Comparison of Client-centered and Interpersonal Focus Upon Anxiety.

An interpersonal therapist's focus upon the affective dimension of behavior may be compared with the client-centered emphasis. In interpersonal psychiatry, the assumption is made that security-operations are largely in the service of avoiding awareness of anxiety. A correlative assumption is that the client will not be likely to recognize and verbalize what he is anxious about, or even necessarily recognize when he is anxious. Thus the interpersonal therapist is as likely to focus upon and express for the patient those anxieties which the patient has not verbalized as those of which he has become aware, e.g.:

> DOCTOR: 'Well, you know I noticed you started telling me so-and-so and then for some reason you got to talking about so-and-so. Have you any idea how it happened? . . . Well, I gather you're anxious. You're uncomfortable. You're worrying about what I think? — or what?' (Sullivan, 106).

In this interpersonal example as in the one from client-centered therapy, the therapist is clearly focusing upon anxiety, but equally clearly he is focusing upon a non-verbal kind of anxious expression.

The patient has not said, 'I am anxious.' The therapist has observed the patient's behavior and interpreted it as expressing anxiety. This difference in focus is represented in Figure 16. Anxiety is focused upon in both approaches, but the client-centered therapist re-expresses the anxiety which the client has verbalized, while the interpersonal therapist calls attention to anxiety which the therapist has observed or inferred. The interpersonal psychiatric emphasis upon non-verbal feelings does not presume that the client will accept what the therapist has said. Whether the client is ready yet to observe his own anxiety would determine whether he could accept the therapist's observation.

The theories have characteristic ways of referring to the client's activity. Interpersonal psychiatry takes insistent note of the client's interpersonal effectiveness. How does he function socially? Is his behavior socially disjunctive or socially skillful? Does he function primarily on a 'security-operation' basis to avoid awareness of anxiety, or does he function in a socially integrative, conjunctive way? Psychoanalytic therapy has a different focus upon activity; the ego-defensive quality of activity is emphasized. What do the client's behaviors mean in terms of the repressed feelings and motives he is trying to avoid recognizing? How does he defend himself against both internal pressures and external threats? Interpersonal psychiatry's emphasis upon activity can be characterized by the quality of *orientation toward others*. Psychoanalysis emphasizes activity in terms of *orientation toward the self*. The activity dimension is theoretically relevant in client-centered therapy only when the client comments upon his own behavior. In interpersonal psychiatry and psychoanalysis, the actional focus is theoretically appropriate when the interviewer observes and comments upon the client's activity or when the client observes and comments upon his own activity.

Psychoanalytic and client-centered examples suggest the contrast in reference to non-verbal and verbalized activities:

> DOCTOR: 'It seems you are having difficulty talking today.'
> PATIENT: 'It does, doesn't it? I know I must be honest and tell you everything but sometimes it's so hard. I don't know quite how to go about it.' (Silence).
> DOCTOR: 'Is it something to do with me?' (Colby, 12).

In this psychoanalytic example, the therapist talks about the patient's non-verbal activity. 'You are having difficulty talking.' Rephrased in psychoanalytic technical terminology, this says, 'I see that you are showing resistance,' which is a description of an ego-defense. By contrast, the client-centered counselor would be philosophically unable to respond in the same way. Perhaps silence on the interviewer's part would be the only acceptable approach. Later, after the client had verbalized his difficulty, the client-centered therapist would be able to say, 'You mean that you try to work on your problems, but it's pretty unbearable sometimes.' The client-centered therapist re-expresses the client's feelings about his activity after the client has talked about it. The analytic therapist comments on the activity itself and implies its ego-defensive quality.

Motivational references are characteristically different in the four theories. Client-centered therapy refers to the client's verbalized motives. If a motive, desire, wish, etc. is talked about by the client, it may also be re-expressed by the therapist. Psychoanalytic therapists are especially likely to infer unconscious motives from symbolic communications. Interpersonal psychiatry infers the non-verbalized search for security in relation to other people. Dynamic relationship therapy infers the non-verbalized desire for wholeness with mother symbols and for autonomous separation.

An exchange from psychoanalysis may be used to illustrate the four motivational emphases:

> CLIENT: (Wearily) 'I have the feeling that nothing is working out or making sense today — it all seems so useless.'
> ANALYST: 'I wonder whom you're angry at?'

In this exchange, the analyst infers that the unconstructive, depressive reaction is a dynamic defense against the client's intense hostility. The motive is the destructive rage which the client feels but cannot readily recognize or express.

An interpersonal psychiatrist might have said: 'I wonder if you're trying to force me to take care of you?' Such a response would suggest that the inferred motive is social control — a maneuver to avoid anxiety and distress by courting dependency satisfactions.

A dynamic relationship therapist might have said: 'You're afraid I don't care enough about you. You want me to give you more attention.' Here the motive is cast in dependency-seeking terms, but is expressed in an affectional dependency rather than a social-control sense.

Each of the three therapies which could legitimately talk about motives in response to this client expression has been illustrated in its idiomatic fashion. It is apparent that the differences in the value systems of the three theories lead to differences in the qualities which they attribute to motivation. By contrast again, a client-centered reference to the motivation in this behavior would have been different. The client-centered therapist would be unlikely to refer to the motive in the client's weary remark, '. . . it all seems so useless,' since no motive was verbalized. The client-centered therapist might have thought, however, 'You'd like to make sense out of things. You want to work through your problems.'

Each theory has its unique motivational emphasis: psychoanalysis upon *symbolic* love-hate instincts; interpersonal psychiatry upon *non-verbal* security seeking and anxiety avoidance; dynamic relationship upon *non-verbal* struggles for affectional unity and separation; and client-centered upon the *verbalized* enhancement of the phenomenal self.

Characteristic emphases upon communication modalities and behavior dimensions occur in each theory. Client-centered therapy refers to the affective dimension of verbalized content. While interpersonal psychiatry includes the verbal mode, it also emphasizes the non-verbal affective dimension and the personal-social meanings of activities. Psychoanalysis includes all of the foregoing in some degree, but relatively emphasizes the symbolically expressed motivation. Dynamic relationship therapy refers to both verbal and non-verbal feelings, but is especially responsive to non-verbalized feelings and motives toward the interviewer.

Exploratory Study of Referential Emphases from Three Sources

A preliminary study provides an empirical comparison of relative theoretical emphases in published psychotherapy protocols (9). Psychoanalytic, relationship, and client-centered sources were sampled in such a way as to provide a picture of the most general emphases in these sources. Group and individual protocols for both child and adult clients were included. Fifty or more therapist verbalizations were drawn from each theoretical source. These samples were classified by interpersonality dimensions and attributed qualities. Communication modalities were disregarded.

The kinds of referential emphases which differentiated among the three theories will be illustrated by sample therapist remarks, then related to their characteristic theoretical sources. The differentiating therapist references were:

Self-perceptions:

Of inadequacy, 'You doubt your ability to do that'; and
Of dependency, 'You think you need someone to help you.'

Perceptions of others:

As attacking, 'It seems to you that your father was pretty critical.'

Activities:

As aggressive toward others, 'You're really jumping on me'; and
As aggressive toward the self, 'You're being pretty rough on yourself.'

Feelings:

Of anger, 'I wonder if that doesn't make you boil'; and
Of depression, 'You must feel pretty bad about that.'

Motives:

Of desire for affection, 'You want me to be more friendly'; and
Of desire for understanding, 'You wish people would understand you better.'

Psychoanalytic therapists were most likely to emphasize the client's self-perceptions of inadequacy, his perceptions that other people were critical, his feelings of hostility, and his depressive feelings. Of special interest is the fact that no single behavior dimension was emphasized by analytic therapists, suggesting that analysts range widely in their responses to the client. More striking, however, is the consistent emphasis upon negative qualities attributed to the client; inadequacy perceptions, criticism from others, hostility, and unhappiness are all intensely negative or unpleasant in attributed quality. The analysts were most consistently responsive to the unpleasant qualities of the client's behavior.

Relationship therapists were most likely to emphasize (a) activities in general, (b) motives about others, (c) critical, aggressive activities, (d) feelings of hostility, and (e) desires for others to be friendly to the client. Of special importance is the selective emphasis upon the current interpersonal transaction and the affectional interaction as suggested by the attributions of client aggression toward the therapist and client wishes for the therapist's affection.

Client-centered therapists emphasized (a) the affective dimension, (b) self-orientation, (c) self-perceptions of dependency, (d) self-criticism, (e) desires that other people would be more understanding, and (f) desires for people in general to be friendly. Especially striking here are the self-emphasis, the focus upon feelings and the generally positive value attributed to specific behaviors.

Generally this study suggests consistency of theory and operation. It should be borne in mind that results have been presented in terms of differences rather than similarities among the theories. The characteristics of therapist emphases not reviewed here are those which the three sources share.

SUMMARY

What interviewers talk about, or their referential operations, is presented in detail. The interpersonality synopsis model is developed for the purpose of defining referential operations in atheoretical terms and relating such operations to theoretical sources. The interpersonality diagram represents symbolic, verbal, and non-verbal modalities; perceptual, actional, affective, and motivational behavior dimensions; and past, present, and future temporal relationships. These are proposed as spatial concepts for representing how an interpersonal message is communicated and what the message is about. Attributed qualities of interpersonality expression are proposed as specifications of behavior meanings. Orientation, tonus, value, status, and control qualities are defined and illustrated. Relative emphases of the four theories are presented by means of the interpersonality model. It is proposed that psychoanalysts are relatively likely to receive communications in the symbolic mode, client-centered therapists in the verbal mode, and both interpersonal and relationship therapists in the non-verbal mode. An exploratory comparison of psychoanalytic, client-centered, and relationship protocols of psychotherapy suggests that psychoanalysis attributes negative value qualities to the client; client-centered therapy emphasizes the affective dimension and attributes positive, self-oriented feelings to the client; relationship therapy is most likely to respond to interpersonal activities and motives, attributing qualities of both negative and positive affectional value to the client. These preliminary data appear to be quite consistent with theoretical definitions of referential operations.

And once again there gather'd a scarce heard
Whisper among them; as it were, the stirr'd
Ashes of some all but extinguisht Tongue
Which mine ear kindled into living Word.
　　　　　　　　　　　　　　—KHAYYAM

XI. Theoretical Interpretation and Personality Integration

The form of therapeutic communication will be considered in this chapter. From the referential structure developed in Chapter X, it becomes possible to clarify the interaction of the therapeutic value system as expressed by an interviewer's operations and the client's potential effectiveness as expressed by the kinds of meanings to which the client is most responsive. How does the interviewer's theoretical understanding of the client interact with the client's own potentialities? Does the interviewer provide a fitting mantle of values which clothes the client's problems in an effective way? Or does the interviewer impose an alien value armor which must be bolted on painfully or else cast aside because it does not suit the client's integration? The present chapter will consider the structure of theoretical value systems in psychotherapy as these are applied in inferential, valuing, and interpretive operations. The relationship of theoretical value systems to the potential structure of client effectiveness will also be considered as a basic determinant of therapeutically effective communication. Do the interviewer's values correspond with the client's potential integration?

To develop a syntax of therapeutic communication, we shall reexamine the four theories by considering the inferential, valuing, and interpretive operations of interviewers and the value integrations of clients. This will provide a basis for a systematic definition of *communication channels,* some of which are relatively *direct* and conversational in form, while others are more *tangential* in expressing the value system of a theory. Having defined such direct and tangential communication channels, we shall return to a detailed exposition of the interpretive operations characteristic of theoretical value systems. Finally, we shall illustrate the interaction of psychotherapy theory and client integration by hypothetical interviews from each theoretical approach.

INTERACTION OF INTERVIEWER'S AND CLIENT'S VALUE SYSTEMS

The psychotherapy relationship is an intermingling of two value systems. Presumably, the interviewer provides an effective, smoothly working integration of values which will assist in mending the conflicted, disrupted, or inefficient functioning of his client. Too often, however, the interviewer fails to 'reach' a particular client. The interviewer's technique, philosophy, or personality are not attuned to the client's 'all but extinguisht Tongue.' The 'living Word' kindled by the interviewer's ear is not rephrased in the client's dialect. A foreign car in the United States encounters similar problems when it needs 'tuning up.' Many garages are not equipped with tools or knowledges which 'fit' the foreign car's problems. The highly skilled American car mechanic may be unable to speak to a strange motor — *interpretations* are inept or there are no tools with which to communicate to the ailing foreigner. The report by Rosenbaum et al. (87) of psychotherapeutic failure in the treatment of religious patients may have similar import, since the value systems of psychotherapists are frequently discordant with religious belief. The question of how helpful a particular psychotherapist is for a particular person in distress may well be a matter of the degree to which the patient and the therapist are able to experience similar meanings. Do they share enough beliefs and attitudes that there is a likelihood of developing mutual acceptance? More hopefully, is the interviewer sufficiently multilingual in value understandings that he can talk with effective fluency to many kinds of clients?

The present chapter reviews characteristic theoretical conceptions of client improvement as these relate to the characteristic interpretive operations designed to promote a client's readjustment. This assessment is intended to delineate the *form* of therapeutic communication. It will consider how each theory's conceptualization of personality effectiveness is represented in the client's value integrations, and how the particular value emphases of each theory are reflected in interpretive operations. The degree of similarity between the client's kind of interpersonality functioning and the kind of interpretations provided by the theory will be considered as a likely determinant of how readily the client responds with effective improvement to the theoretical communication. It will be recalled that this question was raised in Chapter I, where the possibility of a variety of 'good' human adjustments was considered. Figure 1 (see p. 8) portrays the proposition that similarity in the interviewer's and client's value systems will enhance therapeutic communication.

To distill the most characteristic interpretive operations of each theory, it will be essential to neglect many aspects considered in the four theoretical chapters, Chapters IV, V, VI and VII. No systematic recapitulation will be made here. Rather, the cardinal interpretive propositions from each theory will be discussed and represented in the form of interpretive operations most differentially typical of the four theoretical approaches.

WHAT IS THERAPEUTIC COMMUNICATION?

There are at least two crucial variables in the question of how well an interviewer will communicate with a particular client. The first variable may well be the interviewer: Is he able to recognize the kind of personality integration which this particular client will be most likely to achieve? Does he have the personality and theoretical-operation skills which will implement such reconstruction? The second variable may be the client's potential integration: What kind of value system or behavior integration is he most able to develop? How closely does the client's *problem* correspond to the therapist's *tools?* Some possible good adjustments were sketched in Chapter I (cf. pp. 3-4) in which it was proposed that the comfortable paternalism of psychoanalysis, the effective socialization of interpersonal psychiatry, the autonomous creativity of dynamic relationship and the empathic understanding of phenomenology were four relatively different kinds of behavior-value integrations. These four are suggestive of the many possible ways of adequacy in society. Certainly there are other good adjustments, such as a satisfying dependency upon a deity which provides many people with confidence and skills for untroubled life in the midst of turmoil.

The four value integrations derived from an assessment of theories are specifically co-ordinate to the logic of interpretation in each theory. The present chapter will develop an analysis of the problem of theoretical interpretation in relation to the most likely channels of communication with the patient's potential effectiveness. It will be recognized that the interviewer's personality as well as the theory espoused by the interviewer could be examined in the same way. The essential proposal is that therapeutic communication is jointly determined by the interviewer's personality-theoretical-value language and by the degree to which the client's potential personality integration corresponds to the structure of the interviewer's equipment. Does the interviewer have the appropriate attitudes, values, and skills to repair the patient's kind of damage? Are the interviewer's interpretations therapeutically valid for this client?

The variety of definitions and meanings of *therapeutic communication* between interviewer and client will be considered. What communication channels does the interviewer use in *interpreting* the meaning of the client's behavior? How does the personality of the client influence the effectiveness of the interviewer's interpretive responses? In what ways do the interviewer's interpretations and the client's personality integration interact to produce therapeutic change?

INTERPERSONALITY SYNOPSIS OF THEORETICAL INTERPRETATIONS AND CLIENT INTEGRATIONS

It has been proposed that a psychotherapy theory is essentially a value system. Such a value system becomes a basis for describing the interviewer's referential, inferential, valuing, and interpretive operations and for describing the client's adjustment in both ineffectiveness and adequacy terms. Figures 18 and 23 show how each of four theories may be summarized in terms of its characteristic referential emphases. Such referential summaries provide structures in which both the interpretive operations of the interviewer and the value integration of the client may be examined.

Psychoanalytic Interpretations and Psychosexual Integrations

The psychoanalytic value system defines maturity in terms of the conscious acceptance of erotic, aggressive instincts and their integration into a genital-love, parental role in society. Such acceptance and integration are to be achieved principally by the client's becoming acceptingly aware of unconscious meanings which are intruded into behavior in the form of symbolic communications in dreams, fantasies, slips of speech, and unexplained, ego-defensive behavior. Hence, the interpersonality synopsis of referential emphases in psychoanalysis (Figure 22) shows the *symbolic mode* as the principal focus of the psychoanalytic interviewer. The psychoanalyst presumes that the unconscious will become conscious and useful as the client becomes aware of such symbolic meanings. Hence, the psychoanalyst consistently *refers* to such symbolic communications. He *infers* that the symbolic meanings are distorted messages about the contents of the unconscious. He *values* these messages as the most effective means of helping the client to integrate his unconscious erotic, aggressive drives into conscious ego. Therefore he provides interpretations which allow such erotic, aggressive meanings to emerge into conscious verbalization.

Such referential, inferential, valuing, and interpretive operations may be illustrated from the experience of a psychiatric resident who was a client in neoanalytic treatment. This client had difficulties with sexual impotency and intense problems in his study of psychiatry since he was unable to read more than a few minutes at a time and rarely remembered what he had read. He talked about interesting chats he used to have with his mother as she lay in bed with her books around her. He said, 'I wish I could read my mother's *book*.' Noticing that he had said *book* rather than *books*, he wondered why he had made such a slip, but was unable to continue with the thought and shifted to his feeling that he was like his mother and probably meant that he wanted to lie in bed like mother with books around him. This seemed to the therapist to be a protective identification with mother to keep from recognizing incestuous wishes. In later interviews the client talked about his pride in the clean appearance of his books and how he wanted his friends to admire the floridly perfectionistic arrangement of his bookcase. Yet he frequently envied the disorderly array of books and magazines in the therapist's office. Such disorder suggested to him that the therapist had read and knew more books than the client. Finally, the client talked about his disdain for psychologist-therapists who seemed feminine to him. The therapist reminded the client of his earlier wish to 'be in the therapist's book.' The client objected that only an adequately masculine person could be allowed such an honor. At last the client was able to recognize his ambivalent wish to protect and keep his mother's book pure versus his wish to pierce and ravage it. The incestuous wish was accepted. In this series of symbolic communications, the therapist consistently *referred* to the covert meanings of the client's communication. The therapist *inferred* that incestuous meanings were repressed by means of the reading difficulty and the feminine identification. The therapist valued these meanings as a basis for therapeutic improvement. Hence, he interpreted and aided the client's interpretation of the wish to be in both the therapist's and the mother's book. By bringing such meanings into conscious awareness, the reading difficulty was resolved and the impotency abandoned. The client accepted the legitimacy of becoming a sexually mature man. Figure 22 summarizes such interpretive meanings attributed by the analytic therapist.

Interpersonal Psychiatric Interpretations and Social Integration

The interpersonal psychiatric value system defines maturity in terms of positive, socially effective, consensually valid, interpersonal operations. That is, the adequate interpersonal man feels accepted and secure in relation to other people; he behaves in socially integrative, constructive ways, and he is able to see the world in a socially valid form. Such social integration is to be achieved by the client's becoming aware of the interpersonal anxiety which provokes his parataxic distortions and maladaptive security-operations. By learning how he misperceives his own behavior and the behavior of others, he is able to correct it and to become more secure in his relationships to other people. Hence the interpersonality synopsis of interpretive emphases in interpersonal psychiatry, Figures 20 and 23, shows the *non-verbal mode* as the principal focus of the interpersonal interviewer. The interpersonal therapist presumes that the threat of insecurity can be brought into verbal awareness and that distortions in both behavior and perception can be modified constructively as one learns about his anxiety-avoiding techniques. Hence the interpersonal therapist employs his social value system in helping the client to develop interpersonal security and socially valid skills. The interpersonal therapist *refers* to both verbal and non-verbal messages about sources of anxiety, about security-operations, and about parataxic distortions. He *infers* that such non-verbal, socially invalid behaviors are expressions of insecurity. He *values* the client's potential ability to be an effective part of society if the client becomes aware of his distortions and corrects them constructively. Thus, the interpersonal therapist *interprets* the client's behavior in terms of its discrepancy from the social reality. The client is expected to become aware of such discrepancies between his own perceptions and the socially real. He is expected to modify his perceptions and behavior to conform with the consensually valid.

Such referential, inferential, valuing, and interpretive operations may be illustrated by a selection of some other details from the 'reading mother's book' example. This client had experienced that his older sister was his father's favorite. She was considered to be the 'bright' member of the family and was always held up to him as *the* example of a good student. This sister completed her graduate studies with aplomb and excellence. She also spent most of her time 'reading books.' There seemed to be no way that the client could compete. Anyway, he knew that only women read books, since his father had a large library of un-opened, gold-engraved books which were bound in Moroccan leather. Books were for display, not for masculine reading. This client was the mother's favorite. The mother read esoterically, but did not study and was 'an average' kind of person. She was not impressed with studiousness; she reveled in non-accomplishment. The therapist responded to these interpersonal meanings in terms of the client's wanting to be an 'average' student in order to keep his mother's affection. The therapist interpreted the client's feeling that the therapist was a 'feminine-psychologist' as a parataxic distortion to maintain the interest of his 'mother-fiction.' The therapist showed warmth and acceptance toward this client to provide him with a sense of security and to develop his social realism. These operations appeared to provide the client with enough security and maturity that he was later able to explore the 'book' symbolism in an effective way. Figures 20 and 23 summarize the social value interpretive meanings attributed by the interpersonal therapist.

Dynamic Relationship Interpretations and Creative Independence

The Rankian value system defines maturity as the acceptance of wholeness without fear and the establishment of creative autonomy with a minimum of guilt. Such creative independence is to be accomplished by the client's recognition that he can love and be loved without being trapped and that he therefore has the right to be his unique self. Hence the interpersonality synopsis of referential operations in dynamic relationship therapy shows the feeling and motive dimensions of the non-verbal mode as the primary emphasis of the dynamic relationship interviewer. The dynamic relationship interviewer presumes that creative independence will become possible for a client who has experienced fully his needs for unity and his fear of separation. Hence the interviewer *refers* to such non-verbal relationship meanings. He *infers* that the therapist is a mother-symbol from whom the client wants but fears to separate. He *values* both the unity and separation needs as motives which the client must recognize and accept before effective independence can be achieved. Hence, he *interprets* the client's behavior in terms of feelings and motives about the immediate relationship. Such operations may be illustrated by one client's reaction to the interviewer's reminder that the termination of therapy had been set for two weeks hence. Without apparently noticing the implications, the client started talking about his wife's inadequacy as both hostess and cook. He also complained about her insistence on the children eating everything that she set before them. The therapist remarked, 'Apparently you're quite disturbed about terminating therapy. You're afraid you need my support and that your wife will run your life again.' The client's reply: 'I guess that is what I'm talking about—but I'm sure I can handle it on my own.' Thus the dynamic relationship therapist employs his unity-separation value system in helping the client to experience the meaning of contemporary experiences in such a way that he can accept his uniqueness. The dynamic relationship therapist *refers* to non-verbal feelings and motives. He *infers* that such meanings about the relationship are potentially present in the client and *values* these meanings as the springboard to effectiveness. Hence he *interprets* the client's immediate behavior in terms of the relationship to himself as a mother-symbol. Figures 21 and 23 summarize the interpretive meanings attributed by the dynamic relationship therapist.

Client-centered Interpretations and 'Democratic' Understanding

The client-centered system of values prizes the development of a self-accepting, democratically understanding kind of maturity. Such empathy is to be developed from the client's experience in being understood and respected by an empathic counselor. Hence the inter-personality synopsis of referential operations in client-centered therapy shows self-oriented feelings and positive motivations in the verbal mode as the interviewer's principal address to the client. The client-centered therapist supposes that self-acceptance and democratic understanding will develop in the client who is helped to experience fully his own feelings. Hence, the counselor empathizes with and re-expresses the client's verbalized feelings. He *infers* that the therapist is most effective as a second self for the client. He *values* the client's capacity for growth on the basis of such empathy, and hence *interprets* the client's verbal communications only to the extent that he empathizes selectively rather than completely. Since this question of client-centered interpretation requires careful analysis, it will be returned to later (cf. p. 250). Figures 19 and 23 summarize the interpretive impact of the client-centered value system.

In this brief résumé of theoretical interpretations and client personality integrations, it has been proposed that each theory is a value system about the nature of personal maturity. It has also been suggested that client personality may be selectively modified by the interpretations of one value system in contrast to another. Some preliminary research suggests that certain clients are more likely to respond effectively to the interpersonal value system while others are more constructively responsive to the dynamic relationship value system. Furthermore, it seems likely that interpersonal therapy may be most effective at an early stage in therapy with certain clients, and that psychoanalytic therapy may be more appropriate later on. The 'reading mother's book' client may be plausibly understood in such terms.

To illustrate the possible interactions between therapeutic value systems and the value-integrations of particular kinds of clients, we now turn to two exploratory studies which bear upon this proposition. One investigation of 'normals' and one of schizophrenics will illustrate how the therapist's theoretical method and the client's personality integration may jointly contribute to a change in adjustment.

INTERACTIONS OF THERAPEUTIC VALUE SYSTEMS AND THE VALUE-INTEGRATIONS OF CLIENTS

The reactions of 'normal' individuals to contrasting theoretical methods, as reported by Smith and Glad (93), Bourestom and Smith (10), and Glad, Smith, and Glad (42), are suggestive. A dynamic relationship method of group leadership was compared with an interpersonal psychiatric method in the treatment of 'normal' college student groups, in which each individual served as his own control. The intention was to explore the possibility that particular people would show characteristically different reactions to one theoretical method in contrast to another theoretical method. Analyses of the behavioral observations under the two conditions of leadership revealed that certain patterns of reaction were clearly different. For example, one illustrative finding was that those group members who showed consistent withdrawal-avoidant attitudes and reactions under dynamic relationship leader methods showed anxiously friendly, socialized reactions under interpersonal psychiatric methods. These results suggested that the withdrawing, autonomous kind of person prized by Rankian theory was most likely to show such theoretically typical behavior in the presence of Rankian leadership. Furthermore, even though such people were able to respond with sociability and 'friendliness' to the interpersonal psychiatric method of leadership, such socialization appeared to be a self-protective cloak of anxious compliance in order to avoid domination by another, rather than a comfortable acceptance of integration into a friendly relationship. Generally, then, this Rankian kind of personality seemed to show his characteristic autonomy when treated by dynamic relationship leadership; his self-protective sociability was characteristically expressed when social values were imposed upon him by interpersonal psychiatric leadership methods.

Based upon extensive exploration by Ferguson (21) and Hayne (51),[1] therapeutic improvement in two kinds of schizophrenic patient appears to be related to the theoretical method of leadership in group psychotherapy. In a study comparing the reactions of several kinds of schizophrenic patient to three theoretical methods of group psycho-

[1] Results of this inverse factor analysis of therapeutic improvement of schizophrenic patients are considered to be extremely promising by the author, but should not be considered definitive before more adequate cross-validation has been accomplished.

therapy, it was found that the most 'regressed' patients were 'improved' most by the 'symbolic mothering' approach of dynamic relationship methods. The most 'adult' patients were helped to social remission by 'socialization' methods from interpersonal psychiatry. A client-centered empathy with the patient's feelings did not appear to influence therapeutic progress, but did enhance the 'individuality' of these already idiosyncratic patients.

Analysis of the proposition that certain kinds of patient were most likely to 'improve' with particular kinds of method indicated that:

1. The affectively blunted, emotionally regressed patients were most responsive to the dynamic relationship emphasis upon their feelings toward other group members and the therapist. When treated by such an emphasis upon feelings in the relationship, both anxiety and emotionally warm, friendly behavior developed. When treated by other methods, no such improvements occurred. Such therapeutic reactions to the Rankian 'symbolic mothering' seem highly reasonable in patients who have given up socialization in favor of a regressive psychotic withdrawal. Assuming that such patients were withdrawing from their bitter experiences in being rejected and unloved, it might be supposed that the Rankian 'mother symbolic' approach revived some possibility of emotional satisfaction and some hopeful struggle toward normalcy.

2. The anxious-antagonistic schizophrenic patients became most regressed when treated by the dynamic relationship approach, but were most effectively socialized and adjusted when they were treated by an interpersonal psychiatric method. These patients appeared to be actively struggling against the schizophrenic solution of accepting psychotic regression. The 'symbolic mothering' of dynamic relationship therapy appeared to push them in the direction of such a regressive solution. The socialization pressure from interpersonal psychiatric leadership produced more socially effective, mature reactions and thus promoted a reconstruction of their social adequacy and satisfaction.

The difference in reaction of the 'regressed' patients and the more 'mature' schizophrenics who responded well to an interpersonal psychiatric emphasis is reminiscent of Rosen's remark [1] that direct analysis speaks to the child in the schizophrenic while interpersonal psychiatry speaks to the adult. These exploratory studies of the interaction of

[1] From a lecture by John Rosen at Colorado Psychopathic Hospital and on the previously noted assumption that both direct analysis and dynamic relationship therapy are essentially concerned with the mother-surrogate implications of the therapist.

therapist method and patient personality suggest that the therapist's interpretations are likely to be most therapeutically valid — or useful — if they are addressed to the level of meanings which are most characteristic of the particular patient. This proposition is illustrated in several possible interpretations to Rosen's (86) patient, who '. . . felt compelled to discover a transmission . . . more powerful than any known . . . His problem was how to transmit . . . fluid.' It will be recalled (see p. 180) that Rosen proposed the oral interpretation, *'How can you transmit mother's milk to your mouth?'* An interpersonal psychiatric alternative might be, *How can you communicate with others so that they will accept you?* A dynamic relationship response could be, *You're afraid I don't love you enough.* A phenomenological meaning might be, *It's distressing not to be in control.* Rosen's proposition about the therapeutic validity of his oral interpretation to this orally regressed patient seems completely consistent with the two studies cited. The most effective therapeutic communication occurs when the interpretive meanings are close to the patient's current personality functioning. How such concordance of patient and therapist meanings can be achieved requires an assessment of the several possible channels of communication between the therapist's interpretation and the patient's value integration.

DEFINITIONS OF COMMUNICATION CHANNELS

To provide a basis for examining the interpretive values and logics of our four theories of therapy, it seems essential to examine several ways in which communication may occur — or fail to occur. In Chapter X, the interpersonality synopsis model was used to represent the several aspects of client personality to which the interviewer or group leader is likely to address his remarks. There, the problem considered was, What does the interviewer or leader talk about in responding to a client or group? Here, the problem is, How does the interviewer or leader communicate? In approaching this question, the interpersonality synopsis model will again be used as a technical aid. The definition of various aspects of *interpersonality* has great importance in understanding how communication occurs and what its influence will be upon the client's change. The model is repeated with appropriate changes as Figures 17 and 18 to examine the communication question. Figure 17 summarizes the several atheoretical, *direct* channels of communication which will be elaborated in this chapter. The figure is organized in such a way that *direct* communication channels are shown adjacent to consciously (Cs) available content. Tangential or *indirect* channels are shown in Figure 18 as *theoretical inputs.* A theory emphasizes certain potential meanings of the client's functioning such as specific *empathic meanings, symbolic meanings, social meanings,* and

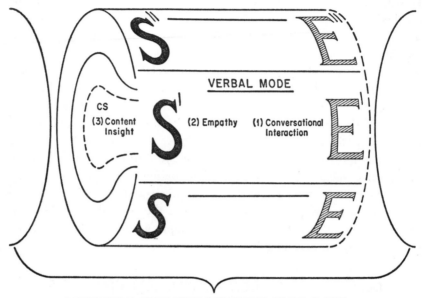

A-THEORETICAL INTERVIEWER PERCEPTIONS OF THE CLIENT

Fig. 17. Interpersonality Synopsis of Relatively Atheoretical, *Direct* Channels of Therapeutic Communication.

relationship meanings. That all such meanings are *theoretically potential outputs* from the patient is indicated by so labeling the unconscious (Ucs) depth perspective of the model. Such *theoretical* potentials may be relatively more or less true of any particular patient.

The problem of how interpretation depends upon the particular theory will be assessed by comparing various *direct* forms of communication such as *conversational interaction, empathy,* and *content insight* with the various tangential or *indirect* forms of communication found in the four theoretical positions. It will be seen, however, that even empathy is theoretically variable, depending upon what aspect of the client's verbalized content the therapist chooses to emphasize. Furthermore, it will be seen that the particular theoretical system results in its characteristic kinds of interpretations as a result of the value integrations proposed by the theory. Thus the psychoanalytic symbolic emphasis upon psychosexual development results in one general kind of interpretation, the social adequacy and consensus emphasis of interpersonal psychiatry leads to a different kind of interpretation, the

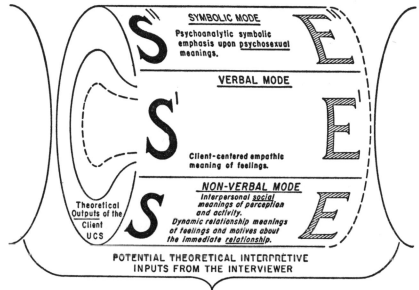

Fig. 18. Interpersonality Synopsis of *Indirect* Communication in Four Theories of Psychotherapy.

union-individuality value of Rankian theory produces another interpretive direction, and even the client-centered phenomenological empathy has potential interpretive qualities depending upon what aspects of the client's content it chooses to emphasize. For simplicity in presenting this analysis of interpretive logics, we shall begin with the least complex concepts — conversation, empathy, and content insight — then consider more complex aspects of interpretation in client-centered, interpersonal, relationship, and psychoanalytic processes.

DIRECT AND INDIRECT COMMUNICATION

The interviewer's response to the client may range from near-conversational remarks such as, 'That sounds as though your war experiences were pretty interesting,' to the tangential, indirect inferences and interpretations characteristic of a particular theory, such as 'When you talk about falling asleep in a conference or being unable to finish a book on psychiatry, you sound so enthusiastic that I wonder whether your defenses are more important to you than being the responsible adult you claim you want to be.' In order to review the problem of communication between interviewer and client, we shall begin with the more direct expressions and move to the more tangential, inferential approaches. The reader will recall, however, that an indirect approach is not necessarily less therapeutically communicative, since the client's personality problem may well be such that apparently remote meanings are the ones which communicate most effectively; e.g. the affectively-blunted, regressed schizophrenics who were seemingly more therapeutically 'open' to the symbolic mothering or *relationship meanings,* while the anxious-antagonistic, relatively more mature schizophrenics were more therapeutically 'open' to *social meanings.* The many channels of therapeutic communication may be summarized as:

A. Direct communication (see Figure 17), such as:
1. Conversation
2. Empathy
3. Content insight
B. Indirect, or theoretically tangential, communication (see Figure 18), such as:
1. Empathic meanings
2. Social meanings
3. Relationship meanings
4. Symbolic meanings.

It will be recognized that the *empathic rephrasing* is most relevant to client-centered therapy; *social meanings* are most relevant to interpersonal psychiatry; *relationship meanings* are most characteristic of dynamic relationship therapy; and *symbolic meanings* are typical of psychoanalysis.

In a sense the problem of communication between interviewer and client can be simplified into the question, Are the interviewer and client talking about the same things? Relationships between what the interviewer talks about and how the client is involved can be summarized as direct and indirect channels of communication. Since the direct forms of communication — conversational, empathic, and content insightful — are likely to occur in any theoretical approach, they will be considered before the theoretical forms.

Direct Channels of Communication

CONVERSATIONAL INTERACTION: When the interviewer says in essence, *We will talk together and see what it is all about,* he is taking a relatively conversational approach to psychotherapy. The interviewer *interacts* with the client in an attempt to develop information and understanding of the client's problems. This approach is characteristic of much psychotherapy and has no particular theoretical kinship, although it is unlikely to occur in client-centered or dynamic relationship approaches. Some samples of near conversational interactions are as follows:

(a) THERAPIST: 'Tell me about your ninth mission.' (46).

(b) PATIENT: 'I just can't think of anything to say. I'm so scared to death.'
DOCTOR: 'What do you think is going to happen?' (109).

(c) PATIENT: 'Just that there is no feeling of . . . well, I mean there is no repulsion, but at the same time there is not that draw. In short, there is neither repulsion nor attraction.'
DOCTOR. 'Now you have said it. What you have said is that from an emotional point of view this situation is quite useless. (109).

In each of these examples, the interviewer is conversationally interactive with the client. In example a, the therapist asks about an experience. In example b, the client says, 'I'm afraid'; the interviewer says, 'Afraid of what?' In example c, the client says, 'I have no feeling about this'; the interviewer replies, 'It's emotionally meaningless.'

In each case the interviewer is essentially interacting with the client. They are talking together about the same things.

EMPATHIC RESPONSES: The therapist may principally wish to communicate that he is quite able to see what the client means and that this meaning is acceptable to him. While such an operation is most typical of client-centered therapy, it is also common in other psychotherapies. It will be introduced here and treated in detail in connection with a theoretical focus upon empathy (cf. p. 250).

The conversational interaction may be close to client-centered empathy. When the doctor said, '. . . from an emotional point of view this situation is quite useless,' he was almost re-expressing the feeling which the patient had just verbalized. The conversational interaction merges imperfectly into the empathic response. A more vividly empathic response is available in the following psychoanalytic excerpt:

The client has been talking intensely about his competition with an older sister who was apparently the father's favorite and with whom he could not successfully compete: 'She seemed to get all the attention and was usually the best student in her class. I guess she's more like my father than I am. I'm an average kind of person like mother — it keeps me out of trouble by being that way — but it really keeps me failing all the time. I just can't seem to learn the things I need to.' The therapist interrupted with, 'You mean that being like a woman protects you from everything except failure — and what you most want is a masculine kind of adequacy.'

This psychoanalytic empathy is essentially an emotional rephrasing of the client's verbal content. It will be noted, however, that such content would be more likely to occur in psychoanalytic than in client-centered treatment.

Since *empathic* responses are most typically client-centered theoretical they will be considered in detail under *tangential* communication.

CONTENT INSIGHT RESPONSES: A client may experience something very different from what he expresses either verbally or gesturally. On such an occasion the interviewer may express insight into and acceptance of such experienced but unexpressed reactions. The interviewer is saying essentially: 'I wonder if this is what you are keeping to yourself?' *Content insight* differs from *empathy* primarily in terms of whether the content has or has not been expressed. In empathy the therapist takes the client's point of view and helps him by re-expressing the essence of what the client has already said. In content insight the therapist sees that there is something the client should say, but for some reason has not been able to talk about. In such an event the therapist provides leads or stimulation to the particular content which he thinks the client needs to verbalize. It will be noted that this content insight is shown in the diagram (Figure 17) as co-ordinate to the consciously available aspects of the client's experience. The therapist has insight into what the client has not said and helps him to say it. The following are examples of such content insights into things the client has not expressed:

(a) *Something about me?* (12)

DOCTOR: 'It seems you are having some difficulty talking today.'

PATIENT: 'It does, doesn't it? I know I must try to be honest and tell you everything but sometimes it's so hard. I don't know quite how to go about it.' (Silence).

DOCTOR: 'Is it something to do with me?'

PATIENT: (Laughs). 'It is. I think the main thing that bothers me is how you will take it. . . .'

(b) *Guilty about something?* (106)

DOCTOR: 'Oh yes, and the payment of exactly 2½ per cent of one's income to this fund for the sick and wounded is never neglected by a good union member, I gather.'

PATIENT: 'Exactly! It's a very important part of membership.'

DOCTOR: 'And one, of course, which you have never violated.'

PATIENT: 'Of course not!'

DOCTOR: 'Well, of course you understand I have no suspicion about you, but your voice sounded odd when you mentioned it, and I couldn't help wondering if it was preying on your mind.'

PATIENT: 'Well, as a matter of fact, early in my journeymanship I actually did pocket a little of the percentage, and it has been on my conscience ever since.'

(c) *At whom are you angry?*

PATIENT: (Wearily) 'I have the feeling that nothing is working out or making sense today — it all seems so useless.'

DOCTOR: 'I wonder whom you're angry at?'

PATIENT: 'That's right, I am mad! But I can hardly think of anyone who doesn't annoy me!'

In each of these examples, the doctor infers that the patient is hiding something that needs to be said but that the client has difficulty expressing. By showing awareness of what the client is keeping back, the interviewer makes verbalization possible. Such content insights will be seen to have more easy kinships with theoretical values in interpretation than do conversational or empathic responses. There is a greater likelihood of a theoretical input from the interviewer since what the client may be keeping from expression is infinitely varied. The interviewer's selection may impose considerable theoretical structure upon the available content. Thus, the *At whom are you angry?* illustration has a clearly psychoanalytic input in terms of psychoanalytic theory of depression. Equally plausible inputs would be available in dynamic relationship terms, such as, *You must be a bit annoyed at me,* or in interpersonal psychiatric terms, such as, *Is it perhaps that you're feeling pretty neglected?* Certainly, content insights may be unrelated to theoretical emphasis, but are likely to be phrased from the interviewer's theoretical value system.

The *conversational interaction,* the *empathic response,* and the *content insight* into unexpressed experience may be relatively devoid of theoretical kinships. They may be reasonably direct forms of communication in which the therapist attempts to develop in both himself and his client an awareness of what problems are present. The therapist provides an acceptance of the possibility of doing something constructive about such problems. *Direct* responses are likely to occur in therapists of any theoretical or personality persuasion.

Indirect or Tangential Channels of Communication

REVIEW COMPARISONS OF THEORETICAL EMPHASIS: Before considering the question of indirect communication channels, it may be well to compare informally a variety of responses of therapists to patients. This may provide sensitivity to the many ways in which a therapist may respond to or 'interpret' his patients.

> PATIENT: 'It wasn't what I thought I *said.*'
> DOCTOR: 'In the nicer style of the art, one might respond *really* to what you feel . . . but . . . I respond more to what I hear.' [1]

This sample from an interpersonal psychiatrist may illustrate a contrast between client-centered *empathic* validity and interpersonal *consensual* or social validity. The client expresses distress that the therapist has failed to understand her true feelings; he has not shown empathy. The therapist expresses his judgment that one must learn to communicate in such a way that others will understand one's meaning. The therapist proposes to the client that she develop consensual skills.

A client-centered criterion of the 'correctness' of an interviewer's remark is that the interviewer provide an empathic summary of what the client has expressed; or, in other words, the client-centered therapist's criterion of validity is empathy. He should synopsize the affective meaning of the client's verbalized content. The interpersonal psychiatrist's criterion of validity is social consensus. The client should learn to express himself in such a way that his views conform with those of his society so that he is understood by other people. Comparison of an

[1] Personal communication from David McK. Rioch.

interpersonal and client-centered reaction to the same patient behavior will help to clarify such theoretical differences.

A patient bristled to Dr. Sullivan about '. . . that day when you called me skinny.' Dr. Sullivan bristled back, 'I beg your pardon?' When the patient elaborated, Dr. Sullivan corrected him, 'I distinctly recall what I said, namely, that you seemed to have suffered your mother's opinion that you were thin' (106). This therapist response is clearly in the interest of *consensual* or social validity. Sullivan has said, *Now look — let us get the facts straight — you have changed my meaning to fit your parataxic picture of me.*

An empathically valid interviewer response to the irritated '. . . that day when you called me skinny,' might be, '*It's pretty annoying to have anyone comment on your thinness.*' Such comparisons propose that there may be many valid ways of talking about or referring to a client's functioning, if by validity we mean, Is it really or potentially present? rather than, Is it accepted by the client as his own meaning? The client-centered interviewer may intend to empathize with the content of what the client is expressing while, to provide another contrast, the psychoanalytic interviewer may intend to talk about the ego-defensive aspect of the client's behavior as in the following interchange:

> PATIENT: '. . . that suggests to me the return of vigour and energy.'
> ANALYST: 'Yes, but what are you denying?' (6).

The interpersonal psychiatrist may intend to describe the patient's socially expressive behavior, as in this excerpt: '. . . you see this little "social oil" — this little self-depreciation, this being hesitant, this asking the other fellow, "Is it all right?," "Isn't that so?," and so on, sounds dreadfully apologetic, as if one were constantly finding it necessary to put out a picture of being very harmless.' (108).

A dynamic relationship therapist may intend to interpret the client's relationship to the therapist; for example, 'Helen, all you want is to have me say you can't do it, isn't it?' (103).

Perhaps the most clarifying contrast is the comparison of the *client-centered* and the *interpersonal psychiatric* approaches. In essence, the client-centered interviewer intends to empathize with what the client *is* saying. The interpersonal interviewer may intend to represent something the client *is not* talking about.

Such a difference may be illustrated further by two sample interactions of client and interviewer:

DOCTOR: 'And when I don't jump and respond to it as you might feel one would to this sort of thing — m-m-m then you do feel sort of doubly let down.'

PATIENT: 'Then you're kind of responding — ah — to what you hear, aren't you?'

DOCTOR: 'Yeah.'

PATIENT: 'It wasn't what I thought I said.' [1]

In a similar situation the client-centered counselor would structure his task as an attempt to empathize with and rephrase what the client is trying to verbalize:

CLIENT: 'It wasn't what I thought I said.'

INTERVIEWER: 'It's distressing to be misunderstood.'

Another comparison will further illustrate the difference:

PATIENT: 'I think that's what I'm saying. I think I go around in my life, sort of half of the time thinking that perhaps I can make it. If I get real depressed, I think "This is too hard," and then I kind of *kill* myself flouncing around doing everything right, and then I get kind of negativistic and get an unknown sort of drag at the feet about doing it when I'm sometimes doing it right. Don't you think?' (Pause)

DOCTOR: (Cough) 'You are asking how to grab hold of this thing, you know —— '

PATIENT: 'Yes, how do we analyze it? How do we get better from that? How do we talk about it?'

DOCTOR: 'One approach to it is to notice it when it happens here — in its detail, and what adjustment you have to make to me . . . where you have to judge me, be careful with me, and do all the right things, be the good patient, and all of that sort of thing. Because I take . . . it that it gets lived out here as it does elsewhere. Here is a convenient place to try to take a look.' (108).

In this example the interpersonal psychiatrist responds to the patient's question with a description, or structuring of the tangential approach that is characteristic of much psychotherapy — i.e. we will not necessarily talk about what you say, we will talk about how you behave and how you relate to me.

The client-centered interviewer might have said to a similar client production: 'You feel pretty perplexed — you'd like someone to tell you how to resolve it.'

In the client-centered alternative, the client and interviewer both talk about the client's uncertainty and perplexity. In the interpersonal

---

[1] David McK. Rioch, personal communication.

psychiatric example, the client talks about her perplexity and uncertainty, while the interviewer refers to her socially expressive behavior, her security-operations — the self of which she may not be aware. To rephrase this difference, we might say that the client-centered interviewer responds to the verbally expressed feelings while the interpersonal psychiatrist refers to the unverbalized behavioral manifestations as well as the verbal content.

Therapeutic communication is most characteristically a result of some theoretical point of view and is usually less direct than social conversation. The interviewer is likely to interpret on the basis of his theoretical logic. Thus he will selectively respond to some particular aspect of the client by *empathizing* with theoretically valuable meanings, by responding in terms of the *social* value of behavior, by maximizing some feeling quality in the immediate *relationship,* or by interpreting the psychosexually *symbolic* meaning of the patient's behavior or verbalization. Such tangential channels of communication have distinctive relationships to each of the four theories. These distinctive qualities are results of the nature of the theoretical systems and the effects which a theoretical value system has upon the therapist's operations. In the following sections we shall examine the four basic kinds of emphasis provided by the theories and consider how such value systems are likely to determine interpretations of the client's behavior.

To recapitulate the interpersonality synopsis of theoretical operations, it is proposed that psychoanalysis refers to the symbolic mode of communication. It infers that psychosexual meanings from the unconscious are conveyed in this mode. It values such erotic, destructive, ego-defensive, and transference qualities, and it provides interpretations which facilitate the client's ability to verbalize consciously and accept such psychosexual symbolisms.

The interpersonal theory refers to the non-verbal mode of communication. It infers that such non-verbal messages have implications for the cultural effectiveness and ease of the client. It values such anxiety, security-operation and perceptual distortion qualities as the most effective springboard to interpersonal adequacy. Hence, it interprets the client's non-verbal communications against the criterion of consensual and social validity.

The dynamic relationship theory refers to the non-verbal feelings and motivations which the client *may have* toward the therapist as an *implicit* mother-symbol. The theory infers that the client's feelings and motives will be fears of rejection, love, and guilt about the therapist, and desires to be an accepted, yet independent, part of the mother-symbol therapist. The therapist values such relationship meanings as the essential ore from which creative autonomy may be forged. Hence he interprets the client's immediate behavior as an expression of such conflicting emotional pulls.

Such interpretive emphases are characteristic of the three theories which allow *interpretation* in psychotherapy. Client-centered theory proposes that the *therapist should not interpret.* Yet, we shall see that the selective kind of empathy prized by client-centered therapy has interpretive implications. The client-centered theory refers primarily to the verbal mode of communication, selecting especially the self-oriented qualities of feelings and the positive qualities of motivation. The therapist infers that such feelings and motives are quintessential to phenomenal self-expansion. The therapist values such self-expansion as the primary process in therapeutic growth. Hence he selectively attends to and empathizes with such positive motive and self-oriented-feeling qualities of the client, providing interpretation by selective emphasis.

In organizing a presentation of theoretical value systems in the interpretation of client functioning, it seems useful to begin with the least complex interpretive approach — client-centered empathy — then consider more complex interpretations from the other theories. Client-centered empathy is a useful starting point since it demonstrates how non-interpretive responses from the interviewer still have the impact of interpretation and communicate the interviewer's value system to the client.

INTERPRETIVE IMPLICATIONS OF CLIENT-CENTERED EMPATHIC MEANINGS: Rogers (83) has proposed that the basic prerequisite of the client-centered counselor is a philosophy of respect for the client's point of view. This philosophy of respect is implemented by the use of empathic responses on the part of the counselor. Essentially the counselor attempts to put himself in the place of the client and to experience the client's feelings in the same way as the client *expresses* his experience. Such a proposal appears more simple than practice is likely to allow. Experience — even at the verbal level — is multidimensional. There are many aspects, dimensions, and qualities of the client's verbalized experience. An example cited earlier from Snyder (98) may illustrate the multidimensional possibilities of empathy.

The client expressed that '. . . I had a dream that disturbed me. It was about this girl I ran around with in high school. I can't remember the exact circumstances. We were talking together, and I said, "I'd crawl on my belly if I thought it would do any good." Then she said, "Go away and leave me alone." ' The counselor elected to respond to the client's directly verbalized *feelings*, and replied, 'You said you felt somewhat disturbed by it.'

This response expressed one empathic emphasis but left a multiple set of possible empathies untouched. Obviously, the counselor could have empathized with the client's perception of himself as a complete failure in the dream, *You were really in a degraded position;* perception of the girl friend, *You found that she rejected you completely;* wishes about his girl friend, *You desperately wanted her affection.* Many other possibilities for empathy are also available in this example. Hence it appears that empathy has interpretive characteristics, since particular aspects rather than all aspects of the client's verbalization are selected for emphasis by the counselor.

The client-centered approach tends to *empathize* with the *client's verbalized feelings about himself* rather than the several other possible foci provided by the client, e.g. '. . . you felt . . . disturbed by it.' That this emphasis is a theoretical value judgment and partly interpretive is suggested by two studies, one reviewed in Chapter X and one to be reviewed here. In Chapter X (cf. p. 227), one study was reported in which the client-centered theory was shown to emphasize *positive motives* and *self-oriented feelings*. These results were considered to be altogether consistent with the self-concept theoretical emphasis upon the '. . . enhancement and maintenance of the phenomenal self . . .' (99) as the core motivational proposition in client-centered therapy. It will be noted that this proposition is basic to a positive form of motivation and an emphasis upon the self. Other sources (83) stress that *verbalized self-feelings* are the important operational focus of client-centered therapy. Hence, Figure 19 summarizes the self-concept theory and the interpretive value emphasis of client-centered therapy by showing that the client-centered therapist emphasizes *verbalized self-oriented feelings* and *positive, self-enhancing motivations* in his empathy with his clients.

That such an emphasis is a form of interpretation as the result of selective attention by the therapist is suggested by a comparative analysis of *empathic* foci reported by Roberts (80) and Ferguson and

Anderson (22). To introduce this study, we will further elaborate some possible types of empathic foci. A sample of client expression from Chapter IX will be used as a basis for constructing seven different kinds of empathic reaction from an interviewer:

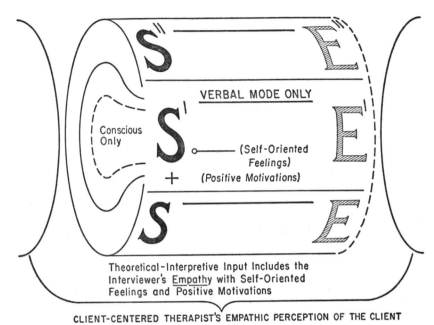

CLIENT-CENTERED THERAPIST'S EMPATHIC PERCEPTION OF THE CLIENT

Fig. 19. Interpersonality Aspects of the Client as Represented in the Interviewer's Client-centered Empathic Meanings.

CLIENT: (In obvious distress and after considerable blocking) 'It seems to me that you could say something about that. I'm all dried up.'

THERAPIST: (Silence)

CLIENT: (Angrily) 'It isn't often I ask you directly to say something. What about it?'

THERAPIST: (Silence)

CLIENT: (Resignedly) 'I see you're not going to give in, and even though I want you to reassure me that I'm all right, I can see this is something I have to get from myself rather than from you. But it sure is disgusting to get up the nerve to ask something directly and get slapped in the face for it.'

This sample provides many possibilities of selective focus in empathy. We shall illustrate seven which could all be considered as empathy with some aspect of the client's expression:

1. Focus upon *positive self-oriented qualities of feelings:* 'You have

some confidence that you can decide for yourself how you're doing.'

2. Focus upon *negative self-oriented qualities of feelings:* 'You're pretty discouraged and angry.'

3. Focus upon the client's *feelings in general:* 'You're pretty upset, sort of disgusted and half-way confident at the same time.'

4. Focus upon *self-oriented qualities of perception:* 'You think of yourself as being pretty helpless and inadequate.'

5. Focus upon *other-oriented qualities of perception:* 'It seems to you that I'm letting you down by not reassuring you.'

6. Focus upon *self-oriented qualities of motivation:* 'You'd rather like to get this reassurance and sense of adequacy from yourself.'

7. Focus upon *other-oriented qualities of motivation:* 'Somehow you'd like me to reassure you.'

Each illustration of possible ways in which the therapist could express something from the client's point of view has a fairly distinctive quality. Each of these 'empathies' expresses something different from every other illustration, yet each is also almost directly represented in the client's verbal production. In the study by Ferguson, Anderson, and Roberts (22, 80), five types of therapist emphasis upon the client's verbal reactions were defined and developed in sample operational terms. They were an emphasis upon: self-oriented feelings, self-oriented perceptions, perceptions of others, wishes about the self, and wishes about others. The reactions of two 'research subject clients' who were treated by each of these five emphases in alternation are suggestive of the interpretive quality of various kinds of 'empathy.' Of first interest was the finding that the clients tended to *follow the interviewer's lead.* They tended to talk about those aspects of the 'phenomenal field' upon which the interviewer focused. Thus, the interviewer's empathy with the client's feelings about himself, e.g. *You feel pretty distressed about that,* increased the client's tendency to talk about himself and to express disturbed feelings.

Other characteristic reactions in the relationship between overt, *verbalized* content and *fantasy* [1] reactions of the clients were of interest. When the interviewer focused upon the client's *perceptions of others,* the overt and verbal reactions of the client were excessively friendly and pleasant. Fantasy-projective reactions, however, were in the opposite direction, suggesting that the overt friendliness was a cover for more disturbed reactions. When the interviewer focused

[1] As measured by the Emotional Projection Test (38, 41).

upon the client's *wishes about other people,* an increase in unpleasant, critical reactions occurred at the overt level. The fantasy-projective test responses were reasonably consistent, suggesting that this emphasis upon wishes about others provoked an integrated kind of hostility reaction.

Generally, the study suggests that 'empathy' is potentially a multiple interviewer method. The self-feeling focus prized in client-centered therapy is the one that characteristically provokes client-centered kinds of reaction. Other empathies appear to produce their own characteristic responses in the client. Thus, it may be that the client-centered 'empathy' is interpretive in that it communicates a particular kind of value system to the client, namely: *Of everything you have expressed, your own feelings are the most important. These feelings I will help you to experience fully!*

INTERPERSONAL PSYCHIATRIC INTERPRETATIONS OF SOCIAL VALIDITY: The essential interpretive premise of interpersonal psychiatry is that the patient should be a comfortably integrated part of his social process. He should recognize his own social stimulus value, he should function in a socially efficient way, and he should be consensually valid in his perceptions — see things as others do. Consequently, the interpersonal therapist's interpretations are largely in the form of social value judgments, such as: *You are a valuable person; You see things differently from the way in which others do; You fail to recognize that your behavior is socially abortive or ineffective.* The value system provided by the interpersonal therapist is clearly social in its emphasis; to be happy you must be an effective part of the interpersonal process. As a result of this social criterion of adjustment, the interpersonal therapist is most likely to talk about the emphases shown in Figure 20 and outlined below:

1. *Perceptual distortions,* and how to correct them, e.g. 'I distinctly recall what I said, namely that you seemed to have suffered your mother's opinion . . .' (106).

2. *Security operations* or interpersonal activities, e.g. '. . . as though you had to put out a picture of being very harmless.' (108).

3. *Feelings of interpersonal anxiety* or the threat of loss of security, e.g. '. . . Well, I gather you're anxious. You're uncomfortable. You're worrying about what I think? — or what?' (106).

In each of these emphases, the therapist expresses a *social value judgment* about the client. All of these judgments impose a pressure toward *consensual validity: You will be effectively adjusted if you see yourself and others in a socially valid form and if you behave in socially effective ways.*

Several comparative studies of interpersonal psychiatric methods have shown that the characteristic effects of interpersonal therapy and

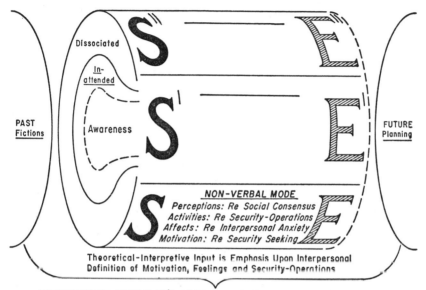

INTERPERSONAL THERAPIST'S SOCIAL-VALUE PERCEPTIONS OF THE CLIENT

Fig. 20. Interpersonality Aspects of the Client as Represented in the Interpersonal Psychiatric Social Validity Meanings.

leadership are improved social perceptions, skills, and affections. Lewis (64) has shown that social consensus, skill, and affection were increased by the use of an interpersonal method of group leadership. Glad et al. (39) have shown that a general result of interpersonal leadership was a more positive perception of others and more friendly social behavior. Harris (48) provided a similar finding in individual interviews, while Ferguson (21) demonstrated the same result with group treatment of schizophrenics. Apparently, the interpersonal value emphasis upon social integration and effectiveness produced congruent processes in both 'normal' and patient groups. Interpretations from the *social values* frame of reference seemed to induce *social adequacy* in people exposed to such interpretation. It will be recalled, however, that this may depend partly on the person's own value-integration. The closer the client is to effective social adjustment, the more likely may he be to respond in a socially integrative way (cf. p. 238).

DYNAMIC RELATIONSHIP INTERPRETATIONS OF MEANINGS OF FEELINGS ABOUT THE THERAPIST: The dynamic relationship patient is considered to be suffering from failure to have effectively differentiated himself from mother-symbols. Every new relationship is a reliving of the old struggle between his wish to be a part of the mother and his attempts to establish a creative independence. As a result of this struggle, he suffers fear of rejection and guilt over his wish to be constructively autonomous. The road to independence must be through an effective acceptance of complete love and unity with a mother-symbol. Thus the dynamic relationship therapist infers that the important meanings in psychotherapy are the client's feelings and wishes in relation to the therapist and in relation to independence. Hence he interprets the interaction of the client with himself in terms of the immediate feelings and motives about the relationship to the therapist. The value integration of creative independence is the essential basis for interpreting the 'living present.' The dynamic relationship therapist is most likely, as shown in Figure 21, to interpret:

1. *Feelings about the therapist*, e.g. 'You want me to tell you what to do,' or 'You're pretty angry at me for not letting you come forever.'

2. *Independence motives*, such as 'You want to explore things by yourself and do something interesting, but you're afraid to strike out on your own.'

In these emphases, the therapist expresses a value judgment about the meaning of the relationship. He *interprets* the client's expressions as meaning something about the struggle between unity and separation.

Comparative studies suggest that the dynamic relationship method results in the behaviors which the theory values. It will be recalled the studies cited earlier (cf. p. 237) showed that one kind of 'normal' group member was individualized by this approach and that the responses of regressed, affectively blunted schizophrenics indicated that they were most effectively treated by such a mother-symbolic method. Harris (48), in individual interviews with 'normals,' found that dependency was the only characteristic reaction to a dynamic relationship approach. Such preliminary evidences suggest that the unity-separation value system of dynamic relationship interpretations is likely to provoke congruent reactions in clients treated by such interpretations.

PSYCHOANALYTIC INTERPRETATIONS OF PSYCHOSEXUAL-SYMBOLIC MEANINGS: That psychosexual maturity is the therapeutic value-emphasis of psychoanalytic theory has been considered in several ways (cf. Chapters I, III, and IV). Essentially, the psychoanalytic patient is expected to become effectively adjusted by reworking and modifying the meanings of his infantile and childhood experiences, by bringing unconscious love-hate conflict meanings into consciously verbalizable control, and by integrating a parental-role attitude into both conscious awareness and personal-social functioning.

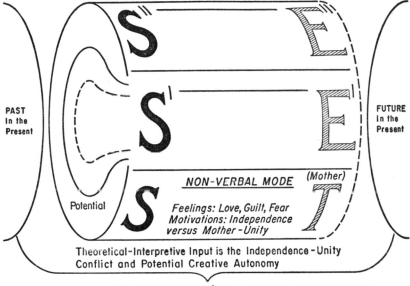

Fig. 21. Interpersonality Aspects of the Client as Represented in Dynamic Relationship Meanings.

Operational aspects of the analyst's behavior in implementing such psychosexual maturation have been elaborated in Chapter IV. Here we may illustrate how the interpretations made by the therapist can be contrasted with interpretations from other viewpoints in terms of the interpersonality synopsis model. Since psychoanalysis is the most complex approach, both conceptually and operationally, it will be necessary to present a more abbreviated picture of it than of the other therapies. Generally, however, psychoanalytic interpretation can be subsumed most completely under the *symbolic mode* of the interpersonality model. In a sense, most of the analyst's interpretations to his patient are an answer to the question, *What is this patient symbolizing?* The analyst's question to a patient (cf. Chapter IV), 'Isn't my asking you to pay me a little bit like your father's requiring you to clean up the trash from his carpenter work?' basically asks, *Do I not partly symbolize your harsh and unloving father?* This interpretation at once included (a) certain aspects of the patient's past problems in terms of his excessive oral regression from the oedipal threat provided by the father, (b) his unconscious, destructive feelings in comparison with his consciously expressed love for his mother, and (c) his potential father-identification. Hence the analyst's interpretation of a similarity between himself and the patient's father had multiple referents and an integrative intention.

Psychosexual symbolism in analytic interpretation may be somewhat simplified to provide specific examples of interpretations. Most psychoanalytic interpretations will have more pervasive roots, or referents, than are found in the more consistently value-determined interpretations provided by other theories. Some systematization is possible, however. This can be in relation to what the symbolic interpretations are primarily about. The interpersonality model of psychoanalytic emphasis in Figure 22 outlines the following summary:

Orientation toward the self, or ego, is emphasized by the analytical therapist, e.g. 'It seemed to you that your father was castrating you when he cut off your hair.'

Parents are emphasized by the analyst, e.g. '. . . father was castrating . . .' or 'You really want to be rocked to sleep as your mother used to do.'

Parents in relation to the therapist or transference meanings are emphasized, e.g. '. . . a little like your father asking you . . . ?'

Symbolic feelings of love and hate are emphasized, e.g. 'Your dream of the truck hitting that professor on the campus — does that remind you of anything about your father?'

The past — especially psychosexual fixations and regressions as these enter into repetitive-compulsive behavior and transference reenactment — is focused upon, e.g. 'You cry bitterly, as though you were being sent to bed without your supper.'

Ego-defensive verbalizations and behaviors are especially emphasized in newer psychoanalytic technique, e.g. in response to the patient's request for 'a happy session today,' the day before he had to make an extremely disturbing visit 'home,' the therapist wondered,

'Certainly, but what is it you're trying to keep from thinking about?'

The ego-defensive interpretations provided by analytical theory can be seen more sharply by contrast to the security-operation interpretations provided by interpersonal theory. An interpersonal interpretation will be rephrased to provide a more typically psychoanalytic meaning. The interpersonal interpretation was:

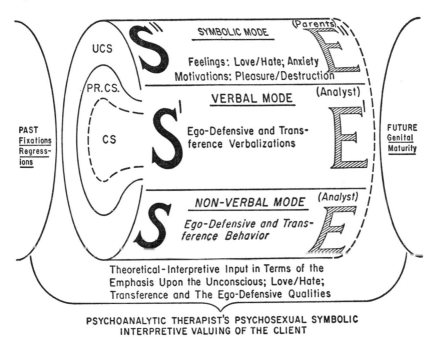

PSYCHOANALYTIC THERAPIST'S PSYCHOSEXUAL SYMBOLIC INTERPRETIVE VALUING OF THE CLIENT

Fig. 22. Interpersonality Aspects of the Client as Represented in Psychoanalytic *Symbolic* Meanings.

'. . . you see this little "social oil," this little self-depreciation, this being hesitant, this asking the other fellow "Is it all right?" and so on sounds dreadfully — hmm — apologetic, as if one were constantly finding it necessary to put out a picture of being very harmless.' (cf. p. 254).

A psychoanalytic rephrasing will suggest more of an emphasis upon the internal problem than upon the social meaning. The psychoanalytic meaning will tend to be more related to transference and regressive meanings than to social maneuvering. It might be phrased as follows: 'This business of appearing so harmless here is reminiscent of how important it was to you to keep out of your father's way. You were so angry at him, and so afraid, that you had to act like a little mouse to control your feelings and not let him notice you.' Consistent with psychoanalytic theory, this ego-defense alternative includes psycho-sexual experiences and transference meanings. This alternative also emphasizes the internal personality process, while the security-opera-tion interpretation emphasizes the interpersonal, social value of the behavior.

Practically no research has been done in assessing the effects of psychoanalytic interpretations as compared to other theories. Ends and Page (18), however, have shown that group psychoanalysis with alcoholics produces changes toward accepting one's self as like one's ego-ideal, which appears to be consistent with the psychosexual ma-turation intention of psychoanalytic theory.

SYNOPSIS OF INTERPRETIVE EMPHASES

Having reviewed the principal values and interpretive operations of the four theories, it becomes possible to make a more compact synopsis. Brief illustrations from each theoretical source will provide a basis for recapitulating the psychoanalytic interpretation of *symbolic* mean-ings, the client-centered emphasis upon *verbalized* self-feelings, the interpersonal psychiatric interpretive valuing of *social* consensus and effectiveness, and the dynamic relationship interpretation of *inferred* union-separation tendencies. These aspects are shown in Figure 23 as a brief summary of the theoretically derived interpretive emphases.

Psychoanalytic Symbolic Emphasis

An example from the psychoanalytic frame of reference is drawn from Durkin's (16) group therapy with mothers of disturbed children. One of the mothers had been asked to free-associate about her brusk refusal to consider a party that another mother had suggested. Durkin mentions that Mrs. B.'s refusal seemed to be related to a brother trans-ference meaning about Mrs. G. When Mrs. B. immediately responded to the party suggestion with, 'No, no, I don't believe in that,' it was understood by the therapist as a gesture which had interested her so much that she had to respond defensively. Her relationship to her brother had necessitated keeping him at more than arm's length when he attempted to be friendly. Mrs. B. was asked to free-associate about this. Mrs. B. said, 'Well . . . let me see — alone — one day my

brothers went sleigh riding and left me alone — but I don't like that —
so why — do I like to be left alone — and I do like to be. I'm always
so terribly busy. It seems I never have free time — only once in a
while. I do lie down for a nap when Fred goes back to school and there
is nobody around — I never can do it if there's anybody around no
matter how tired I am. . . . Well, I don't know why — oh, oh, I just
remembered about my brother and the crib — I felt awfully lonely

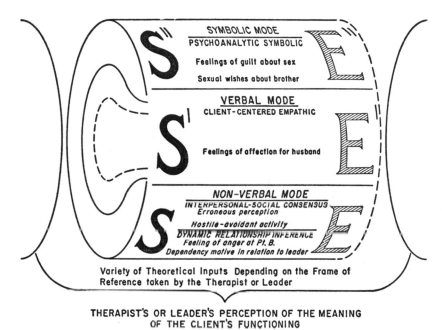

SYMBOLIC MODE
PSYCHOANALYTIC SYMBOLIC

Feelings of guilt about sex

Sexual wishes about brother

VERBAL MODE
CLIENT-CENTERED EMPATHIC

Feelings of affection for husband

NON-VERBAL MODE
INTERPERSONAL-SOCIAL CONSENSUS
Erroneous perception
Hostile-avoidant activity
DYNAMIC RELATIONSHIP INFERENCE
Feeling of anger at Pt. B.
Dependency motive in relation to leader

Variety of Theoretical Inputs Depending on the Frame of
Reference taken by the Therapist or Leader

THERAPIST'S OR LEADER'S PERCEPTION OF THE MEANING
OF THE CLIENT'S FUNCTIONING

Fig. 23. Interpersonality Synopsis of Clinical Examples from the Four Theoretical
Sources.

in the mornings those days. I used to wish he'd come.' At this point
Mrs. B. became completely blocked.

Dr. Durkin intervened, saying, 'Perhaps you don't approve of what
the little girl must have been thinking about when she lay alone in
bed?' Mrs. B. responded, 'Oh, I don't know — I was lonesome and
maybe — oh, I don't know.' The patient seemed quite embarrassed so
the therapist attempted to help her through her difficulty by saying, 'I
think it would be natural to wish that the brother would come, but feel
pretty naughty about it.' In these two psychoanalytic therapist responses, Dr. Durkin has represented the fantasy symbolic implications

of the material rather than the verbalized content or the non-verbal expressions of distress in the situation.

Certainly the psychoanalytic theory tends to promote the therapist's emphasis upon such indirect, symbolic meanings of associative fantasy. This oversimplification is intended to show the psychoanalytic emphasis rather than to represent completely the psychoanalytic method. The *psychoanalytic symbolic* emphasis is shown in the feelings and motives dimensions of Figure 23.

Client-centered Verbalized Self-Feelings Emphasis

From client-centered therapy we might take an example from Hobbs's transcript of group therapy (54). One of the members of the group, Kay, had expressed: 'I had a perfect relationship with him. One of the kind where each went 90 per cent of the way and it adds up to 50 per cent. And one of the things I think helped to do that: we had to depend upon each other, because we lived a long time in a foreign country. We had no outside forces and we depended entirely upon each other.' The leader responded, 'You had a very warm relationship. He was almost your whole life.' It will be noted in this sample that the leader has attempted to summarize the emotional content or attitude in the client's verbalization. There is no attempt to suggest a symbolic meaning but simply to re-express the client's verbalized feelings. This leader emphasis is represented in Figure 23 as the client-centered empathy with the feelings which the client has verbalized.

From a psychotherapy research group with paranoid schizophrenics the following material was represented by the leader from a client-centered approach:

Patient D. said, 'Do you feel angry at someone you like? How do you act when you like someone?'

Patient W. said, 'I don't like anybody in particular.'

Patient B. said, 'You never like anybody?'

Patient W. said, 'I've never liked anybody very much.'

The therapist responded from a client-centered approach to Patient W., 'You've never felt close to anyone and it annoys you to have anybody try to become better acquainted with you.'

This response is more elaborated than usual in client-centered therapy. It has been found that with paranoid schizophrenics it seems necessary to go a bit beyond what is produced, since feelings tend not to be verbalized. In the interpersonality model, the description of this patient could be represented as empathy with the patient's verbalized feelings of annoyance.

These illustrations show how the client-centered counselor's and leader's responses to the client may be located in the verbalized mode of the interpersonality diagram. The feeling dimension of the patient's verbal production is especially emphasized.

Interpersonal Psychiatric Consensual Validity Emphasis

Moving down the *interpersonality* diagram we can now illustrate the non-verbal emphasis in interpersonal psychiatry. Interpersonal psychiatry is most likely to emphasize the perceptual distortions, activities which appear to be security-operations, and feelings of interpersonal anxiety. Sullivan said to a patient, 'You seem to have copied your mother's paranoid psychosis with some improvements on it' (106). This representation of the patient would be located in the perceptual dimension of the non-verbal mode as in Figure 23.

An example of an interpersonal psychiatric emphasis from the paranoid schizophrenic group illustrated above is shown in the following sequence:

Patient J. says, 'I would like to ask you a question, Mr. W. What is your occupation?'

Patient W. says, 'I worked on a truck for a year.'

Patient J. says, 'You had to get up early in the morning?'

Patient W. says, 'Yeah.'

Patient J. says, 'You had to talk to people, didn't you?'

Patient W. says, 'Umm-huh.'

The therapist made this comment, 'Mr. J. is trying to be friendly and understanding, but apparently, Mr. W., you're refusing to respond to him.' This therapist's representation located Mr. W.'s behavior in the activity dimension of the non-verbal mode as shown in Figure 23.

The interpersonal psychiatric approach tends to emphasize non-verbal communications of interpersonal perceptions, activities, and feelings rather than the verbalized expressions of feelings and attitudes or the fantasy implications of associative material. This is a relative rather than an absolute emphasis since the interpersonal psychiatrist may range across the spectrum of interpersonality.

Dynamic Relationship Wholeness and Independence Inferences

Moving to the middle of the non-verbal mode in Figure 23, we may locate the dynamic relationship therapist's emphasis upon the patient or group interactions at the level of inferred feelings and inferred motivations. To illustrate this, we shall continue with the same transaction as has been used to illustrate a client-centered and an interpersonal psychiatric emphasis from the paranoid group.

Patient B. says, 'You would like other people to like you, wouldn't you?'

Patient W. nods his head and says, 'Sure, we all feel like that.'

The therapist responds to Patient W., saying, 'But you are a little annoyed when we show any interest in you. Mrs. B. is being very friendly and you are irritated at her.' In this representation of Patient W. the therapist has principally addressed himself to an inference about the immediate emotional response to another member of the group. This emphasis upon the part of the therapist is shown in the feeling dimension of the non-verbal mode, Figure 23.

The dynamic relationship therapist is also likely to focus upon and emphasize motives about the relationship. He is likely to talk about what the group members want in relation to other people in the group. A sample at this level from a teaching session is as follows:

Group member E. says, 'Why do I have headaches all the time?'

The leader replies, 'You'd like me to cure your headaches.'

This leader response is shown in Figure 23 as a dependency motive in relation to the leader.

We have attempted to illustrate differences in operational emphasis by therapists from four theoretical sources. The reader will recognize that these are intended to be relative rather than absolute emphases. Such differences in theoretical operations are a reflection of the interpretive value judgments of the four theories.

Interaction of Therapist's Interpretations and Client's Personality

In attempting to examine the joint effects of the client's value integration and the therapist's value system in interpretation, we have examined successively (a) some kinds of people who are especially responsive to particular kinds of interpretation, and (b) four theoretical types of emphasis in interpretation of client functioning. The proposition has been expressed and partly supported that the degree of similarity between the client's current personality organization and the therapist's theoretical value system will contribute to the amount of therapeutic communication that takes place. This proposition is tentative but has garnered some research support. How it might be likely to work in practice will be illustrated in a series of hypothetical interviews from each theoretical position. Rosen's direct analysis is also included as a plausible approach to the problem. The reader may well consider which theoretical method would seem to be most appropriate for this client.

HYPOTHETICAL INTERVIEW SERIES

We have considered that theories influence therapist operations and client behavior. To illustrate the interaction of theory and client, a set of four hypothetical interview series has been constructed around material from a psychoanalytic interview. Each of the hypothetical interviews begins at the same place in the published source. The purpose of these protocols is to suggest how the same client production may lead to different interpretations by the therapist and how, as a consequence, the therapy movement and direction may be modified. Some of these interpretations 'sound' more therapeutically valid than others. The first series is an actual sample from a psychoanalytic interview. This sample focuses somewhat insistently upon sexual motivation, but illustrates the psychoanalytic symbolic emphasis.

Psychoanalytic Sexual Emphasis

Berg (6) presents a relatively orthodox psychoanalytic protocol from a male patient who came to him afflicted with stomach trouble of psychogenic origin. In an early session, the following exchanges occurred:

> PATIENT: 'I have a friend called Gladys, who has recently got married. The dream was that I went to her house, and she had a whole table laid out with food, as though the articles of food were wedding presents. I told her, "Do you know the way this table is laid out has some special psychological significance?"'

The patient goes on to say:

> 'The dream just serves to reflect my present condition — food-conscious. In the centre of this table there was a special dish of fish. The dish was special and the fish in it was special, and it was in the centre.

'I lifted it up to see what sort of legs the dish had, or else to see what sort of fish it was.

'I don't want to believe what you say about this pain being of psychological significance. To me it is a purely physical pain.'

ANALYST: 'Free association to your action in the dream, lifting the dish?'

PATIENT: 'I just had to see how the fish was laid out, the way that fish was lying there on a big dish. I always look at things. I always search for details. The whole table was arranged like a table of wedding presents, and the most prominent thing was the fish. I wanted to know if it was on a dish with legs or whether it was flat.'

ANALYST: 'What are your thoughts about Gladys?'

PATIENT: 'I am envious a little. I have taken her out in the past. I think she might be a suitable match.'

ANALYST: 'And after the wedding you go to her house?'

PATIENT: 'Yes, and I see all this food that I cannot have so easily.'

ANALYST: 'When you say you are envious, what are you envious of in connection with her? What would you like?'

PATIENT: 'I'd like to be able to eat food. Of course, *you* mean that I'd have liked to have married her, but I tell you that it is not a matter of sex at all. When I get better from my stomach trouble I shall probably have the problem of impotence to wrestle with, if you keep suggesting that I am impotent.'

'I admit I had curiosities about Gladys, and that I was envious of her marriage. Now "lifting up" suggests to me lifting up her frock.'

ANALYST: 'What is the food connected with a wedding?'

PATIENT: 'Sex, of course. But *I* was interested in the dish.'

ANALYST: 'Whether it was a dish with legs or not?'

PATIENT: 'The fish was the biggest thing there, on a nice big table.'

ANALYST: 'What is the biggest thing at a wedding?'

PATIENT: 'It is sex, of course. A man lifts up a frock to see the girl's legs. Sex, of course.'

ANALYST: 'What is the biggest thing in your life?'

PATIENT: 'It is food.'

ANALYST: 'And the dream tells us it is sex.'

(Silence)

ANALYST: 'What are you thinking about?'

PATIENT: 'I was thinking that, when I get well, the biggest problem in my life will be impotence.'

ANALYST: 'So you are making this fuss about food in order to disguise from yourself the idea of impotence and your castration phantasy. Your dream is interesting in that it shows that sex is being disguised under a symbolism of food.'

This psychoanalytic protocol demonstrates insistently that the theoretical approach determines what aspects of the total behavior the therapist will comment upon and draw inferences about. In this case sexual motivation is the therapist's focus. Most of the analyst's remarks draw the client's attention to the probable sexual motivation behind both his dream and his symptoms. Therapeutic movement in such a brief excerpt cannot be considered in any detail, but a strong resistance to and a tendency toward beginning acceptance of erotic motivation is noted in the client's objection that the analyst will precipitate impotency. To a degree then, the client accepts the theoretical framework of the analyst and over a period of time might understand and modify his difficulties in terms of their psychosexual dynamics.

Client-centered Empathy Focus

Assuming a different theoretical approach, it might be expected that a characteristically different kind of interview development would proceed from the same starting point. As will be recalled, the client-centered approach focuses upon the client's verbalized perceptions, with special interest in their affective and valuing qualities. Under this interviewer condition something like the following sequence might develop from the same client.

CLIENT: 'I'd like to be able to eat food. Of course, *you* mean that I'd have liked to have married her, but I tell you it is not a matter of sex at all. When I get better from my stomach trouble I shall probably have the problem of impotence to wrestle with, if you keep suggesting that I am impotent.'

COUNSELOR: 'You're afraid that you'll get another problem just as bad if you work through this one.'

CLIENT: 'No! I'm afraid you'll talk me into another problem.'

COUNSELOR: 'You feel that you're not allowed much independence here.'

CLIENT: 'Well I do have the impression that you try to force your ideas on me and don't have much respect for what I think.'

COUNSELOR: 'It's pretty frustrating to be told what to think.'

CLIENT: 'Yes, it is. Somehow it seems that people are always trying to tell me what to do. They treat me as if I had no judgment of my own. Well — maybe I haven't. Maybe I invite people to dominate me.'

COUNSELOR: 'You wonder whether you force people to treat you like a child?'

CLIENT: 'That could be it. I always have felt that people try to push me around, they don't respect me, but maybe that's the way I want it somehow. Maybe I want to be taken care of so I can avoid any responsibility.'

COUNSELOR: 'In a way you want to be dominated.'

CLIENT: 'Yes — I guess so. But it sure makes me mad when people take it that way. I really want to be a responsible person — I'm just afraid to be, I guess.'

COUNSELOR: 'You're pretty mad at people who take advantage of your compliance.'

CLIENT: 'I sure am. Whether I invite it or not they don't have to be so uppity. I really ought to try to be myself a little more, though, and not try so hard to please other people. It doesn't do any good.'

COUNSELOR: 'In a way you really want to accept yourself — but you're not sure you can.'

CLIENT: 'Oh, I don't know — maybe I can work at being a more self-reliant person. At least you seem to accept me and respect me.'

The therapeutic movement illustrated in this client-centered series is obviously different from that in the psychoanalytic sample. The client moves from resistance to the external control he has attributed to the counselor to a dawning recognition that this may be his own distortion. Perhaps he has the capacity to accept selfhood and develop his independent way of being responsible for himself. This abbreviated illustration shows much faster movement than a real process of client-centered counseling, but essentially represents the form of that process.

Dynamic Relationship Inferred Feelings and Motives

The dynamic relationship therapist, approaching the same material, would be likely to assume that the patient's relationship to mother, and his inability to break the apron strings, would result in his struggling with the unity-separation problem in the interview. In such an event the therapist would focus upon the client's feelings about his relationship to the therapist. Such an interview might proceed as follows:

PATIENT: 'I'd like to be able to eat food. Of course, *you* mean that I'd have liked to have married her, but I tell you it is not a matter of sex at all. When I get better from my stomach problem I shall probably have the problem of impotence to wrestle with, if you keep suggesting that I am impotent.'

THERAPIST: 'You're pretty annoyed at me.'

PATIENT: 'Not especially annoyed — just that I don't quite accept your point of view.'

THERAPIST: 'It seems that I'm trying to control you?'

PATIENT: 'It sure does — I've tried all my life to be independent — then I come to you and you try to force your ideas on me.'

THERAPIST: 'You don't want me to tell you what to do?'

PATIENT: 'Well, I guess I do in a way — I want you to help me — but I'm afraid you'll force me to do as I'm told.'

THERAPIST: 'You really want me to take care of you — but that threatens your own freedom?'

PATIENT: 'That seems to be it. Somehow mother always demanded obedience in return for anything she gave me. I wonder if that's what my dream meant — I'm afraid that I won't get any love if I don't become impotent?'

THERAPIST: 'It sounds as if you want me to help you decide what your dream meant.'

PATIENT: 'It does, doesn't it? One minute I'm mad at you for trying to control me — the next minute I ask you to tell me what you think. Apparently I feel two ways about you.'

THERAPIST: 'You want my support and understanding — but want freedom at the same time.'

PATIENT: 'That's it — I want to be taken care of but I don't want to be stifled. On the other hand, I don't want to be so different and obnoxious that you won't like me.'

THERAPIST: 'It's pretty important to you for me to like you as long as I don't smother you. I guess you're also saying you don't trust me very much.'

PATIENT: 'Not exactly — it's just that I don't know how far I can trust myself with you. Mother always took over and made decisions for me if I gave her the slightest edge — and of course I always did I was so afraid she wouldn't love me if I stepped out of line.'

THERAPIST: 'You want me to assure you that I'll accept you whether you agree with me or not.'

PATIENT: 'You sure hit it there. If I could expect some acceptance whether I thought the same things as you or not, I guess I could be a little more comfortable about being different. That way I might really accomplish something — at least for myself.'

In this focus upon feelings about the relationship, the therapy process goes on apace in terms of a struggle between uniting and separating attitudes toward the therapist. The outcome of the process is most plausibly one of establishing constructive independence with a minimum of guilt.

Interpersonal Social Values Emphasis

The interpersonal therapist would emphasize somewhat different aspects of the client's behavior and would be likely to induce a different process. The theory assumes that the social role or 'security-operations' are interpersonal maneuvers designed to avoid the recognition of anxiety about being unloved. On this basis the interpersonal therapist is likely to select the verbal, gestural, and temporal cues that suggest the client's techniques for avoiding awareness of anxiety. One form that the interview might take under these conditions would be the following:

PATIENT: 'I'd like to be able to eat food. Of course, *you* mean that I'd have liked to have married her, but I tell you it is not a matter of sex at all. When I get better from my stomach trouble I shall probably have the problem of impotence to wrestle with, if you keep suggesting that I'm impotent.'

THERAPIST: 'Is it possible that you believe I said you are impotent? I see that you are attacking me because you think I said that. We might wonder how you developed this curious idea.'

PATIENT: 'You told me I am — you said I am afraid of marriage.'

THERAPIST: 'As I recall, I wondered whether you let Gladys go because you were afraid you wouldn't satisfy her?'

PATIENT: 'Well that's what you meant then — that I'm impotent — isn't it?'

THERAPIST: 'Do you suppose that you're criticizing me because you suffered from your mother's low opinion of you and must fight anyone who reminds you of it? I don't share her opinion.'

PATIENT: 'I know you don't — but it seems to me I've proved that I'm as capable as anyone, whether mother loved me or not.'

THERAPIST: 'I wonder if you let Gladys go because you believed that no woman's affection could be trusted. You accuse her as well as me of calling you impotent, when you really mean that you can't bear to accept your mother's rejection?'

PATIENT: 'Well — maybe. I guess I react to both you and Gladys in pretty much the same way. I can't stand the idea that someone will disapprove of me. So I guess I try to avoid sticking my neck out. There's no point in asking for it.'

THERAPIST: 'You mean that you keep from getting clipped by just not expressing your opinion. Perhaps you've never learned to express your own ideas in such a way that others are not affronted. Just a moment ago you *literally accused* me of calling you impotent. Perhaps you're pretty aggressive when you want to say something important.'

PATIENT: 'They won't listen to me if I'm not aggressive, and they clip me if I am. I don't see any way out except by just keeping my thoughts to myself.'

THERAPIST: 'But that's uncomfortable too — even now I notice almost a tear in your eye, as though you feel you're a complete failure. Personally I think you can do a great deal to make yourself more comfortable and socially effective. I have confidence in you.'

PATIENT: 'Yeah — whatever I do you seem to see something the matter with it — you just pick me to pieces.'

THERAPIST: 'I'm sure that seems to be true — I'm trying to help you see your difficulties and your possibilities — that's pretty painful sometimes.'

In this series the emphasis is upon developing an understanding of the dynamics of interpersonal behavior, and upon developing social effectiveness in place of social withdrawal. The course of therapy movement in these exchanges is discernibly in the direction of a developing awareness of the social self and a developing concern about being socially effective and comfortable.

Orally Symbolic Direct Analysis

Finally we may end this series of samples by illustrating another psychoanalytic approach which chooses a different focus from that used in the excerpt cited from Berg. Rosen's direct analysis proposes that sexual symbolism may really be a screen for oral symbolism. To quote Rosen (86), 'A male patient felt compelled to discover a transmission which would be infinitely more powerful than all transmissions known to automotive engineering. . . . His problem was how to transmit . . . fluid.

'It was easy enough to understand this from a genital point of view as a transmission of semen, but the effect on the patient's psychosis was dramatic when we made an oral interpretation, *"How can you transmit mother's milk to your mouth?"* The patient's confirmatory response was, "My mother thought I always needed a vacation." Therapist: "Anything to get rid of you." '

The symbolism in schizophrenia, then, is oral for Rosen, regardless of the vehicle. Let it be emphasized that this is his proposal about schizophrenia — not psychopathology in general. However, let us follow a hypothetical course of therapist-patient interchange with the same sample to which the other frames of reference have been applied, since the symbolism in Berg's patient is so clearly oral.

PATIENT: 'I'd like to be able to eat food. Of course, *you* mean that I'd have liked to have married her, but I tell you it is not a matter of sex at all. When I get better from my stomach trouble I shall probably have the problem of impotence to wrestle with, if you keep suggesting that I am impotent.'

THERAPIST: 'How can you get mother to feed you if you've got a penis?'

PATIENT: 'My mother always said she had wanted a girl when I was born.'

THERAPIST: 'She didn't want to give milk to anyone else with a penis.'

PATIENT: 'She tried to force me to be like a girl, and I've had to work pretty hard to satisfy my own demands for masculinity.'

THERAPIST: 'You can't see how you can expect mother to love and feed you unless you're a girl.'

PATIENT: 'She couldn't stand having another boy — I had to make some concessions.'

THERAPIST: 'It doesn't matter what she wanted, because I'm your mother now and I don't want a girl, I want a boy. I wouldn't love you unless you have a penis.'

PATIENT: 'You mean you love me whether I'm a girl or not — my mother wasn't so good natured — and how can I believe you?'

Obviously the direct analysis approach cannot move rapidly with the kind of patients it is applied to. However, it should be noted that in the sample excerpt we have used, direct analysis would come closest to approaching the symbolism at the level where the patient would accept it as his own meaning. Attention should also be directed to the close similarity between direct analysis' symbolic interpretations and dynamic relationship's hypothetical substratum. Both approaches address themselves to the symbolic relationship to mother. Direct analysis *expresses* such symbolism, dynamic relationship therapy *assumes* it to be present in the meaning of the therapeutic relation.

SUMMARY

The characteristics of therapeutic communication are considered in relation to social conversation on the one hand, and theoretically determined interpretation on the other. Thus it is proposed that conversational interaction, empathy, and content insight are close to both social conversation and theoretical interpretation. Some research evidence is presented to suggest that the degree to which theoretical interpretation works depends upon the degree of similarity between the client's personality and the therapeutic theory. In considering this question of 'therapeutic fit,' an analysis is presented of the psychosexually symbolic interpretive emphasis of psychoanalytic theory, the interpretive aspects of client-centered empathy, the social validity coercion of interpersonal psychiatric interpretation, and the unity-separation pressures of the dynamic relationship interpretation of feelings and motives about the therapist. On the assumption that the theory determines the form of therapeutic communication and the structure of the client's personality determines the degree to which a particular form of communication is effective, a series of hypothetical interviews is constructed to show the likely differences in the processes of change engendered by four approaches to therapeutic interpretation.

And the Word became
flesh and dwelt among us
—JOHN 1: 14

XII. Science, Shibboleths, and Shrines

In seeking a more simplified account of meanings and processes in psychotherapy, this chapter contrasts research results and concepts from the four theoretical sources. As a result of this assessment, it will be seen that a conceptual simplification of psychotherapeutic diversity is feasible. Skillful psychotherapists provide two essential conditions for the client's readjustment. These conditions are:

1. *A positive, rewarding atmosphere.* The skillful therapist produces an interpersonal atmosphere which is very like the warmth of any good human relationship and is the most appropriate condition for effective learning.

2. *An integrated set of adjustive values.* Some kind of value integration which provides both cultural acceptability and personal effectiveness is implicit in any therapeutic relationship. The four theoretical value systems reviewed in this book may be used to illustrate such possible kinds of behavior-value integrations. The psychoanalytic value of *psychosexual maturity* is likely to produce an integration of *paternalistic* behavior and attitudes. The interpersonal psychiatric value of *social satisfaction and skill* will lead to a *socialization* kind of integration and adjustment. The Rankian value of *autonomous creativity* provides an integration in terms of *constructive individuality.* The client-centered philosophy of *empathic* respect for the client encourages the development of a *democratically understanding* kind of effective adjustment.

Research results from several points of view are brought together to suggest that improvement in any successful psychotherapy may be understood as a joint function of the favorable conditions for learn-

274

ing provided by a warm interpersonal relationship, and the effectively adjustive system of values provided by the therapist's personality and theory. Successful psychotherapy may be conceptualized simply in the proposition that *under favorable conditions of learning, one is most likely to adopt those values and skills which are available in the learning situation.*

A SEARCH FOR SIMPLICITY [1]

Science founders upon its shrines but charts new lands when freshly driven by doubt and inspiration. One task of science is to provide better maps — to simplify its constructs and broaden their explanatory value — to the end that larger bodies of fact may be included in a smaller body of explanation. Thus it seems essential that the assessment of psychotherapy presented in this book be examined for its parsimony. Not strangely, it appears that looking at psychotherapy from several viewpoints provokes uncertainty about the finality of any current perspective. If behavior is selectively modified by the idiom of each therapy, some more efficient conception than any current theory should emerge from such diversity. Is there any way that various processes of modification can be given a common conceptual framework? One theory is accused of supposing that 'There is only one kind of psychotherapy. . . anything else is a covering up or ameliorative procedure' (50).

From such an accusation psychoanalysis should be able to defend itself by efficient explanation of personality modifications engendered by any other set of theoretical operations. If psychoanalytic theory and therapy is the only 'true' science of psychotherapy, then its propositions should be most effective for conceptualizing personality modification in general. How conveniently does psychoanalytic theory account for the methods and results of other approaches to personality change? The author's intention in this chapter is to make a simplified account of psychotherapy. For heuristic purposes we may do this by exploring the value of psychoanalytic theory in understanding other theoretical viewpoints and data.

[1] This chapter is modified from 'An Operational Conception of Psychoanalytic Therapy and Leadership,' a paper presented at the University of Kansas Fourth Annual Institute on Research in Clinical Psychology, *Conceptual Bases for Research in Group Psychotherapy*, April 8, 1957 (mimeograph distribution to participants).

Theoretical Simplification — An Illustration

Theoretical versatility engenders some operational nimbleness and much doubt: Is this fountainhead the true source? It seems likely that a common subterranean source may gush ritual wine at the alter of Oedipus, cool waters in the oasis of independence, champagne at the table of understanding, and beer at the bar of friendship. The possibility of theoretical simplification may be illustrated from an experience in brief psychotherapy. The client, a research engineer, provided valuable psychoanalytic clues. He told of his disappointment in his father's refusal to answer questions about sex. This meant to him that father must not have accepted his capacity for manhood. He told of his pleasure in building things for the comfort and delight of his mother. He recognized a relationship between his scientific curiosity and his mother's interest in wandering through the woods with him. Such clues might have led to the king's road of psychoanalytic interpretation and modification. The therapist's theoretical versatility, however, produced a wider variety of understandings, interpretations, and descriptive reactions to this client. For example, the client improved his ability to get along comfortably with a chronically disturbing neighbor. This change seemed to result from a recognition that the neighbor was overzealous in his affection toward the client in the same way that his father had been. The client became more effective in managing a somewhat flirtatious wife. This seemed to result from an interpersonal recognition that his own pride in her ubiquitous charms and his satisfaction in her 'esthetic display' value to other men contributed to her affectional gregariousness and to his fear of desertion. The client's inability to complete much of his creative work was discussed in relation to his feelings that esthetic interests are feminine and involve competition with women. Hence he feared that such interests would lead to rejection by mother, wife, and therapist. Assuming the dynamic relationship approach, the therapist was able to work with many aspects of this threat in the immediate relationship and provide a valid experience of acceptance for the client so that he developed considerable pleasure in his 'creative' interests and their personal-social value. Empathic clarifications of the client's feelings were proposed by the therapist and seemed to help him recognize and accept such feelings. Everything that has been said about this client could be expressed in psychoanalytic form and would thereby gain integration. The client has been intentionally described in more variegated ways — as diverse reactions to theoretically varied operations.

Psychoanalytic theory has produced so many crucial insights into human personality and change that its concepts are justifiably enshrined. Unfortunately the psychoanalytic shrine is a procrustean bed [1] upon which many observations must be fitted, trimmed or stretched. The likelihood of observing and understanding interpersonal processes and change has been limited by such couching. In the example cited it seems reasonable that the client's change in ability to relate to the neighbor who was a father-transference figure can be understood in psychoanalytic terms. This perceptual-behavioral change is equally lucid as an instance of the interpersonal psychiatric conception of correcting a parataxic distortion. The client's improved ability to handle jealous feelings and to modify his wife's flirtatiousness seems aptly clear in interpersonal psychiatric terms. [2] That the nature of the human environment itself is modified by one's perceptions is a datum which psychoanalytic theory does not easily predict. The client's increased comfort in creative endeavor and his ability to complete creative work is readily predicted from dynamic relationship theory but somewhat tortuously derived from psychoanalysis (7).

Sensitivity in clinical psychotherapy, as well as both precision and scope in accounting for present data and predicting new insights, may result from the invention of constructs which will account for the multiform phenomena of personality change. In seeking simplification of a greater complexity than psychoanalysis proposes, it may have heuristic value to examine our four theories from a single frame of reference. Since psychoanalysis is the most confidently embracive theory, it will be used for this purpose.

PSYCHOANALYSIS REVISITED

If a runaway slave tore a golden bough from Diana's sacred tree, he won the right to battle for her Kingship. If he vanquished and

---

[1] The 'bed' metaphor is deliberate and perhaps theoretically valid in defining the likely horizons of psychoanalytic theory. It is perhaps no accident that ego-analysis is less likely to occur on the couch than is id-dream analysis. As psychoanalytic method has forsaken the 'bedroom' and moved into the 'living room' its theoretical scope has broadened to include life. Conversely, the therapist who occasionally employs the couch in alternation with face-to-face interviews will recognize the intimate importance of such differences in physical arrangements.

[2] Although existential theory (not reviewed here) may be even more appropriate to this instance.

killed Diana's incumbent, his prize was a grimly frightened defense against other would-be Kings. Prowling around Her tree, ready with drawn sword, he must be vigilant against the moment when another slave might seek the crown. Perpetually he must peer into the darkness, rain or sleet, for if he '. . . snatched a troubled slumber it was at the peril of his life. The least relaxation of vigilance, the smallest abatement of his strength of limb or skill of fence, put him in jeopardy . . .' (26).

On the same theme, Lewis Carroll has written:

> And hast thou slain
> the Jabberwock?
> Come to my arms
> my beamish boy . . .

The Oedipus problem and its mismanagement can be found in fable, ritual, poetry, and life. Oversimplified, this problem is: How can one comfortably achieve a parental role without symbolically killing the father and without perpetual fear of retribution for such unjust manhood? How can one become an effective parent-figure in our society? Psychoanalytic theory and therapy concern themselves intensely with this problem. In order to produce a manageable simplicity, this aspect of psychoanalytic theory will be applied to a theoretical exploration of the psychotherapy and leadership of groups.

Group process illustrations rather than individual therapy examples will be used to probe the explanatory value of psychoanalysis outside of its native habitat — the intimately personal couch.

What produces personality change in psychoanalytic treatment has been pondered by many authors. Braatøy (11) comments, '. . . by not inquiring about factors which are close to consciousness — the analyst informs the patient that he is not interested in those factors. . . .' Landis (60) complained rather bitterly about the lack of freedom in association, since the analyst interpreted contemporary associations as expressions of resistance. Wood (111) described how he learned to anticipate what the analyst was going to comment on and thus was able to carry the process forward with less help. The writer's own analyst suggested termination at the point where I knew what he was going to say. 'It seems to me you don't need much more help,' he said at that point. 'You're doing most of the work yourself now.'

Such descriptions of psychoanalysis suggest that psychotherapy may be conceptualized in terms of selective learnings. That is, the patient or group member is exposed to particular kinds of selective interest and descriptions from his therapist or leader and learns to reorganize himself in those terms. The studies cited in earlier chapters (cf. pp. 4, 13, 159, 237, 255) provide research support for this proposal. The process of change in personality may be largely a function of the method employed by the therapist or leader. To some extent this appears to be true regardless of the kind of patient or group member with which the leader is dealing. For example, the writer's clinical impression in being analyzed and his clinical impression of colleagues observed in analysis suggest that the process of becoming an analyzed personality is partly one of adopting a parental attitude about one's self, of assuming a more authoritarian attitude and role or, to express it in psychoanalytic terminology, of becoming a genital character. This is consistent with psychoanalytic theory; that is, the psychoanalytic theory proposes that maturity is a function of the degree to which one has developed acceptance of, and controls over, his instinctual erotic-aggressive drives and has learned to express these in personally satisfying and socially efficient ways. This is to be accomplished, at least partly, by accepting sexual maturity and assuming a parental identification picture of oneself. In contrast to this psychoanalytic process, client-centered investigators have observed that the person who already has a fairly democratic, understanding relation to people is likely to become adjusted most quickly in client-centered therapy. The relatively authoritarian personality tends not to improve when he is treated by a client-centered approach. The method of therapy tends to produce particular kinds of personality results, but its efficiency in producing such results may be associated with the personality integration of the patient or client at the time he enters therapy (cf. Chapters I and XI).

A relatively psychoanalytic personality integration might provide a better beginning point for therapeutic success as a function of psychoanalysis than would a personality integration that is not consistent with the psychoanalytic goal. The client-centered method seems more likely to produce effective personality modification in those people who are already on the road toward a phenomenological life philosophy. Rank's conception of personality modification implies such theoretical selectiveness when it proposes that proper candidates for psychotherapy are those who are engaged in a struggle between wishes to be themselves, independent, creative, autonomous individuals, versus wishes to be parts of mother-society and to fit into the normal pattern of living. Such people can be helped in treatment as a function of the fact that they are already concerned about how to become autonomous, separate selves. While visiting at the Chestnut Lodge, mecca of interpersonal psychiatry, the writer was impressed with the way that staff members seemed to epitomize Sullivan's conception of effective adjustment. These people were comfortably warm individuals who glowed, without exuding, with a quality of friendliness and interest. I have wondered whether this is a result of the interpersonal psychiatric value system. Certainly some of the research reviewed in earlier chapters supports the proposition that personal adequacy according to interpersonal psychiatric criteria is produced by methods of therapy consistent with interpersonal theory.

To examine the theoretical economy of psychoanalysis in explaining data from other theoretical sources, it seems necessary, first, to review some psychoanalytic concepts. It has been suggested that the theory proposes special ways of conceptualizing personality disturbance and a special way for patients to become mature in any social milieu (cf. p. 65). The psychoanalytic theory defines characteristic operations in psychotherapy. It also provides a conceptual framework for group leadership along psychoanalytic lines. Furthermore psychoanalytic theory has special ways of defining criteria for valuable personality modification and effective group functioning.

Psychoanalysis postulates that maladjustment is a joint function of excessive psychosexual fixations and ego deformations which leave the personality with insufficient energy reserves and reality skills for coping with crucial experiences. This is especially related to the problem of how one fails to become an emotionally mature, genital character or a parental figure. Maladjustment is in part a failure to model one's self effectively after one's same-sex parent. Conversely, the mature personality is an emotionally integrated parental figure.

Psychoanalytic Process in a Client-centered Group

From a non-psychoanalytic source the possible psychoanalytic process of maturing is suggested by a member of Hobbs's group-centered psychotherapy (54). This is Jane. She started in the therapy group with the statement that she wanted to work on the problem of dependence and independence because there was a great deal of conflict between her and her husband. She said she felt strongly about not taking money from her family because her relationship with her parents was not good. Her relationship to her in-laws was quite impossible. She felt she would be enslaved to her mother-in-law for the rest of her life if she and her husband accepted help from her in-laws in his college career. In a self-appraisal written before the group therapy began, she said that she couldn't stand the way that mother-in-law 'idolizes my husband.' 'I feel as though I were back in my own home playing second fiddle.'

Generally Jane's condition at the beginning of group-centered therapy could be described in psychoanalytic terms as a conflict with her husband as a result of oedipal transferences. The psychodynamic oedipal problem is further suggested by her masculine identification. This can be understood as a hysterical identification with father as a protection against an erotic attachment. Even though Hobbs's group was strictly non-analytic in intention and operation, Jane's modifications can be understood in a psychoanalytic conception.

After the fourth meeting of the group Jane wrote in her diary that Mary's remark about hostility feelings made her realize that she actually loved her mother, but that her fear of being like mother was so intense that she wouldn't admit this affection. There is considerable material in the transcription of the sessions and in diary entries to indicate that the process of becoming adjusted was related to the acceptance of a feminine identification. This was accomplished partly by identifying with other members of the group. Immediately after her first group meeting she wrote, 'The most outstanding reaction I had was my feeling of identity and sympathy for Kay.' In an interview two months after termination, her process of psychosexual maturation is suggested by her saying, 'It's a funny thing. I'm not very old, but I don't feel as young as I felt in February. I was only 23. I'm still only 23 but in February I felt about 16. I feel older now.'

It requires little reworking in this group-centered process to see Jane's changes in psychoanalytic conceptual terms. Whether improved economy is achieved by this reworking may be questioned. It should be recognized that Hobbs presents Jane as one who profited only moderately from the group-centered therapy because he wanted to show a middling example. One might even conjecture that this example may be related to Rogers's observation that the more authori-

tarian kind of personality tends to profit little from the phenomeno-
logical-empathic approach. In any event it is easy to read psychoanalysis between Jane's lines. This sample from Hobbs can be used
to illustrate a process of personality modification according to psychoanalytic theory. Certainly it is as middling an example of psychoanalysis as of phenomenology. Jane will be left hanging in conceptual
mid-air at this point, since no firm conclusions about her theoretical
fit seem feasible.

Classical Psychoanalytic Process

A more classic example of psychoanalytic change can be drawn
from the chapter on psychoanalysis in this book (cf. Chapter IV). The
case review there presents the process of becoming a parent-like
figure. The process included the working through of feelings about
father and the adoption of a modified acceptance of identification
with the father. The patient had come into analysis with intense feelings of bitterness and even hatred toward his long-dead father.
There was an interminable process of interpreting transferences
which the patient attached to the therapist. For example, during the
first few months the patient felt that he was not allowed to smoke in
analysis even though the analyst was smoking cigars during the whole
period. The patient developed very positive attitudes or transferences
toward the therapist (mother-surrogate), and extremely negative
attitudes toward the therapist (father-surrogate). The analyst's interpretation of the transference included calling the patient's attention to some of the differences and similarities between the therapist's
role and the father's role. The therapist might say, 'Isn't my asking
you to pay me like your father requiring you to clean up the trash
from his carpenter work?' The process of change towards an acceptance of identification with father is discernible in this particular psychoanalytic process.

*It can be said conceptually, and in some experiences of the process,
that psychoanalysis produces a parental role acceptance.* How is such
emotional integration of a parental role to be achieved? In individual
treatment, the analysis of resistance and the transference are nuclear
operations. They become the basis for the patient's giving up his infantile fixations, adopting a more genital role, and in a sense identifying with the parent-surrogate-therapist. In group processes, the same

psychodynamics have been identified with modifications appropriate
to the more life-like setting of a group.

The understanding of culture dynamics through psychoanalysis has
been suggested by a number of social scientists. Money-Kyrle (68)
has generalized the transference phenomenon to all kinds of social
group formation. The model of group formation according to him is
not the family as it really is but as it appears in fantasy. The real family tends to consist of only *two* parents and their children. The imaginary family which determines a group's structure and process, however, contains four parents (and perhaps six). There are the good,
wise, protecting father; the bad, ogreish, punishing father (and perhaps some vestige of the real father, who is good, bad, and realistic).
Then there are the giving, loving, tender mother; the depriving, rejecting, unloving mother (and perhaps some semblance of the good-
bad, objective mother of reality). In a therapy group process the
sibling-like members of the group relate to these six parents and the
other competing, voracious, frightened offspring in much the same
ways as a family of children vie with each other for parental affection,
gang up together for mutual protection, and share their horrifying
intimacies for mutual catharsis. Under such theoretical conditions how
is the process of becoming adjusted to be accomplished? Psychoanalytic theory proposes the ideal conditions of psychotherapy for both
individuals and groups. That is, the psychoanalytic method of free-
association on the part of the patients and transference and resistance
analysis on the part of the therapist are the conditions which presumably will implement most adequately the process of psychoanalytic
maturing. Devoted psychoanalysts have tended to propose that the
most effective conditions for group therapy are those which are most
similar to individual analysis. For example, Foulkes (25) says and
illustrates that the therapist's implicit structuring of the psychoanalytic
group should be, 'This is not only a leaderless group, but also an aim-
less group.' The difference from individual treatment is that 'the dynamics observed under the group analysis are *operative in the same
way as in life itself*.' Durkin (16) agrees that psychoanalytic group
therapy is essentially similar to individual treatment (cf. p. 260). The
psychodynamic basis is in the transference phenomenon and its ma-
nipulation. The libidinal and hostile drives toward leader and members
provide the essential basis for the leader's interpretation of transfer-

ences and resistances. The advantage of group over individual treatment lies in the broader repertoires of defenses and in simultaneous investments of contradictory transference attitudes. Slavson's (92) description of analytic group psychotherapy is essentially similar. It is psychoanalysis in a group, where the emphasis is upon the individual's experiencing and working through his unfortunate fixations, his maladroit ego deficiencies, and 'through a glass darkly' his parental images.

An *internal, relatively individual process* is explicitly emphasized in the psychoanalytic way of becoming adjusted. The leader and the sibling members of the analytic group provide each separate member with an opportunity for reproducing, re-experiencing, and working through emotionally corrective experiences on that long, long libidinal trail. It is plausible that a psychoanalytic-like process of personality transformation would occur under such psychoanalytic-like treatment conditions. The author is reasonably convinced that this kind of process does occur as a function of psychoanalysis. Whether the same or other processes result from other therapeutic leaderships is an important scientific question. We may consider this question by examining from the psychoanalytic viewpoint some processes of therapy induced by other theoretical methods.

Illustrations of Psychoanalytic Understandings of Group Process

A *dynamic relationship teaching session* with psychiatric residents and clinical psychologists [1] will illustrate the possibility of explaining interpersonal processes in a non-psychoanalytic group. This session was intended to illustrate reactions to a Rankian approach in group psychotherapy. In order to make the experience meaningful to the students and to reduce somewhat the threat of exposing one's self to professional colleagues, the leader asked the members to assume psychodramatic roles of patients with whom they were well acquainted. As a warming-up process in developing these roles, the leader engaged in a brief psychodramatic episode with one of the residents, then used this episode as a basis for a discussion of how vividly one may experience an assumed role. The group process developed under these conditions is fairly representative of the results of an emphasis upon the immediate emotional relationships. More specifically, this process

[1] From Colorado State Hospital. The author wishes to thank John Miller, M.A., Carol Estrada, M.A., and Alfredo Mateos, M.D., for permission to use these excerpts.

may be examined from the psychoanalytic point of view by illustrating the reactions of group members.

Member A gives a plausible psychoanalytic reaction of identification with the leader. A takes the role of a drug addict whom he had seen in group therapy over a period of about six months. A's behavior in this group is equally plausible in Rankian or psychoanalytic-theoretical terms:

A said, belligerently, 'Now I don't know what this is going to do for me. I want out of here, see. I just don't want to stay here, that's all.'

The leader said, 'You're pretty angry at me for having you come to this group.'

During this early part of the session, A was extremely critical of the leader, insistent upon his right to be himself, and dubious about the leader's ability to be of any value to him. The leader's response to A was principally in terms of A's demand for direction and his anger at the therapist. Later, A became more agreeable and began to consider co-operating.

A said, 'I have been in psychotherapy before. I know what it is and how the psychiatrist will do. He will discuss problems. Tell you what is going on and he'll work with you and sympathize and give you answers.'

The leader responded, 'It seems to you that I really don't care about you.'

A said, 'You don't care, nobody cares, this whole hospital is a lot of baloney. They don't care. They don't care if I stay here a year, ten years. If I don't stay here, they don't have a job.'

During this middle phase A became more agreeable with the therapist but tended to attack another member of the group who will be considered later. Generally A seemed to accept the therapist more and to consider the possibility that his independence was safe in this group. The leader responded primarily to A's pride and to his resistance to control.

During the final phase of this meeting, A became quite warm toward the therapist.

A said, 'What makes you guys at this stinking hospital think you can do any good?'

The leader responded, 'You are a very critical person.'

A reacted pleasantly, 'Of course I'm critical.'

The leader described A's expressive behavior, saying, 'I noticed you smiled when you said that.'

At this point A became quite friendly and accepting. He said, 'Well, I am rather proud of it, I'm me. I don't want to be like other people. After all I am an individual, and why should you or anybody else tell me I have to be like the other guy?'

During this latter phase the members began to vie for the leader's attention. This competitive reaction may be construed to indicate that the group members had accepted the leader as a parent-surrogate. In characteristic ways they sought his interest and attention. Member A joined in this sibling rivalry, being the one who appeared to identify with the therapist by seeking his counsel. The conversation turned to the question of whether the therapist was married and how he got along at home. Another group member, B, inquired, 'How do you get along with your wife?'

A joined in, 'Not only that, maybe he can teach us how to get along with our wives?'

Later A summarized, 'Yeah, have you botched up your life? Do you understand our problems or have you had problems that you could sympathize with us or what?'

These reactions of A could be understood from the psychoanalytic frame of reference as a partial acceptance of identification with the therapist and a partial expression of willingness to take counsel and support from the 'good father.'

Particularly noteworthy in A is the fact that his behavior in this group was most characteristically the kind that Rank conceptualizes. That is, A was an excellent example of the struggle for independence, selfhood and resistance to affectional control. From a Rankian point of view this could be understood as an insistent expression of opposing will which has not yet been transformed into creative, constructive selfhood. The experience of being understood and accepted in the group appeared to make it possible for A to accept some affectionate interest from the therapist and become less insistent upon his independence. From a psychoanalytic interpretive approach A's movement in this illustration could be understood in terms of first responding to the controlling, demanding, coercive mother transferences in the therapist and attempting to throw off such controls. Upon discovering that the controls which he attributed to the mother-transference meanings were not evidently present, Member A began to respond to the good-father transference meanings and to accept a partial identification with the father. Both the dynamic relationship and the psychoanalytic explanations seem to be reasonable summaries of A's behavior.

Member B can be seen psychoanalytically as an orally fixated personality. He assumed a very different relationship to the leader than A had taken. B immediately presented a demanding, dependency role in playing the part of a chronic alcoholic. There was a considerable challenge in B's demands upon the leader. He said, 'Can you cure my alcoholism? You can't! Just the only thing I need is Antabuse. Give me Antabuse, and I will be out. It seems that you don't like what I say. Do you? Yeah. You just think. You just look at me.'

The leader replied to this and other responses in the group by saying, 'You want me to tell you what to do and how you can get better except that you doubt that you need to get better.'

During this beginning, B was relatively critical of the therapist but with somewhat less intensity than A had shown, and for apparently different reasons. B expressed doubts that the therapist was interested in him, and expressed some fear of the therapist's displeasure. In one sense B seemed to be seeking but not expecting oral dependency gratification. The therapist responded to B by expressing B's dependency wishes and his cynicism in relationship to the leader.

During the middle phase of this meeting, B continued his dependency demands with somewhat less bitterness, but began to question the leader's competence. The leader had said, 'Apparently all of you have this feeling that I am not able to do anything to help you.' B said accusingly, 'The only thing is — are you being paid to do this?'

In a sense it appeared that B was testing the leader's competence and affection as well as insisting upon dependency satisfactions. There seemed to be a suggestion that B felt the therapist had accepted and could help him, but wondered whether this would happen. This expectant attitude became strikingly clear in the final phase of the meeting.

During this last phase B appeared to have discovered that affection might be available from the leader. B gave some characteristic expressions of the meaning of affection to him in terms of a family structure.

B interrupted A at one point, saying, 'Why don't we shut up for a while and let the leader talk to us and say what he thinks? We have been talking and we don't know anything.'

In partial response to B the leader said, 'I notice now that after having really lambasted me, you are trying to get me to talk to you, that you are no longer as angry as you were.'

Later, B said, 'Are you going to help us?'

He joined in wondering about the therapist's marital status and affections, saying, 'How do you get along with your wife?' Later he said, 'If you can get along with her, you can get along with us. We want to know what the old lady's like so we can know what you're like.' The leader responded, 'You have the feeling that if I can get along with someone else I might be able to do you some good.'

It appeared that Member B's involvement in the family rivalry was of a different quality than that of A. B seemed concerned about the leader's affectional capacity: 'Were his breasts sufficient?' That is, there was the impression that B felt that the leader could accept him as a person and be of some value to him if the therapist had a capacity for intense affection. In other words, the condition that B was trying to clarify was essentially 'Are you a good husband and father so that a person such as I could expect to be a happy child?'

Psychoanalytically this process in B seems to be consistently a search for dependency gratifications with a movement from initial expectation of rejection and deprivation to a dawning question whether affectional supplies could be available with this leader. It will be observed, however, that B was responding to the therapist in terms of mother transferences throughout the meeting. He was consistently seeking evidence and assurance of affection. He made quite clear that it was mothering affection that he sought when he expressed the hope that the leader was a good father who could provide him with a good mother. In psychoanalytic terms it appears that the patient whom Member B was representing tended to be fixated and to function at an oral-dependent gratification level with the hope for continual affectional supplies from mother-transference figures. It will be observed that B's personality process is readily understandable in Rankian relationship terms even though it fits quite neatly into psychoanalytic oral fixation terms. In dynamic relationship theoretical terms, B is quite simply an example of the wish to remain a protected part of the mother-surrogate. Both the psychoanalytic and Rankian explanations fit the illustration. The Rankian synopsis seems somewhat more compact.

Member E is the best psychoanalytic example of oedipal conflict. She dramatized a girl from one of her own therapy groups. E quickly took the side of the leader, was relatively uncritical, but tended to ask for *medical advice* from the *psychologist*-leader. She attacked other members of the group rather than the leader. The leader responded primarily to E's annoyance at other group members and to her ambivalent seeking and rejection of the leader's help. E said in the early phase, 'That's the trouble with everybody here at the hospital. Now here's this man that is trying to help us and everybody thinks that they are fine and don't need help. Why do I have headaches all the time?'

The leader responded, 'You'd like me to cure your headaches.'

During the middle phase of the meeting E began to establish more positive relationships to other group members. Generally this was an attacking, defensive relationship in response to their criticism of her. She continued to seek the leader's advice. The leader's response was principally in terms of pointing up her demands for medical help.

B said to E, 'So you like it here?'

E said, 'No, I don't like it here but I think there must be some reason.'

The therapist interjected, 'All of you apparently have this feeling that I am not able to do anything to help you.'

E replied, 'How come you are always telling us what we think?'

Later E expressed distress about the lack of interest on the part of the hospital staff, saying, 'And you see the trouble is, like on the ward, you never get to see the doctor.'

It appears that E is indirectly requesting interest and affection from the leader. Earlier her demands for attention had been more forthright.

During the final phase, E was a central figure in the sibling rivalry for the leader's attention. Her reactions were characteristically different from those of both A and B, tending to have an erotic, almost seductive quality. Following A's comment, 'Well, yeah, maybe he can do something,' E said, 'Yeah, but he's like all the other doctors. He doesn't answer questions. You know, a lot of the doctors here just aren't interested.'

The therapist responded, 'I have the feeling that you think I have no interest in you either.'

E introduced the question about the family background of the leader, saying, 'Are you married?'

The therapist replied, 'You seem to be becoming interested in me as a person.'

E attempted to deny this, saying, 'Well, just — this has something to do with your interests.'

The therapist replied, 'That is, if I'm married I couldn't be interested in you.'

E replied, 'Well, your wife might get jealous.'

Finally she asked, 'Does your wife know you are doing this?'

E's relationship to the leader was very different from those of A and B in terms of the meaning of the family situation. E had seemed to be courting the therapist-father-transference figure's erotic interest in her. That is, in spite of the leader's principal address to the symbolic mothering problem, E was responding to the oedipal conflict problem in her own role. She responded to the group leader as a father-transference-figure and appeared to experience both an oedipal interest in him and a feeling of threat from competing with the mother. In this group it would appear that E's behavior could be best understood in terms of a psychoanalytic formulation. Member A and Member B are reasonably understood in the Rankian framework even though they can be construed to fit the psychoanalytic conception.

Such a comparison of the psychoanalytic and dynamic relationship explanations of the behavior of three group members provides credence for psychoanalytic economy. To a degree A's movement from rebellion and individuality to willingness to cooperate and accept counsel from the leader may be construed as a developing sense of identification with the leader. B's insistent dependency and bids for affection seem psychoanalytically understandable in terms of mother transferences toward the leader. E's erotic, seductive behavior and her competitive concern about the leader's wife seem understandable as an oedipal transference re-enactment. This development of sibling-like competitiveness for the leader's interest is quite consistent with psychoanalytic theory. In making such a psychoanalytic summary of the reactions of these group members, it will be recognized that a Rankian summary is equally cogent for every member except E.

Psychoanalytic concepts can be applied to the therapeutic structuring of unorthodox kinds of therapy groups. The value of such concepts may be illustrated in the treatment of a group of adolescent girls.[1] This group was conducted by a male psychiatric resident and a female clinical psychologist. There were seven girls ranging in age from thir-

[1] Abstracted from a review prepared for the author by Carol Estrada, M.A., Clinical Psychologist at Colorado State Hospital.

teen to twenty years. All but one of the girls had been in a state hospital for a period of from one to two years. Three of the girls had been
diagnosed as schizophrenic, three as sociopathic personality, and one
as a schizoid personality. The group met two separate hours per week
over a period of seven months. During initial meetings, the two therapists attempted to handle the group on a relatively conventional psychoanalytic group basis. Becoming discouraged after a couple of un-
productive months, they consulted the writer as to possible ways of
improving the situation. Earlier research had suggested (cf. pp. 237,
238, 255) that an address to *ego-defenses* (or security-operations, characteristic of the interpersonal psychiatric approach) tends to be symbolically likely to have father-transference meanings, while an address
to the interpersonal or *relationship feelings* of the group (characteristic of the Rankian approach) tends to have mother-symbolic transference meanings. Therefore the suggestion was made that the therapists attempt to implement a family-symbolic situation in this group
by discontinuing their interest in the associative productions of the
girls and focusing primarily upon the group process as it emerged in
immediate experience. To make the family meaning more specific it
was suggested that the male therapist, Dr. P., implement his father-
transference role by addressing himself primarily to the social behavior
defenses and interpersonal activities of the girls. It was suggested that
the female therapist, Mrs. E., implement her mother-transference
meanings by addressing herself to the emotional interactions and implicit feeling expressions in the group process. With this increased
structuring of a family-like situation, the group appeared to make better progress. They became interested in the therapists themselves and
asked many personal questions about them and their families. They
expressed an interest in Mrs. E.'s recent marriage and talked a great
deal about the fact that Dr. P.'s wife was going to have a baby. During
this period questions about sexual behavior were raised by the girls.
The therapists tried to discuss these frankly and accept the attitudes
expressed about them. Of special interest throughout the series was
the fact that the girls were most likely to express anger and hostility
toward the female therapist and most likely to express affectionate or
even seductive attitudes toward the male therapist. This occurred in
spite of the fact that the female therapist took the more accepting,
understanding role.

During the seven months, six of the girls made evident improvements in adjustment. While a conventional method of group analysis did not appear to work in this group with these therapists, a modification related to psychoanalytic theory did seem effective. Of special interest in the psychoanalytic conception of transference is the fact that even though the mother-surrogate was most understanding and accepting, she was the principal target of the girl's hostility. Even though the father-surrogate was more authoritarian, distant and cold, he was the principal target of the girls' affectionate and seductive expressions. These reactions are entirely consistent with the psychoanalytic conception of oedipal transference meanings. An equally reasonable explanation would be that Mrs. E.'s acceptance made the girls feel safe in expressing hostility toward her, while Dr. P.'s distance made it seem necessary to placate him and protect against his anger. Certainly studies by Smith and Woodward (95) and Shearn, et al. (91) (cf. Chapter IX) make this simpler presumption reasonable.

Such illustrations of psychoanalytic explanation and structuring of group processes demonstrate considerable credibility in the application of psychoanalytic postulates to the explanation of non-analytic group processes. They do not demonstrate that the best explanation of such processes can be made in psychoanalytic terms. Except for Subject E in the dynamic relationship teaching group, a somewhat more efficient summary than the psychoanalytic one could easily be made.

Processes of change in personality as these result from interpersonal psychiatric, dynamic relationship and client-centered approaches, will now be reviewed. The question is: Do psychoanalytic concepts provide an efficient explanation of reactions to non-analytic therapy or leadership?

CLIENT-CENTERED THERAPY

Phenomenological theory, operations and effects as presented by Rogers and his co-workers (83, 84), may be summarized as: (a) a philosophy which prizes the individualities and private worlds of its clients; (b) operations which provide empathic understandings and respect; and (c) predictions that the clients' growth potential will lead to more integrated acceptance of themselves and more empathic understanding and acceptance of others.

The client-centered group approach has demonstrated (Hoch, 55) that the process of improvement is associated with increases in positive statements and attitudes about the self and increases in tendencies to plan and face problems constructively. Clients who benefit most from group-centered therapy are those who begin the process with empathic leader-like, healing responses (Gorlow, 45). Studies by Lewis (64), Page (72), Jeffers (56), and Glad, et al. (39) showed that client-centered group treatment had characteristic effects when compared with a two-factor learning and an interpersonal psychiatric approach. A group treated by the client-centered approach developed more positive attitudes toward each other in the group,[1] but did not change their reactions to people outside of their group. In a projective test they expressed more comfortable and accepting attitudes toward people in general.[2] Such improvement in acceptance of self and others is altogether consistent with client-centered theory (cf. Chapter VII).

A direct comparison of client-centered group therapy and psychoanalytic group therapy was made by Ends and Page (18). Examining processes of improvement in hospitalized chronic alcoholics, these investigators compared client-centered, psychoanalytic, two-factor learning and an atheoretical discussion group to evaluate the kinds of processes of change induced by each. Clearly different kinds of change [3] were induced by the four methods:

(1.) In client-centered treatment, there were improvements in the 'healthiness' of the client's acceptance of himself. These improvements suggested that the client develops a realistic self-picture, both in terms of modifying his ideals and improving his acceptance of capacities and limitations. The client-centered approach was effective in producing a social remission (with seven out of the fifteen patients treated by client-centered methods remaining 'greatly improved' for 1½ years of follow-up).

(2.) In psychoanalytic treatment there was a different kind of improvement in which the patient's acceptance of himself changed but his ideals were unmodified. The implication of this kind of change is that the patient is freed from some of his inhibitions and tends to accept himself as being the kind of person he wants to be. While such a change was undoubtedly valuable — as shown by the fact that six of the fifteen analytic patients had no further alcoholic episodes in the

---

[1] As measured sociometrically, Lewis (64).
[2] As measured by the Emotional Projection Test (38), Jeffers (56).
[3] As measured by various indices in Q-sorts of Self and Ideal Self.

following year and a half — the authors concluded that it was a somewhat unrealistic quality of change. The modification toward accepting the self was less coordinated than the process in client-centered treatment.

(3.) The two-factor learning approach was deleterious in its effects.

(4.) The social discussion, control group was apparently more harmful than beneficial in its effects.

This study suggests that the client-centered approach in group treatment is effective in producing an integration of the self. It also suggests that psychoanalytic group therapy is effective in increasing one's self-acceptance without modifying one's ideals.

Client-centered group therapy, then, appears to produce more positive feelings, a greater degree of closeness to others within the group, a greater degree of comfort and freedom in one's affective life, ability to face problems constructively, and an integration of attitudes and ideals about the self. These changes occur with minimal, if any, attention to either symbolic meanings or interpersonal behavior in the group.

The results of client-centered group treatment may be reconsidered in psychoanalytic terms. Hobb's Jane (described earlier, cf. p. 280) can be seen as a hysteric-like reaction to an oedipal attachment to father. This case, however, does not illustrate a client-centered product. A theoretically idiomatic process of change is expected in the client-centered group approach.

How would psychoanalysis account for client-centered changes? Bortree and Glad's (9) research (cf. p. 225) offers some implications for this question. Their comparison of psychoanalytic, relationship, and client-centered interviews showed that analytic therapists were most likely to respond to negative qualities in the patients. Client-centered therapists were most likely to emphasize the positive qualities of the client. The client-centered approach accentuates the positive — especially the positive aspects of feelings. Both theoretically and empirically, the good, the true, and the beautiful in the client's verbalizations are emphasized. This finding is consistent with the self-structure conception of motivation in terms of the enhancement and maintenance of the phenomenal self. The therapist not only accepts and re-expresses the client's feelings and attitudes, but tends to selectively emphasize the more constructive and positively valued aspects. Psychoanalytically this positive emphasis might be considered 'a covering-up or ameliorative procedure,' a support for the ego by avoiding the more painful erotic and destructive instinctual life. This positive emphasis may be considered a supportive approach to ego-strengthening.

The client's negative expressions are supposedly acceptable to the client-centered therapist but apparently they are less emphasized in operational terms. More generally, psychoanalysis might explain client-centered results as the integration into conscious ego of erotic, aggressive, and conflictual impulses. This integration is achieved by an accepting awareness from the mother-father-surrogate therapist even though the symbolic implications of the material are neglected. The disturbing feelings of the client become less disturbed and more adequately integrated because the therapist allows these to come into conscious awareness without threat or retaliation in the interview. On such a basis it might be considered that the malforming and mouth-warming experiences of childhood are reworked and restructured in the client-centered approach through a kind of immediate experience of acceptance which makes the process tolerable and reintegration possible. The corrective emotional experience occurs in vivo rather than in retrospect. Symbolic meanings are not integrated but new experiences change the meanings of an outdated past.

This attempt at psychoanalytic explanation does not satisfy the author. A more economical conception would consider the client-centered process as a learning to reorganize one's self in the terms that are provided by the therapist or leader. The product of client-centered therapy should be more consistently similar to the product of psycho-analytic therapy if the two processes could be explained in psycho-analytic terms.

INTERPERSONAL PSYCHIATRY

Interpersonal psychiatry proposes that the individual is a function of his relations to other people. Effective adjustment consists of experiencing an integration and belongingness in an interpersonal process. Research has tended to support the proposition that interpersonal psychiatric methods enhance the development of a socialized, integrated, and friendly individual. One series of studies (cf. p. 255) demonstrated that a method derived from interpersonal psychiatry resulted in improved interpersonal relations, affections, and skills. Subjects treated by the interpersonal approach became better liked and liked others better, both within their own group and in the larger group of students from which they were drawn. They became more realistic in their evaluation of each other and in general learned to behave in more friendly, accepting ways. They developed more friendly, affectionate attitudes in fantasy. Similar interpersonal improvements occurred in another comparative study of interpersonal psychiatric method and dynamic relationship method on 'normal college students.' [1] The interpersonal psychiatric method tended to produce interpersonal adequacy and friendliness.

An interpersonal psychiatric method in treatment of paranoid schizophrenic groups has consistently increased the socialization skills of psychotic patients (21).

However, it appears (as reviewed in Chapter XI) that the interpersonal psychiatric approach is more effective with the marginally psychotic, disturbed-antagonistic patients than with the more 'regressed' psychotic adjustment of affective-blunting. Generally, the studies on interpersonal psychiatric methods suggest that both college students and marginally schizophrenic patients become more effectively socialized as a result of an address to their interpersonal operations.

Explaining these socialization phenomena in terms of psychoanalysis, it seems necessary to consider 'security-operations' and 'ego-defenses' as relatively cognate conceptions. That is, the psychoanalytic conception of ego-defenses involves the assumption that behavior is symptomatic of the ego's methods of excluding unacceptable wishes and anxieties from awareness. The interpersonal psychiatric conception of security-operations postulates that behavior is in the service of avoiding the recognition that other people refuse to respond with affection and tenderness. Expressive behavior is characterized in interpersonal psychiatric terms as defenses against the fears of rejection and insecurity. The emphasis is upon their interpersonal meaning and intent. Psychoanalysis describes such expressive behavior in ego-defense terms. That is, psychoanalysis considers these to be techniques that the individual uses for excluding disturbed meanings from awareness or repressing them into the unconscious. Such ego-defenses implement repression and finesse one's libidinal requirements upon the world in a sufficiently attractive form that they will be acceptable. To

[1] Smith and Glad (93); Glad, Smith, and Glad, Virginia (42).

a degree it is possible to consider *security-operations* and *ego-defenses* as cognate terms. Both expressions describe the personality's management of its relation to the environment.

The interpersonal psychiatric operations of the therapist-leader in the studies referred to have generally described the social behavior of the individual in the group. Under these conditions group members have developed social skill, affection, and a greater awareness of other people. They have been able to modify their interpersonal skills, perceptions, and affections. Such therapist operations might be described psychoanalytically as a diluted form of ego-defense analysis in the group situation. The results are plausible as part of the psychoanalytic conceptual structure in such terms. That is, the therapist's address to the social expression in the group might be considered as a group form of ego-defense analysis with an opportunity for trying out new ego-skills.

This explanation of interpersonal psychiatric results neither simplifies nor clarifies. A psychoanalytic rephrasing does not add to understanding. A simpler explanation is that the individual learns those things which he is taught. In these groups he was exposed to interpersonal skill opportunities. He learned such skills.

DYNAMIC RELATIONSHIP THERAPY

Dynamic relationship theory postulates an ambivalent struggle between one's wishes to achieve competent, unique, artistic, selfhood and one's wishes to remain a comfortable, integrated part of mother-society. In this struggle the individual experiences fear of desertion by mother-society and guilt over his wishes to withdraw. Some research illustrates the pragmatic reasonableness of the theory. An interview study conducted by Harris (cf. p. 256) suggested that dependency was a characteristic behavior reaction of normal college students when they were being interviewed by a dynamic relationship method. In Smith et al. (cf. p. 237), the dynamic relationship portion of his study of normal students illustrates the Rankian prediction. The same people who respond to dynamic relationship operations with anxiety, desires to be left alone, and perceptions of others as friendly but confused, are most sociable in the interpersonal psychiatric condition. Such anxious independence as relationship therapy provokes is transmuted into friendliness by the interpersonal psychiatric method. Yet these students remain uncomfortable in their interpersonal friendliness. It appears that people who express the characteristic expectations from dynamic relationship theory are able to socialize when appropriate conditions are provided, but that they are uncomfortable about this interpersonal control. It almost seems that socially conforming but anxious people are the very ones Rank prizes. They do not want to be a part of the social process. They wish to be their unique selves even though this is uncomfortable.

The reactions of affectively-blunted and disturbed-antagonistic schizophrenics suggested (cf. p. 238) that the most regressed patients were helped by dynamic relationship therapy, but that the more marginal adjustments were disturbed rather than helped by this method. If we assume with Rank that the process of becoming adjusted depends upon experiencing both comfortable acceptance and comfortable withdrawal from the mother-society-therapist, these paranoid-schizophrenic response data become psychodynamically plausible. The affectively withdrawn schizophrenic is able to respond more adequately to the dynamic relationship emphasis because the therapist has addressed himself to the emotionally disturbed, regressive nucleus of the psychosis. That is, the therapist addresses the patient's difficulty in emotional relationships to mother. Similarly the disturbed-antagonistic patient may become most psychotic when addressed by symbolic mothering because the therapist provokes those infantile, regressive feelings which this patient is trying to avoid.

Dynamic relationship theory is certainly a plausible representative of the oral fixation problems of psychoanalytic theory. It is intriguing in this connection that Bergler's (7) discussion of *The Writer and Psychoanalysis* comes to essentially the same conclusion that Rank arrived at with his modified conception of personality. That is, in both conceptions, creativity results from the problem of how to resolve the difficulties centered around separation from the mother figure. Thus the assumption in Rank's theory that personality disturbance is a function of separation threat and need for individuality may reasonably explain the data of the paranoid schizophrenic responses and the normal college student responses which were illustrated, as well as the processes of creative individuality.

Rank's method and theory fit the psychoanalytic conceptual system. The adequacy of explaining all personality phenomena on the basis of the oral-separation-anxiety problem is unconvincing. The psycho-analytic conception of oral fixation of libido and its attendant problem in deprivation and affectional withdrawal threat seem sufficient for Rank's theoretical needs. There is still the question of economy: per-haps the kind of process of change which Rank's theory produces is characteristic of his theory and not as essentially characteristic of psy-choanalysis. That is, the group or the patient treated by dynamic rela-tionship therapy may be most likely to respond in the direction of an increasing acceptance of individuality, creative potential, and legiti-mate uniqueness because these are the values presented to him. In other words, the client may value his uniqueness because the therapist or leader has valued it.

'IMPROVEMENT' BY ADOPTING THE THERAPIST'S VALUES

That the patient may improve by adopting the therapist's values is suggested in some excerpts from a terminal meeting of a group of six paranoid schizophrenics.[1] Five of these six patients were either dis-charged or about to be discharged from the hospital in social remis-sion. One patient had apparently made little progress. The group was discussing what they thought had helped them to improve.

Mr. E. is saying, 'That's right. I'm pretty sure that's why I was afraid to go out by myself and I was afraid to walk on the street. Afraid to go into crowds.'

Miss F. said, understandingly, 'You mean you were afraid someone would punish you for those thoughts — or just afraid something would happen?'

E. responded, 'Afraid that something would happen.'

Mr. R. said, 'It was just an illness that — the same as everybody else in this group had and we're not ashamed to talk about.'

The therapist, still trying to help Mr. M., who had been unrespon-sive in the group, said, 'I wonder if Mr. M. doesn't feel as though his problem might be quite different from anybody else's in the group. He might think that we would consider there is something very wrong about it if he does talk to us.' (Mr. M. doesn't answer.)

Mr. R. said, 'You shouldn't feel that way, Mr. M. We are all exactly in the same boat. Maybe we had the same experiences so I wouldn't

[1] Treated by the author at Colorado Psychopathic Hospital.

feel ashamed to talk about it. As a matter of fact it makes you feel better to get it off your chest. You're just pushing it back into your mind and it will be there for a long time, if you don't get it off your chest.' (Mr. M. doesn't respond.)

Miss F. says to the group, 'I think it is very hard for Mr. M. to think that he has had any mental illness.' Then turning to Mr. M. she continues, 'But you don't have enough confidence in us to tell us about it?' (Mr. M. sighs.)

Miss F. continues, 'Perhaps you still have the feeling we are prying into your business.'

Mr. M. responds, 'No.'

Miss F. continues, 'Maybe you just have doubts in your mind that we can be of any help to you. So there doesn't seem to be much point in telling us.' (Mr. M. nods.)

The therapist says to Mr. M., 'Have you had the feeling that your situation is much different than anybody else's?'

Mr. M. replies, 'I'm not saying that it wasn't the same.'

The therapist says, 'I wonder if you're not saying that, just because that is what I expect.'

Mr. M. responds, 'No, after all — we are all more or less alike.'

Mr. R. says, 'Well, it makes me feel good that you can talk to a bunch of people that are in the same predicament. If you talk to someone else, they wouldn't understand, whereas everybody in the group here understands.'

This excerpt illustrates that the members of this once psychotic group have tended to adopt the therapist's role in trying to help the less effectively adjusted member of the group to some satisfactory improvement. In a sense the group members have accepted themselves in a way that is similar to their perception of the leader's relationship to the group members. Psychoanalytically this might be *identification* with the leader. In interpersonal psychiatric terms, it would more likely be called *imitative* behavior on the basis of having learned to see themselves as potentially understanding, friendly, comfortable people through a series of reflected appraisals from the leader. From the client-centered, empathic point of view it would be likely to be described as the development of understanding and interest in others as a result of having developed a *more integrated and embracive understanding of the self*. From a dynamic relationship approach it might be expressed as the bringing back of one's creative *insights to enrich society.* In any event the patients tend to become therapist-like in their relationship to other patients. Gorlow (45), in investigating group-centered psychotherapy, has shown that those clients who were best adjusted before therapy began were most quick to assume 'healing' kinds of empathic attitudes toward other group members. Gorlow also found that those who improve most are the ones who adopt leader-like ways of expressing themselves.

SELECTIVE LEARNING OF A VALUE SYSTEM: It appears reasonable that the assumption of the leadership philosophy and role which are characteristic of a particular theory is associated with the process of becoming adjusted in that theory. Rosenthal (88) demonstrated a similar phenomenon. Patients who improved in psychotherapy made changes in the direction of adopting their therapist's moral values, while those who failed to improve did not assume the morality of the therapist. Whether this rather general process in psychotherapy is best described as the psychoanalytic process of achieving a parental role may of course be questioned. That it tends to be so in psychoanalytic therapy is quite clear. That it is a process of parental role adoption in other therapies can be *illustrated* if one systematically assumes a psychoanalytic frame of reference. Perhaps a simpler way of unifying these divergent phenomena is to propose that one learns those values, techniques, and systems of integrating himself to which one is exposed. One learns to assume a parental role if this is a central value in the process he is engaged in by the therapist. One learns to accept one's own feelings and the feelings of others if this is the emphasis made in therapy. One learns to experience oneself in social interaction terms and to value other people as part of his organization if this is the interpersonal emphasis made in the therapy of which he is a part. One learns to accept one's creative individuality and one's indebtedness to others in terms of this uniqueness if an emphasis upon such a value is made in the psychotherapy transaction.

SUMMARY

A psychoanalytic perspective has been applied to the explanation of personality modification processes. Some psychoanalytic propositions considered about therapist and leadership meanings were transference and the process of becoming a genital character, or assuming a parental role. These were proposed as nuclear concepts in psychoanalytic therapy, leadership, and personality growth. There is illustrative evidence that such processes occur in both psychoanalytic and nonanalytic groups. Yet in the search for conceptual simplicity, it may be questioned whether the Holy Grail of personality change is more like a swamp-fire will-o-the-wisp than like the analytic conceptual structure. It is possible to force the results of other theories into the analytic system, but the search for simplicity suggests that local conditions of theory strike provincial fires. A more unifying explanation than psychoanalysis seems possible. Since the personality results of theory seem idiomatic, it is likely that patients and group members integrate themselves in the terms provided by the therapist-leader. They adopt the leader's way of thinking about themselves and become adjusted in his idiom:

1. Psychoanalysts enhance a genital-parental integration by selective response to the sexual and transference symbolic aspects of the personality.

2. Client-centered therapists promote emotional understanding, self-acceptance and awareness of others by providing emotional empathy to the client.

3. Interpersonal therapists facilitate skill in social relations, consensual validity and interpersonal security by responding to such interpersonal aspects of the client.

4. Dynamic relationship therapists nurture pride and satisfaction in one's unique autonomy by accepting and encouraging the uniting and separating gestures of the client.

Clinical impressions and research results suggest that such theoretically prized outcomes are empirical products of the theories.

Psychoanalysis provides a conceptual schema into which these several processes may be fitted. A simpler, more efficient conception is that the client is most likely to learn the personality integration presented by the therapist-leader.

And hast thou slain
the Jabberwock?
—CARROLL

XIII. Commentary on Clinical Problems
in Psychiatric Practice BY ROBERT H. BARNES, M.D.

Director of Educational Services, The Greater Kansas City Mental Health Foundation [1]

Contributing a chapter to this book on research issues in psychotherapy is not an easy job for a psychiatrist. A first inclination is to write a 'critical review,' praising the author for 'original and provocative insights,' yet viewing with some agitation an excursion into clinical problems by one who 'cannot fully appreciate the subleties of the doctor-patient relationship,' etc. This would be completely inappropriate in a work demonstrating so deep an appreciation of the individuality of human needs. One might then attempt a review of the pertinent literature. However, professional dignity will not allow such a drab compilation to appear side by side with the refreshingly original thought and labor which Dr. Glad, with the help of his colleagues, has brought together here. This is indeed a pioneer effort toward a rational research approach to various psychotherapies and their consequences. To psychiatry, and the practice of psychotherapy, the implications are tremendous.

CLINICAL DIFFICULTIES

Many psychiatrists, and I cannot entirely exclude myself, will have read this book with considerable discomfort. First, it suggests that we may need to broaden our approach to the understanding of personality

[1] I wish to express my appreciation to my colleague, John H. Cumming, M.D., for his numerous helpful suggestions during the preparation of this chapter.

functioning and vary our techniques in psychotherapy from patient to patient. Any work which implies a professional myopia will stir up anxieties and animosities. Further, a work derived from and proposing research in psychotherapy will lead to discomfort in those of us who practice clinical psychotherapy from a training background in the descriptive and anecdotal analysis of individual patients in a prolonged and intimate doctor-patient situation. The implication that we may have exhausted the new yield from the old approach — no matter how tremendous the theoretical and applied yield may have been in the last half century — is disconcerting. Particularly so since most of us are limited by training and clinical opportunities to this approach. Information derived through controlled research experimentation and statistical analysis is frequently beyond the clinical psychiatrist's knowledge or interest, and thus may be viewed with disbelief and alarm.

A further source of discomfort to the psychiatric clinician in reading this work will be related to the doubt it casts on the exclusive use of any one frame of reference in the diagnostic and psychotherapeutic approach to patients. Clinical practice of psychotherapy is not easy, and there are many failures and disappointments along the way. Part of our 'character armoring' against this consists of a 'security-operation' in mastering a consistent frame of reference which works best for the individual psychiatrist and psychotherapist. The implications of this book are such as to shake the security of a parochial approach to mental illness in general and the disturbed patient in particular.

CLINICAL PROMISE

Since neither time, inclination, motivation, nor the pressure of practice permits the clinician to relearn readily his approach to clinical problems or submit his basic beliefs to careful re-evaluation, the best use of this commentary may be to place the implications of Dr. Glad's work in a clinical setting and apply them to a few selected, individual problems.

Dr. Glad's basic hypothesis is that 'improvement' in psychotherapy is a function of both 'the theoretically derived method of treatment' and the 'personality organization' of the patient. Thus the closer the patient's basic existent personality to the goals of the therapist and the technique of therapy derived therefrom, the sooner might the patient be expected to 'recover,' with recovery defined in terms of achievement of the therapist's goals.

In actual therapy situations this gives rise to a number of problems. In evaluating the personality of the patient, we are concerned both with (a) the personality weaknesses and poorly functioning defenses, with the resulting anxiety, hostility, and lowered self-esteem; with (b) the *personality strength* and *assets* — the relatively smoothly functioning adjustment patterns. Thus we encounter a person whose interpersonal relationships are generally good, but whose sexual adjustments in a marital situation are very poor and seem clearly based on unresolved oedipal conflicts. In such a situation, by psychoanalytic procedures, a relatively effective 'cure' may be effected. The procedure chosen would have been based more on an analysis of the patient's unresolved problems — thus *personality deficits* — than on his basic assets. This person might have been closer to being a *socially mature* individual than a genitally or *psychosexually* mature person. But we chose to correct the defects rather than strengthen the assets per se. In practice we have come to find that such an approach often leads to a relief of anxiety, etc., and more effective functioning in terms of personal comfort. To put this in Dr. Glad's terms, we may frequently encounter situations in which the person may be closer to effective functioning in terms of *socialization criteria* but may only achieve satisfactory relief of anxiety, lack of self-esteem, etc., via the much longer route toward a psychosexual identification by 'transference operations,' derived from psychoanalysis. The shortest path may not always offer a satisfactory 'cure.' Thus as clinicians we may feel a greater need to evaluate the personality weakness and sources of anxiety, hostility, and depression, than the assets or strengths.

An analogy from medical practice may be in order. An individual with chills, fever, weakness, and bloody sputum accompanying a tubercular lung lesion gains tremendously from measures (diet, rest, limited exercise, and other environmental changes) designed to strengthen his body, but specific therapy (of I.N.H., Streptomycin, lobectomy, etc.) aimed directly at the tubercular lesion may be necessary before 'cure' can be attained. The analogy seems fitting for the 'oedipal' type problem outlined above — a situation in which a relatively specific focus for maladjustment (focus of psychosexual fixation) exists. Here, however, we can only achieve 'cure' when the person relates or identifies well enough and can develop sufficient insight to work with his problems in a transference situation. This demands a degree of 'ego strength,' 'psychological awareness,' intelligence, etc., which is unusual in the general run of emotionally ill people.

The greatest problem for psychiatry is to be found in non-focal emotional illness. Most emotional problems are *not* relatively focal, but involve extensive disturbance in all levels, with little responsibility, individuality, creativity, social effectiveness, etc. In addition, the ability, at least initially, to relate closely and work 'within the transference' effectively is negligible. 'Psychological awareness' and insight are also limited. Here, then, an evaluation of the personality assets is of prime importance, and finding the shortest route to a functioning level of adjustment is imperative. In this framework 'cure' may have a broader meaning, ranging from only minor functioning improvement to extensive advances in effectiveness, socially, individually, creatively, and psychosexually.

An analogy from physical medicine may be helpful. A paraplegic with a transverse thoracic lesion of the spinal cord will never regain effective use of his legs, so our focus is to concentrate on his assets — his arm, shoulder, and hand strengths and uses to which these can be put in aiding his mobility — rather than placing extensive effort on leg braces, remedial leg exercises, etc., in a vain effort toward normal use of his legs — a desirable but unattainable goal.

CLINICAL ILLUSTRATIONS

The following brief case summaries may serve to illustrate the potential clinical applications and values of Dr. Glad's conceptualization:

IMPROVED SOCIALIZATION: *R. E. L.*, a highly successful lawyer in his late forties, was referred by his local internist after a six-month illness, featured by severe anxiety and depression. The anxiety was vague and diffuse and largely expressed in the form of physical feelings of extreme bodily discomfort ('tension'), accompanied by some tachycardia and systolic blood pressure elevation. Depressive ideas were related by the patient to discouragement, 'because I feel so awful' and 'because I can't care for my wife and girls.' Previous treatment, beginning elsewhere five months previously, had consisted of a course of electroconvulsive therapy, followed by chlorpromazine, coupled with brief, supportive interviews. This did not prove significantly helpful.

The patient was highly intelligent and friendly. He gave a very detailed account of his difficulties and at all times was the 'ideal patient,' prompt and courteous to all personnel, including the psychiatrist, even though the latter frequently would not agree to his requests for medication. The patient remained in the hospital for three weeks and was subsequently followed for one year on an out-patient basis.

Background history indicated that the patient was the middle son in a sibling group of three boys. The family was lower middle class, with the mother having relatively high social and economic ambitions for her sons. These had been fulfilled by all three, although to the greatest extent by the patient, who was probably her favorite. However, the patient never felt really close to either parent. Socially the patient had been friendly and mixed well in school, but had dated very little. His wife was his first girl friend and they married after he finished law school. He expressed great concern regarding the economic deprivation he had 'forced her to face' early in their marriage and placed great emphasis on the economic success he had achieved 'for my family.' Sexual adjustment, according to the patient's evaluation, had been fairly satisfactory until the illness, although a 'heavy work schedule' had cut down on the frequency of their sexual relations for some years. The patient remained completely unable to express anything but the most positive feelings toward his wife, who was in fact a charming and adequate woman who took over readily during the patient's illness.

The success strivings in this man were tremendous and his professional performance at a very good level. He labored under the pressure of being a lawyer who 'had never lost a case.' He did every job well and was consequently overwhelmed by work in his law firm and by countless church and community jobs. His chief recreation had been golf, which was played with his same meticulous concern and was thus not a source of relaxation in the least. In fact, the first warning of impending breakdown came several years previously on the golf course, when he was overcome by what appeared to have been an acute anxiety attack with strong fears of death. This was repeated on two subsequent occasions. These attacks seem to have been related to coronary attacks sustained by several professional acquaintances of the patient's while they were playing golf.

Without attempting a descriptive or dynamic formulation at this point, we see this tremendously 'oversocialized' (to use this author's value judgment) man, breaking down under the strains of this 'over-conforming' behavior, which brought only responsibility and little basic gratification. Making this sort of value judgment — i.e., that this man was 'oversocialized' — a prolonged attempt was made to help the patient with *feelings* toward his wife, his mother, his father, his brothers, his two young girls, and toward the therapist. The history, which the patient supplied readily, was replete with situations in which strong negative feelings must have existed and were probably directly related to the symptomatology, yet never could this well-controlled, 'overly socialized' man express antagonism. Despite more than one hundred hours of therapeutic contacts during the year, at no time could the patient express any negative feelings toward the therapist.

Slowly and painfully the patient began to talk about his work, his fears of not doing a good job, his inability to say 'no' to community and civic pressures, etc. Eventually he could talk about his fears in court in front of the judge, but never about any feelings toward his father. Such was the pattern — and slowly the patient improved, but largely along lines of *'better' or more complete socialization* — never in terms of self-understanding, greater individuality, or creativity, or in terms of any psychosexual growth or maturity. Yet his anxiety, tensions, and depressive feelings gradually disappeared.

Clinically it would appear this man could *not* have been effectively treated by empathic understanding of his feelings, by attempts to explore his needs for individuality and creativity (as great as these may have been), or by working through a transference situation. The therapist's initial goals for this patient were quite different from the patient's own, and only as the therapist began to see the impossibility of imposing the goals he saw for this man and began to accept the patient's tremendous strivings toward 'improved interpersonal operations' was progress made. Or so it would seem. Had the therapist sensed this earlier and shaped his 'theoretically derived method of treatment' more readily to the 'personality organization of the patient' (to use Dr. Glad's concepts), the course of therapy might have been greatly shortened. This is an unanswered question. And it will raise the problem in every good psychotherapist's mind of when do you continue to struggle with the resistance toward a 'working through' and when do you vary your goals to bring them closer to the patient's basic personality functioning. Dr. Glad's future work may well illuminate this very crucial question. Up to now most of us 'feel our way through,' changing our techniques and goals only after long effort with the patient, or early or late cross the patient off as 'not a candidate for psychotherapy.' Maybe there is a better way of deciding this early, for the good of the patient and the peace of mind of the therapist. Dr. Glad's thesis points strongly in this direction and may therein represent a major advance in clinical psychotherapy.

INDIVIDUALITY: The next case is presented even more in outline but should serve to raise similar problems from a slightly different standpoint:

M. B. H. was referred for psychiatric evaluation by a sensitive female internist who felt she detected more than the usual 'adolescent adjustment problem' in this seventeen-year-old high school senior. Mary had experienced a 'fainting feeling' two months prior, while taking a bath. She immediately became concerned that she had epilepsy and became very preoccupied, anxious, and depressed. She related this concern to the fact that her mother's younger sister had severe seizures, was psychotic and had to be intermittently hospitalized in the State Hospital. On one occasion the aunt had reportedly seized a meat cleaver and in the patient's presence had threatened to 'cut up my mother with a butcher knife.' Recently the patient herself had a recurrent dream in which a woman in brown hacks the patient's mother to pieces before the patient's eyes.

Mary is an only child, closely attached to a friendly but anxious and hypochondriacal father 'who comes home every night with something new, either cancer or a heart attack.' Mother is a bland, apparently rather ineffectual person, toward whom the patient never expresses many feelings consciously, positive or negative. In early childhood Mary developed severe asthma which necessitated the family moving to Florida. In various ways this isolated her from other children — 'Their mothers thought I had whooping cough or something terrible.' She had no close girl friends, and became more and more of a 'tomboy.' Even in high school she continued to dress and act like a boy.

With this background, the patient asserted herself vigorously in a number of ways. She tried to out-do the boys — both in semi-delinquent acts and in sports — becoming one of the top girl basketball players in her state. Other children admired her for her independence and 'guts.' She established close and lasting relationships with the important older people in her environment — teachers, Y.W.C.A.

staff, coaches, etc. She became active in all sorts of school activities —
plays, student government, debating, Junior Prom Committees, etc.,
etc. On graduation she was chosen as the outstanding girl in her class
in a large, metropolitan high school. Her scholastic performance was
equally good, and she showed exceptional talents in a number of lines.
While her superficial social relationships with peers had become quite
good, she had few close friends and her relations with boys featured
an admixture of competitiveness and admiration and were generally
unsatisfactory for her.

I will add little further regarding the case other than to comment
on the tremendous degree of lowered self-esteem and anxiety that
made one wonder how she functioned at all, let alone at the high level
she did. Interestingly the patient was able to leave her family and
move from the South to begin college in a fashionable Northern girls'
college, where she soon became class president.

Approaching this case from the standpoint of Dr. Glad's analysis,
we would emphasize the strong trends toward individuality and independent creativity. The surface personality is that of a strong individ-
ualist, striving with a high degree of success for her place in the world
and on top of it. From this standpoint, then, one might attempt to carry
out a therapeutic approach aimed toward achieving goals nearest to
these salient, existing personality patterns of the patient. Thus what
Dr. Glad refers to as a *dynamic relationship* approach would seem to
offer the best therapeutic 'fit.'

Again the clinical psychotherapist will raise many questions. What
of this girl's distorted psychosexual orientation (basically homosex-
ual), which may serve to cut her off from satisfactory and meaningful
relationships with men? What of her tremendous attachments to her
father and hostilities toward her mother? I suspect that part of the
answer would be that these problems, too, can be worked through
effectively in the dynamic relationship frame, albeit differently than
they might be in an interpersonal or in a psychoanalytic approach, and
I suspect that Dr. Glad would hypothesize that these problems could
be more effectively, if not deeply, worked through by an approach
which emphasizes pre-existing personality strength in setting the goals.

This also brings up the matter of changing goals during the therapy.
Taking Mary's case as a point of discussion, the therapist might well
set the initial goals along 'dynamic relationship' lines, seeking to
strengthen the patient's functioning capacity by way of a route nearest

her basic strivings for achievement and individuality. Very conceivably as such goals are achieved, and the patient reaches greater 'maturity,' by these standards, she may perceive a need for further help toward other goals. At this point the new goals might best be achieved by psychoanalytic techniques, by a degree of working through of the psychosexual problems in the transference, for example. Thus, 'growth' in therapy may lead to both a change in goals and in the basic therapeutic approach. To an extent, this may be implicit in much psychotherapy in practice — changes in technique as the patient progresses — but generally when this is done it is without any careful planning or analysis, and rather the result of empathic and often unconscious processes within the therapist, in his response to changes in the patient. Dr. Glad suggests, in effect, that a more open-minded analysis of the patient, his desires and needs, might lead us to more conscious and deliberate changes of goals and techniques, even as therapy progresses.

OBJECTIVE ANALYSIS OF CLINICAL PSYCHOTHERAPY

This chapter has represented an attempt to review Dr. Glad's value integration hypothesis in the light of the type of clinical problems seen in psychotherapeutic practice. It is a most intriguing and promising hypothesis, and one which can only be worked out by further painstaking research, statistical analysis, and follow-up. Here, too, is an area that this book should serve to open further. It introduces a methodology for the study of change during therapy — a method that is as free as possible from a dependence, in the evaluation of the results of therapy, on our subjective, wish-fulfilling judgments, which fill our literature with unreproducible, descriptive reports. So skeptical are most psychotherapists of reports evaluating 'social recovery,' 'improved adjustment,' 'better reality awareness,' and the like that we judge most clinical literature in psychotherapy not on the basis of reported *results* but on our appreciation of the techniques or of our agreement with the author's acumen in elucidating the dynamics of the therapeutic techniques he is describing. Imagine the results in medical therapeutics if we were to evaluate a new antibiotic in pneumonia solely on the basis of the author's discussion of the host-organism-antibiotic interrelationships with no consideration as to therapeutic efficacy. In medical therapeutics we have ways of measuring and reporting results, and there we have moved along rapidly in building up an effective therapeutic armamentarium. In psychotherapy our ways of measuring and reporting results are so crude and unreliable that we largely ignore reports of results of psychotherapy. Dr. Glad has moved a long way toward solving this problem. This should not only help him in the further working out and reporting of his basic hypothesis to others, but should lead to the application of this methodology to other clinical problems in psychotherapy, group and individual.

This chapter has underlined some of the potentialities of Dr. Glad's value integration approach in clinical psychiatric practice. The utility of this approach in the training of psychiatric residents and others in psychotherapy should be investigated. It would early emphasize to the trainee the importance of establishing goals in therapy, of evaluating the personality characteristics, strength, and assets of the patient in the setting of goals, and present a rational background for doing this. Further it might facilitate learning by presenting the trainee with a number of readily learnable maneuvers, giving him a degree of security which our current and often unstructured instruction in beginning psychotherapy fails to do. These possibilities need careful exploration.

Finally, practicing psychiatrists and psychotherapists would be well advised to keep this hypothesis in mind currently in their own work and to 'test' it from time to time on selected cases. This may prove nothing 'scientifically' but may produce dividends in the development of one's own therapeutic viewpoint and techniques, and may pave the way to much needed advances in psychotherapeutic procedures. As Freud (32) wrote in 1919, 'We are but a handful of people, and even by working hard each one of us can deal in a year with only a small number of people. Against the vast amount of neurotic misery in the world, the quantity we can do away with is almost negligible.' Hopefully the applications of this work may help to correct this situation, often as true today as in 1919.

Bibliography

1. Alexander, F., and French, T. M. *Psychoanalytic Therapy*. New York: Ronald, 1946.
2. Alexander, F. *Psychoanalysis and Psychotherapy*. New York: Ronald, 1956.
3. Allen, F. H. *Psychotherapy with Children*. New York: Norton, 1942.
4. Appel, K. E. Psychiatric therapy. In J. McV. Hunt (Ed.), *Personality and the Behavior Disorders*. Vol. 2. New York: Ronald, 1944. Pp. 1107–63.
5. Bales, R. F. *Interaction Process Analysis*. Cambridge, Mass.: Addison-Wesley, 1950.
6. Berg, C. *Psychotherapy, Practice and Theory*. New York: Norton, 1948.
7. Bergler, E. *The Writer and Psychoanalysis*. Garden City, New York: Doubleday, 1950.
8. Bortree, D. W. An operational comparison of client-centered, relationship, and psychoanalytic therapies. Unpublished master's thesis, Denver Univer., 1956.
9. Bortree, D. W., and Clad, D. D. Operational differences in therapist formulations and patient statements in client-centered, relationship, and psychoanalytic therapies. *Rocky Mountain Psychologist*, 1956, 1: 3. (Abstract)
10. Bourestom, N. C., and Smith, W. L. A comparison between fantasy productions and social behavior in experimental group psychotherapy. *Group Psychother.*, 1954, 7: 205–13.
11. Braatøy, T. F. *Fundamentals of Psychoanalytic Technique*. New York: Wiley, 1954.
12. Colby, K. M. *A Primer for Psychotherapists*. New York: Ronald, 1951.
13. Coleman, J. U. The initial phase of psychotherapy. *Bull. Menninger Clinic*, 1949, 13: 189–97.
14. Dollard, J., & Miller, N. E. *Personality and Psychotherapy*. New York: McGraw-Hill, 1950.
15. Durkin, Helen E. Dr. John Levy's relationship therapy as applied to a play group. *Amer. J. Orthopsychiat.*, 1939, 9: 583–97.
16. Durkin, Helen E. *Group Therapy for Mothers of Disturbed Children*. Springfield, Ill.: Thomas, 1954.
17. Dymond, Rosalind F. An adjustment score for Q-sorts. *J. Consult. Psychol.*, 1953, 17: 339–42.

18. Ends, E. J., and Page, C. W. A study of three types of group psycho-therapy with hospitalized male inebriates. *Quart. J. Stud. Alcohol.*, 1957, 18: 263–77.

19. Eysenck, H. J. The effects of psychotherapy: an evaluation. *J. Consult. Psychol.*, 1952, 16: 319–24.

20. Fenichel, O. *The Psychoanalytic Theory of Neurosis*. New York: Norton, 1945.

21. Ferguson, R. E. An investigation of behavior of chronic schizophrenics in experimental group psychotherapy. Unpublished Ph.D. thesis, Denver Univer., 1956.

22. Ferguson, R. E., and Anderson, J. N. An investigation of client behavior as a function of specific therapist formulations. Unpublished master's thesis, Denver Univer., 1951.

23. Fiedler, F. E. The concept of an ideal therapeutic relationship. *J. Consult. Psychol.*, 1950, 14: 239–45.

24. Fiedler, F. E. Factor analyses of psychoanalytic, non-directive, and Adlerian therapeutic relationships. *J. Consult. Psychol.*, 1951, 15: 32–8.

25. Foulkes, S. H. *Introduction to Group-Analytic Psychotherapy*. New York: Grune & Stratton, 1949.

26. Frazer, Sir J. G. *The Golden Bough*. New York: Macmillan, 1935.

27. Freud, S. *New Introductory Lectures on Psycho-analysis*. New York: Norton, 1933.

28. Freud, S. *A General Introduction to Psycho-analysis*. Garden City, New York: Garden City, 1943.

29. Freud, S. *The Interpretation of Dreams*. New York: Basic Books, 1955.

30. Freud, S. *An Outline of Psychoanalysis*. New York: Norton, 1949.

31. Freud, S. *Dictionary of Psychoanalysis*. New York: Philosophical Library, 1950. (N. Fodor and F. Gaynor, Eds.).

32. Freud, S. Turnings in the ways of psychoanalytic therapy, *Collected Papers*, Vol. 2. London: Hogarth, 1950.

33. Fromm-Reichmann, Freda. Transference problems in schizophrenics. In S. S. Tomkins (Ed.), *Contemporary Psychopathology: A Source Book*. Cambridge, Mass.: Harvard Univer. Press, 1943. Pp. 371–80.

34. Glad, D. D. Identification of therapist behavior units as a basis for experimental investigation of psychotherapy. *J. Colo-Wyo. Acad. Sci.*, 1951, 4: 67–8. (Abstract)

35. Glad, D. D. Theories, operations, and behavioral feedbacks in interview process research. *J. Colo-Wyo. Acad. Sci.*, 1955, 4: 56–7. (Abstract)

36. Glad, D. D. An operational conception of psychotherapy. *Psychiat.*, 1956: 19, 371–82.

37. Glad, D. D. *Interpersonality Synopsis*. Book manuscript in preparation for publication.

38. Glad, D. D., et al. *The Emotional Projection Test*. Missoula, Mont.: Psychological Test Specialists, 1956.

39. Glad, D. D., Lewis, R. T., Page, C. W., and Jeffers, J. R. Improvement

in psychotherapy — a function of therapy methods and performance measures. *J. Colo-Wyo. Acad. Sci.*, 1953, 4: 49–50. (Abstract)

40. Glad, D. D., and Shearn, C. R. An emotional projection test. *Percept. Mot. Skills*, 1956, 6: 1–12. (Monogr. Suppl. 1)

41. Glad, D. D., Singer, Margaret T., Glad, Virginia, Shearn, C. R., and Krause, L. F. Dynamics of behavior and fantasy in the Emotional Projection Test. Tentative title of manual in preparation for publication.

42. Glad, D. D., Smith, W. L., and Glad, Virginia M. Behavior factors reactions to leader emphases upon feelings or social expressions. *Int. J. Soc. Psychiat.*, 1957, 3: 129–32.

43. Glover, E. Lectures on technique in psychoanalysis. *Int. J. Psychoanal.*, 1927, 8: 311–38, 486–520.

44. Glover, E. Lectures on technique in psychoanalysis. *Int. J. Psychoanal.*, 1928, 9: 7–46, 181–218.

45. Gorlow, L. Nondirective group psychotherapy: an analysis of the behavior of members as therapists. Unpublished Ph.D. thesis, Teachers College, Columbia Univer., 1950.

46. Grinker, R. R., and Spiegel, J. P. *War Neuroses.* Philadelphia: Blakiston, 1945.

47. Group for the Advancement of Psychiatry. Research in individual psychotherapy. *Circular Letter No. 223*, Sept. 10, 1951.

48. Harris, V. W. Factors in the interaction of therapist methods and client behavior. Unpublished Ph.D. thesis, Denver Univer., 1955.

49. Hartley, R. B. An exploration of the influence of therapist behavior upon paranoid schizophrenics in group therapy. Unpublished Ph.D. thesis, Denver Univer., 1954.

50. Hathaway, S. R. Clinical methods: psychotherapy. In C. P. Stone and D. W. Taylor (Eds.), *Annual Review of Psychology.* Vol. 2. Stanford, Calif.: Annual Reviews Inc., 1951. Pp. 259–80.

51. Hayne, M. L. An inverse factor analysis of behavior of paranoid schizophrenics. Unpublished Ph.D. thesis, Denver Univer., 1958.

52. Hayne, M. L., Glad, D. D., and Ferguson, R. E. An inverse factor analysis of behavior in paranoid schizophrenic groups. *Rocky Mountain Psychologist*, 1956, 1: 4. (Abstract)

53. Healy, W., Bronner, Augusta F., and Bowers, Anna M. *The Structure and Meaning of Psychoanalysis.* New York: A. A. Knopf, 1930.

54. Hobbs, N. Group-centered psychotherapy. In C. R. Rogers (Ed.), *Client-centered Therapy.* Boston: Houghton Mifflin, 1951. Pp. 278–319.

55. Hoch, E. L. The nature of the group process in non-directive group psychotherapy. Unpublished Ph.D. thesis, Teachers College, Columbia Univer., 1950.

56. Jeffers, J. R. Therapeutic change as measured by projective techniques: an exploratory study. Unpublished master's thesis, Denver Univer., 1955.

316   BIBLIOGRAPHY

57. Joel, W., and Shapiro, D. A genotypical approach to the analysis of personal interaction. *J. Psychol.*, 1949, 28: 9–17.
58. Karpf, Fay B. *The Psychology and Psychotherapy of Otto Rank.* New York: Philosophical Library, 1953.
59. Kubie, L. S. Discussion. In Margaret Brenman (Chairman), Research in psychotherapy round table, 1947. *Amer. J. Orthopsychiat.*, 1948, 18, 92–118. Pp. 92–5.
60. Landis, C. Psychoanalytic phenomena. *J. Abnorm. Soc. Psychol.*, 1940, 35: 17–28.
61. Leary, T. *Interpersonal Diagnosis of Personality.* New York: Ronald, 1957.
62. Levy, J. Relationship therapy. *Amer. J. Orthopsychiat.*, 1938, 8: 64–9.
63. Lewin, K. *Field Theory in the Social Sciences.* New York: Harper, 1951.
64. Lewis, R. T. An analysis of group cohesiveness as a function of different types of group therapy focus. Unpublished Ph.D. thesis, Denver Univer., 1952.
65. Lippitt, R. *Training in Community Relations.* New York: Harper, 1949.
66. Meehl, P. E. Psychotherapy. In C. P. Stone and Q. McNemar (Eds.), *Annual Review of Psychology.* Vol. 6. Stanford, Calif.: Annual Reviews Inc., 1955. Pp. 357–78.
67. Menninger, K. A. *A Manual for Psychiatric Case Study.* New York: Grune & Stratton, 1952.
68. Money-Kyrle, R. Varieties of group-formation. In G. Roheim (Ed.), *Psychoanalysis and the Social Sciences.* Vol. 2. New York: International Universities Press, 1950. Pp. 313–29.
69. Morris, C. W. *Signs, Language and Behavior.* New York: Prentice-Hall, 1946.
70. Muenzinger, K. F. *Psychology: the Science of Behavior.* New York: Harper, 1942.
71. Mullahy, P. The theories of H. S. Sullivan. In P. Mullahy (Ed.), *The Contributions of Harry Stack Sullivan.* New York: Hermitage House, 1952. Pp. 13–59.
72. Page, C. W. A comparative study of three types of group psychotherapy formulations. Unpublished Ph.D. thesis, Denver Univer., 1952.
73. Porter, E. H. *Introduction to Therapeutic Counseling.* Boston: Houghton Mifflin, 1950.
74. Powdermaker, F., and Frank, J. D. Group psychotherapy with neurotics. *Amer. J. Psychiat.*, 1948, 105: 449–55.
75. Raimy, V. C. The self-concept as a factor in counseling and personality organization. Unpublished Ph.D. thesis, Ohio State Univer., 1943.
76. Raimy, V. C. Clinical methods: psychotherapy. In C. P. Stone and D. W. Taylor (Eds.), *Annual Review of Psychology.* Vol. 3. Stanford, Calif.: Annual Reviews Inc., 1952. Pp. 321–50.
77. Rank, O. *Truth and Reality.* New York: Knopf, 1936.
78. Rank, O. *Will Therapy.* New York: Knopf, 1936.

79. Rank, O. *Beyond Psychology*. Camden, N.J.: Haddon Craftsmen, 1941.
80. Roberts, W. D. An investigation of changes in responses to the Emotional Projection Test as a function of specific therapist formulations. Unpublished master's thesis, Denver Univer., 1953.
81. Rogers, C. R. *Clinical Treatment of the Problem Child*. New York: Houghton Mifflin, 1939.
82. Rogers, C. R. *Counseling and Psychotherapy*. Boston: Houghton Mifflin, 1942.
83. Rogers, C. R. *Client-centered Therapy*. Boston: Houghton Mifflin, 1951.
84. Rogers, C. R., and Dymond, Rosalind F., (Eds.). *Psychotherapy and Personality Change*. Chicago: Univer. of Chicago Press, 1954.
85. Roosa, J. B. The use of semiotic descriptions of group therapy to determine inter-observer reliability and descriptive differences between recorded and written protocols. Unpublished master's thesis, Denver Univer., 1951.
86. Rosen, J. *Direct Analysis*. New York: Grune & Stratton, 1953.
87. Rosenbaum, M., Friedlander, Jane, and Kaplan, S. M. Evaluation of results of psychotherapy. *Psychosom. Med.*, 1956, 18: 113–32.
88. Rosenthal, D. Changes in some moral values following psychotherapy. *J. Consult. Psychol.*, 1955, 19: 431–36.
89. Ruesch, J., and Bateson, G. *Communication*. New York: Norton, 1951.
90. Seeman, J. A study of the process of nondirective therapy. *J. Consult. Psychol.*, 1949, 13: 157–68.
91. Shearn, C. R., Glad, D. D., and Thompson, E. F. Leader's warmth in influencing group process. Tentative title of article in preparation for publication.
92. Slavson, S. R. *Analytic Group Psychotherapy*. New York: Columbia University Press, 1950.
93. Smith, W. L., and Glad, D. D. Client reactions to therapist operations in controlled group situations. *Group Psychother.*, 1956, 9: 18–34.
94. Smith, W. L., Glad, D. D. and Woodward, D. Differences in client reaction to variations in therapist expressive behavior. *J. Colo-Wyo. Acad. Sci.*, 1951, 4: 69–70. (Abstract)
95. Smith, W. L., and Woodward, D. H. An investigation of subject reactions to interviewer affective variations. Unpublished master's thesis, Denver Univer., 1952.
96. Snyder, W. U. An investigation of the nature of non-directive psychotherapy. *J. Gen. Psychol.*, 1945, 33: 193–224.
97. Snyder, W. U. (Ed.). *Casebook of Non-Directive Counseling*. Boston: Houghton Mifflin, 1947.
98. Snyder, W. U. Client-centered therapy. In L. A. Pennington & I. A. Berg (Eds.), *An Introduction to Clinical Psychology*. New York: Ronald, 1948. Pp. 465–97.
99. Snygg, D., & Combs, A. W. *Individual Behavior*. New York: Harper, 1949.

318   BIBLIOGRAPHY

100. Stavern, H. Discussion. In P. Mullahy (Ed.), *The Contributions of Harry Stack Sullivan*. New York: Hermitage House, 1952. Pp. 87–97.
101. Strupp, H. H. An objective comparison of Rogerian and psychoanalytic techniques. *J. Consult. Psychol.*, 1955, 19: 1–7.
102. Sullivan, H. S. *The Psychiatric Interview*. New York: Norton, 1954.
103. Taft, Jessie. *The Dynamics of Therapy in a Controlled Relationship*. New York: Macmillan, 1933.
104. Thorne, F. C. *Principles of Personality Counseling*. Brandon, Vt.: Journal of Clinical Psychology, 1950.
105. Van den Berg, J. H. *The Phenomenological Approach to Psychiatry*. Springfield, Ill.: Thomas, 1955.
106. White, Mary J. Sullivan and treatment. In P. Mullahy (Ed.), *The Contributions of Harry Stack Sullivan*. New York: Hermitage House, 1952. Pp. 117–50.
107. White, R. K. *Value-Analysis: the Nature and Use of the Method*. New York: Society for the Psychological Study of Social Issues, 1951.
108. Will, O. A., and Cohen, R. A. A report of a recorded interview in the course of psychotherapy. *Psychiat.*, 1953, 16: 263–82.
109. Wolberg, L. R. *The Technique of Psychotherapy*. New York: Grune & Stratton, 1954.
110. Wolff, W. Fact and value in psychotherapy. *Amer. J. Psychother.*, 1954, 8: 466–86.
111. Wood, A. B. Another psychologist analyzed. *J. Abnorm. Soc. Psychol.*, 1941, 36: 87–90.

Name Index

Alexander, F., 4, 90, 190
Allen, F. H., 128, 135, 137–8
Anderson, J. N., 252–3
Appel, K. E., 17, 46

Bales, R. F., 43
Bateson, G., 22
Berg, C., 178–9, 265, 271
Bergler, E., 298
Bortree, D. W., 190, 294
Bourestom, N. C., 237
Braatøy, T. F., 188–9, 278

Colby, K. M., 10, 43, 177–8, 182, 223
Coleman, J. U., 43
Combs, A. W., 151
Cumming, J. H., 303

Durkin, Helen E., 92, 125, 132, 134, 136, 195, 260–61, 283
Dymond, Rosalind F., 31, 159

Ends, E. J., 260, 293
Estrada, Carol, 284, 290
Eysenck, H. J., 40, 46

Ferenczi, S., 79
Ferguson, R. E., 237, 251, 253, 255
Fiedler, F. E., 5, 44, 46
Foulkes, S. H., 283
Frank, J. D., 24, 32
French, T. M., 90, 190
Freud, S., 4, 6, 79, 83, 90, 100, 110, 127, 312
Fromm-Reichmann, Freda, 98, 172

Glad, D. D., 31, 190, 237, 255, 293–4, 296
Glad, Virginia M., 237, 296
Glover, E., 79, 84
Glover, J., 79
Gorlow, L., 293, 301
Group for the Advancement of Psychiatry, 24

Harris, V. W., 255–6, 297
Hartley, R. D., 207
Hathaway, S. R., 21
Hayne, M. L., 237
Hobbs, N., 262, 280–82, 294
Hoch, E. L., 292

James, W., 55
Jeffers, J. R., 293
Joel, W., 213, 218
Jones, E., 79

Kant, I., 150
Karpf, Fay B., 125, 127–8
Keely, H. W., 207
Kierkegaard, S., 155
Kubie, L. S., 24

Landis, C., 180, 278
Leary, T., 214
Levy, J., 90, 92, 125, 132, 134, 136, 141, 184, 190, 194
Lewin, K., 213, 218–19
Lewis, R. T., 207, 255, 293
Lippitt, R., 12

Mateos, A., 284
Meehl, P. E., 25
Menninger, K. A., 214
Miller, J. S., 284
Money-Kyrle, R., 283
Morris, C. W., 213
Muenzinger, K. F., 214
Mullahy, P., 100

Page, C. W., 260, 293
Porter, E. H., 43, 147, 150, 154, 156–7, 159
Powdermaker, F., 24, 32

Raimy, V. C., 16, 22, 153
Rank, O., 4, 6, 45–6, 59–60, 123–5, 127–8, 130–31, 135, 137, 140–41, 144, 147, 149, 153, 190, 279, 286, 298–9

319

Subject Index